THE NEW WORLD OF WORK

THE NEW WORLD OF WORK

Labour Markets in Contemporary Ireland

Edited by
Gerry Boucher *and* Gráinne Collins

The Liffey Press
Dublin

Published by
The Liffey Press Ltd
Ashbrook House, 10 Main Street
Raheny, Dublin 5, Ireland
www.theliffeypress.com

© 2005 Individual contributors

A catalogue record of this book is
available from the British Library.

ISBN 1-904148-81-6

Printed in Spain by GraphyCems

CONTENTS

LIST OF FIGURES AND TABLES

List of Figures

List of Tables

ABOUT THE CONTRIBUTORS

Gerry Boucher is a Lecturer in the Department of Sociology, Queens University Belfast. He has worked on EU Commission funded research projects on topics concerned with national and regional development, labour market flexibility, higher education and racism.

Josephine Browne is the head of school at the School of Business and Humanities Dun Laoghaire Institute of Art Design & Technology. She has a long history of research into industrial relations.

David G. Collings is a member of the Human Resource Management Research Group in the Kemmy Business School at the University of Limerick and an Irish Research Council for the Humanities and Social Sciences, Government of Ireland Scholar. His current research interests include human resource management and industrial relations in multinational organisations with a focus on global staffing.

Gráinne Collins is an economist working in the Employment Research Centre, Department of Sociology, Trinity College Dublin. In the past she has worked on poverty measurement, social exclusion issues and the quality of training and working life for employees in the service sector. Her current work focuses on turning Dublin into a "learning city" for all its citizens.

Catherine Conlon is Research Co-ordinator at the Women's Education, Research and Resource Centre, University College Dublin where she directs a number of applied social research projects. Her areas of interest include gender and social policy, equality issues and issues in fertility management, pregnancy and motherhood.

Tony Cunningham is a lecturer in the Department of Adult and Community Education, NUIM. He is currently completing his PhD thesis *Career, Masculinity and the Managerial Labour Process,* which is funded by the IRCHSS. Other research interests include issues of citizenship and democracy in a consumer society.

Michael Doherty is a Lecturer in Law in Dublin City University. He is a law graduate of TCD and Queen's College, Cambridge and was called to the Irish Bar in 2002. His research is sponsored by the Irish Research Council for the Humanities and Social Sciences.

Margret Fine-Davis is Senior Research Fellow in the Centre for Gender and Women's Studies, Trinity College, Dublin. She is Director of the Work-Life Balance Project under the EU EQUAL Programme, which is piloting innovative solutions to flexible working and social inclusion, as well as studying attitudes to work-life balance in the Irish population. She recently completed a collaborative study of working parents with colleagues from France, Italy and Denmark entitled *Fathers and Mothers: Dilemmas of the Work-Life Balance.*

Lidia Greco is a lecturer in sociology of economic and labour processes in the Faculty of Political Sciences at the University of Bari, Italy. She has previously worked in the UK and in Ireland, in the Department of Sociology, Trinity College.

Patrick Gunnigle is Professor of Business Studies in the Kemmy Business School at the University of Limerick. His current research interests include industrial relations in greenfield sites, human resource management in multinational organisations and trade union recognition and organisation.

İ. Emre Işık is Associate Professor at Mimar Sinan University in Istanbul, Turkey. He was previously a lecturer in NUI Maynooth on social theory, migration and multiculturalism. He has published works in Turkey on social theory, identity and on the sociology of the body and health, and is a co-editor of the Turkish sociological journal, *Toplumbilim.*

Carol MacKeogh is currently Lecturer in the School of Business and Humanities in the Dun Laoghaire College of Art Design and Technology. From 2001 to 2003, she was the full-time research fellow at the STeM centre, Dublin City University, working on the SIGIS project.

Niall Moran is a post-graduate student in the Department of Sociology, NUI Maynooth and is an affiliate member of NIRSA. He is currently completing his PhD thesis *Anti-Racism in Ireland: A Social Movement Perspective* which is funded under the Royal Irish Academy's Third Sector Research Project. His research interests include social movements, racism and anti-racism, social integration, and the sociology of the subject.

Michael J. Morley is Assistant Dean (Research) and Senior Lecturer at the Kemmy Business School at the University of Limerick. His current research interests include international human resource management with particular reference to expatriate adjustment and the flexibilisation of working practices.

Aileen O'Carroll is a Lecturer in the Sociology Department at University College Dublin. Her main interest is the organisation of working time within the software industry in Ireland. She also is interested in the gendered organization of work.

Joan O'Connor is a researcher with Women's Education, Research and Resource Centre (WERRC) in UCD. She has worked on commissioned research projects for the Equality Authority and the Higher Education Authority. She is currently principal researcher on a project commissioned by the Gender Equality Unit, Department of Education and Science.

Sara Parsons (former Researcher at the WERRC, UCD) is Assistant Research Officer at the National Crime Council an independent body providing policy advice to the Minister for Justice, Equality and Law Reform. Her main interests are crime prevention, the social construction of crime and social deprivation.

Paschal Preston is Director of the STeM centre and Professor in the School of Communication, Dublin City University.

Valerie Richardson is a Senior Lecturer in the Department of Social Policy and Social Work in University College Dublin. She has been a member of the European Network on Policies and the Division of Unpaid and Paid Work and is the Irish representative on the European Observatory on the Social Situation, Demography and the Family. Her research interests are family policy and child care policy and practice.

FOREWORD

Work matters in Ireland. Today more people are at work in Ireland than for over a hundred years — certainly if "work" means working for money in the formal economy. Mass immigration has replaced mass emigration as a defining characteristic of our population structure. Although pockets of unemployment remain, in most of the country the normal experience is of full employment. And finally, at least for younger women, a paid job is now the norm.

Not only are more people working, but the experience of work appears to have changed. It is part of the common sense of contemporary Ireland that the Celtic Tiger boom means that, whether we like it or not, we are all working harder than ever before. At least in popular imagery, a lackadaisical if charming *mañana* culture has been replaced by a go-getting entrepreneurialism.

In this context it is surprising that the social analysis of work remains undeveloped within Irish academic institutions. Although Irish economic growth has been based on high technology industry and services, there is no social study of technology — unlike in most other small European countries. Certainly, there is well developed work in employment relations, especially at the University of Limerick and at University College Dublin, while the Irish Labour History Society continues to challenge the occlusion of labour from national historiography. Yet work itself — arguably still the most important aspect of people's lives — remains intellectually marginalised.

The Employment Research Centre (ERC) at Trinity College Dublin is one attempt to change this. We bring together social scientists from sociology, political science and economics. This book originated in a symposium on "Working in Ireland" which we organised in July 2003. Hopefully it will contribute to a greater understanding of the realities of employment in Ireland today.

James Wickham
Director
Employment Research Centre
Trinity College Dublin

Chapter 1

IRISH NEO-LIBERALISM AT WORK?

Gráinne Collins and *Gerry Boucher*

1. INTRODUCTION

This book adds to the growing critical literature on the Celtic Tiger era by looking at market dominance over Irish society. We do this by looking at the experience of work in contemporary Ireland. Work has come to fundamentally shape our lives, defining, among other things, who we are, how much income we have, what we are entitled to and how much free time we have to spend with our children. The book follows workers off the factory and company floor, looking at how time with their families is moulded around the working day. It looks at how work is individualised and solidarity fragmented; how workers devise strategies to confront these changes in managerial authority and social control; how they reinvent their identity in the new high technology and service workplaces; and how immigrants are integrated into or excluded from Irish society through work.

The economic dominance of society through working in Ireland is explored through a series of studies, based on qualitative and quantitative research, focusing on work-life imbalances, broadly understood to include economic and social imbalances between work and home, at the workplace and in the labour market. This broader understanding is referred to as life-work imbalances to distinguish it from the more specific term of work-life balance between the workplace and the home. In particular, the studies examine the dynamic of gendered relationships at work and between work and home; changing collective and individual relationships and identities in global Irish workplaces; and the evolving relationship between the state, employers and immigrant workers in the Irish labour market. These themes are central to understanding the dramatic changes in the Irish employment landscape during the Celtic Tiger Partnership era and to the increasing neo-liberal dominance of Irish society.

2. IT'S SOCIETY, STUPID

In the 1992 Presidential campaign in the United States, Bill Clinton used the slogan, "It's the Economy, Stupid" to highlight the importance of domestic as opposed to foreign affairs. During the subsequent Clinton years the Republic of Ireland rode the coat-tails of the American new economy and successfully attracted a disproportionate level of American foreign direct investment (FDI) to the European Union. This investment greatly contributed to the Celtic Tiger and transformed the economic and social landscape. Too far, argue some: Ireland may have jobs galore but at what cost to the social fabric? "It's the Economy, Stupid", rings overly simplistic in post-Celtic Tiger ears: both economy and society matter.

In 2005, with the continuing lacklustre performance of the American economy, this book questions the extensive role and negative societal impacts of the neo-liberal market model and the jobs created. The rhetorical question of whether Ireland should be oriented more towards "Boston or Berlin", asked by the Tanaiste Mary Harney in 2000, has been answered in practice by Ireland's policy flight over the Atlantic towards Boston, undoubtedly on Ireland's reorganised "low cost" national airline. The book does not necessarily argue for a reorientation towards "Berlin" with its overtones of low economic growth and high unemployment, but for a critical examination of what is actually happening in Irish workplaces. The slogan for Ireland at the beginning of the twenty-first century should be neither Boston nor Berlin but "It's Society, Stupid". As the results of the local and European elections in 2004 made clear to Fianna Fáil and particularly the Taoiseach, Bertie Ahern, the social matters again. What we need now is a period of catching up with ourselves, redressing the market dominance of society by finding the right balance between working in the economy and living in society.

The Irish concentration on jobs at all costs is not hard to fathom: cultural policies dominated economic policies up to 1957 and were based on the idea that Ireland could survive on her own — virginal, pure, Gaelic, rural and Catholic. Touting for work would have been simply despoiling! Because of this, the Irish experience of work has been more defined by the lack of work and the subsequent need to emigrate. It is hard to credit that the official unemployment rate in 1993 was 17 per cent and that Ireland remained a country of net emigration until 1996.

As Irish people exited, the policies slowly changed and in the second phase from 1958 to 1986 the state dominated. The state promoted economic and social development by gradually opening the country to external influences including attracting foreign direct investment and EU-influenced policy making. Internally alliances were forged between indigenous economic actors, a welfare state (of sorts) was built and the state pushed the country towards a liberal pluralist culture.

In the third phase from 1987, the economy was in ascendance. The state, working, paradoxically, on a European national partnership model, incorporated the trade unions and business elite (the social pillar was added later) under the rubric of social partnership. At the same time the state itself shrank. It pulled back from promoting services, confining itself to a regulatory role and gradually decreased in size relative to GDP. This had the effect of institutionalising an American neo-liberal market model in the country which was driven by global manufacturing and services firms. During this phase, Ireland experienced an unprecedented employment revival (Auer, 2001) consuming jobs like Ireland's life depended on it, heedless of the consequences.

Arguably, the social experiences of unemployment and emigration at individual, family, community, organisational and national levels shaped Irish attitudes towards work during this period and the official unemployment rate fell to 3.7 per cent. Much of the current Irish fetishism with "economic growth" and the "market" can be traced back to the social reality that, for the first time in modern Irish history, the economy created not only enough jobs for Irish people, men and women, but for returned Irish emigrants and, in many sectors, immigrants too.

Given the recent social experiences of unemployment and emigration, it is not surprising that attitudes like "any job is a good job" prevailed, particularly if one had a higher paying, higher skill full-time job in, for example, an American high technology or financial services firm. At the same time, there was a palpable sense that the boom could not last, that American companies would not stay and that unemployment and emigration would return soon. This led to contradictory attitudes expressed in electoral support for the neo-liberal government which demonstrated a wish for an open economy and at the same time xenophobia and racism aimed primarily against non-EU and non-white immigrants since in Ireland "Irish jobs are for Irish people".

Many authors have highlighted aspects of the Celtic Tiger Partnership era, its outcomes and aftermath, drawing on a number of perspectives and viewpoints: hagiographic, critical, personal, speculative, empirical, comparative and historical (Allen, 2000; Coulter and Coleman, 2003; Kirby, 2002; Kirby et al., 2002; MacSharry and White, 2000; Nolan et al., 2000; O'Hearn, 1998; O'Toole, 2003; Sweeney, 1999, 2004; Travers, 2001). Within this body of literature, there is an emerging critique of the Celtic Tiger in terms of its negative social and cultural outcomes with respect to issues such as class, gender, income inequality, relative poverty, social expenditures, public services, racism, consumerism, individualism and materialism. The strands of this emerging critique provide a detailed empirical basis at the national level for an argument in support of social concerns against "more markets". A separate literature highlights the inherent contradictions of the government trying to be both neo-liberal and partnership orientated at the same time (Boucher and Collins, 2003; Teague and Donaghey, 2003).

However, these accounts that draw attention to the social consequences of Ireland's economic growth have neither taken a hard look at the jobs created nor examined the consequences of those jobs for the people doing them and for their families. Following the attitude that any job is a good job, there has been an obsessive focus in Irish policy on simply increasing participation in the workforce, whether of women, the long-term unemployed, older people, the disabled and, where deemed necessary, immigrants. There has been less policy concern about work-related issues such as the actual working conditions, changes in the organisation of work, work-life balance, the lack of unionisation in the sectors of job growth and the limited extent of enterprise partnership in private sector firms and public sector bodies despite research in these areas (see, for example, D'Art and Turner, 2002).

Even when national policy-making has turned its attention to these issues, for example in the national partnership agreements, policy has been largely ineffective in addressing important social issues like child care, work conditions for service workers and immigrants, trade union recognition and partnership at work. This shows the inability of the national partnership process, and the unwillingness of the government to use its power and authority, to challenge the economic dominance of firms and entrepreneurs in Irish society. The dominant attitude appears to be that if it isn't regulated by EU law and as long as foreign and indigenous firms create jobs, the government will kowtow to managerial prerogative over most workplace issues.

Thus, significant issues in the internal society of firms with wide-ranging implications for Irish society practices remain largely internal private affairs subject solely to the economic interest of firms. These issues include: the individualisation of the employment relationship and remuneration; the substitution of the visible hand of management with the social conformity imposed by fellow employees in work teams; and the gendered nature of work structures. In this sense, the *laissez-faire* Irish workplace, increasingly dominated by global American neo-liberal market practices, has been the economic driver of not only the Celtic Tiger but of Ireland's changing socio-cultural identity and practices oriented around individualism, consumerism and materialism (Kirby et al., 2002; O'Connell, 2001).

3. Gendered Life-Work Imbalances

Of all the ways that Irish society has changed perhaps the most dramatic is the shift of women into the labour market and the knock-on effects of this shift on the gender contract between Irish men and women. Women's labour force participation rates have rapidly increased from 34 per cent in 1993 to 48.8 per cent in 2003 (CSO, 2003) with the average growth in the proportion of women of working age in the labour force increasing by over 6 per cent per year between 1991 and 2000 (Collins and Wickham, 2004). By 1997, Irish women's participation rates had even surpassed the EU average for those women in their early 20s and were near the EU average for the 25–34 cohort: 70 per cent in Ireland compared to 73 per cent for the EU as a whole (*ibid*). Significantly, relative to other EU countries like The Netherlands or the UK, the growth in women's jobs has been in full time and not part-time jobs; however, the absolute number of women working part-time continues to grow.

Further, the patriarchal assumption embedded in the Irish Constitution that women are going to stay at home when they have children is no longer matched by Irish social reality. Thus, the participation rate of married women is 47.8 per cent, and among couples with children, 50 per cent have both adults working compared to 43 per cent where one adult works (CSO, 2002). This means that a child under five has a one in two chance that his or her mother works (*ibid*). These changes in working patterns have clear social implications for women, their partners and children.

In other EU states such as in the Nordic countries and France, the state has stepped in to help the family and provide child care, either directly through state provision or indirectly through providing finance. In the Nordic countries, state policy has been increasingly directed towards changing national gender cultures and gender relations in families, encouraging fathers to participate equally in child rearing and domestic work through, for example, education and generous parental leave acts (Crompton, 1999). This has led the Nordic countries towards a model of the gender division of labour and gender relations based on dual earners and carers (*ibid*). To the extent that there is Irish state policy in this important area linking the economy and society, it can be characterised as a dual earner and marketised carer approach.

Despite a National Childcare Strategy largely devised through the partnership process, the Irish state has mainly left the provision, regulation and payment of child care to families or to be arranged on a *laissez-faire* basis at the firm. Thus, entrepreneurial child care centres, a quasi-market of paid child minders and nannies, paid and unpaid relatives, and the informal economy have flourished. Further, Irish parental leave legislation is shorter in duration, is unpaid, and is more voluntaristic in its application than most other European countries, particularly those at Ireland's level of development. Thus, in this crucial intersection between the economy and society for the country's continued socio-economic development, the Irish state's limited and fairly ineffective intervention has perpetuated the neo-liberal economic dominance over society. These issues are addressed in more detail in Fine-Davis's chapter on work-life balance (Chapter 2), Richardson's chapter on the division of paid and unpaid work (Chapter 3) and Collins and Browne's chapter on Irish fathers with working partners in a semi-state body (Chapter 4). Greco's and Preston and MacKeogh's chapters supplement these studies with analysis of women's experiences in the software industry specifically (Chapter 5) and the Irish ICT sector in general (Chapter 6).

4. LIFE-WORK IMBALANCES IN GLOBALISED WORKPLACES

The contradictory relationship between Ireland's economic development strategy, based largely on American-led FDI and the country's European style national partnership process, raises one of the central tensions between the economy and society in contemporary Ireland. There have been six national agreements since 1987: the Programme for National Recovery (PNR) from 1987 to 1991; the Programme for Economic and Social Progress (PESP) from 1991 to 1994; the Programme for Competitiveness and Work (PCW) from 1994 to 1997; Partnership 2000 from 1997 to 2000; the Programme for Prosperity and Fairness from 2000 to 2003; and Sustaining Progress from 2003 to 2005.

On the one hand, these national social partnership agreements (particularly the first four) are widely credited with providing a stable macro-economic environment that attracted American high technology and services FDI and drove the Celtic Tiger boom (O'Hearn, 1998). Through its multiplier effects this drove the market services-based employment revival (Barry, 1999). Further, the basic trade-off of the initial agreements between wage moderation and industrial peace for tax concessions and fiscal rectitude contributed to stabilising the country's finances, maintaining a low inflation rate and boosting productivity while increasing real disposable income (Hardiman, 2000). The agreements and EU legislation also led to some much-needed regulation of the generally unregulated Irish labour market in areas like part-time work, health and safety, a minimum wage and the attempt to extend partnership to the enterprise level. From this perspective, there has been a positive interrelationship between the Irish development and partnership strategies resulting in a virtuous circle of economic and employment growth with a consensually agreed balance between the economy and society with respect to work related issues.

From another perspective, Ireland's European social democratic veneer and the few positive social outcomes of the partnership process have masked the extent and breadth of the transformation of the Irish economy, polity and society along neo-liberal lines. This neo-liberal transformation has been largely driven by Ireland's economic dependency on American firms and uncritical adoption of the American neo-liberal model by the Irish policy-making and business elite. The institutionalisation of the neo-liberal model in Ireland is reflected, for example, in the shrinking of the Irish state and in negative social outcomes. Thus, Ireland is the only EU country in which both income inequality and state expenditure as a percentage of GDP approach US levels, while Ireland's social expenditure as a percentage of GDP remains the lowest in the EU despite the country's massively increased wealth over the Celtic Tiger period (Boucher and Collins, 2003; Timonen, 2003). An increasing share of this wealth has gone to firms as profits and to the middle and upper classes to be spent on conspicuous consumption; it has not been saved, reinvested in the social infrastructure or redistributed to create greater socio-economic equality (Allen, 2000).

This contradiction at the national level between the outcomes of European style national partnership and American style economic neo-liberalism is reproduced at the firm level through organisational work practices such as human resources management (HRM), ISO 9000 standards, total quality management (TQM) and delayered management devolved to work teams. These practices were adopted first by US subsidiaries, spread to their Irish suppliers and were adopted by indigenous companies, particularly in the high technology and ICT sectors. These practices have been advanced too in the public sector, for example, in the Strategic Management Initiative and enterprise partnership in the national agreements since 1997. In the "ideal type" of these corporate practices, the workforce is non-unionised and the employment relationship, remuneration, task responsibility and work identity are individualised. At the same time autonomous company cultures based on outward conformity to these values and practices are reinforced through the social pressure of work teams. While managerial prerogative remains paramount in these firms, it is often exercised indirectly through setting tasks and

monitoring the output of the teams; individually through performance evaluations and salary reviews; and suddenly through
disciplinary procedures, firings, lay-offs and closures.

Arguably, the social goal of these firms is to create a self-
sufficient company culture, isolated from the rest of society, in
which employees are company citizens, first and foremost, whose
rights are the freedom to have individual work autonomy and
whose duty is individual responsibility for their work tasks. Beyond those required by law, social rights to non-pay entitlements
such as pensions, leave or stock options are subject to managerial
and company discretion and are normally based on performance
and the individual work contract. In these non-unionised workplaces, political rights in company decision-making are minimal
beyond the immediate tasks of the work team, except for those
required by law such as European Works Councils in large multinational firms established in two or more EU countries.

There are at least three major contradictions that arise from the
intersection of the culture and practices of these neo-liberal firms
with those of the European style national partnership process. The
first is a basic contradiction between the isolationist, individualist
and global capitalist orientation of these firms and the intended
solidaristic, neo-corporatist democratic and national orientation of
the partnership agreements. The second is that the spread of these
neo-liberal work practices and values through private sector
firms, public organisations and employees to families, communities, the electorate and decision-makers undermines the liberal
political and social values of national democracy, equality and
solidarity. In turn, this undermines support for the national
agreements and more broadly for the sovereign Irish state. The
third is that attempts to introduce these work practices and values
to older private sector unionised firms and public sector bodies
are a direct challenge to the internal society and culture of these
organisations based on an Irish version of industrial democracy in
which workers' rights and duties are linked both to their national
civil, political and social citizenship rights and to Irish national
culture.

At the same time, it is important to stress that individualism and the new global work practices are largely neutral factors with respect to these contradictions. Thus, individualism can take many forms with, for example, the emphasis on individual autonomy and responsibility being central in historical terms in Europe to the emergence of a liberal public sphere and civil rights. In an Irish context, the spread of this form of individualism in Irish private and public behaviour may be a welcome change from previous social practices such as communal conformity and corruption in which neither autonomy (like the freedom to express opinions or to act differently from communal beliefs and norms) nor responsibility for one's actions were predominant (Inglis, 1998). Similarly, consumption individualism can lead to consumers demanding better value for money. Given Ireland's relative economic underdevelopment and lower standard of living prior to the economic boom, it is perhaps not surprising that many Irish people have responded to the country's sudden wealth and their new affluence by striving for a lifestyle they thought Americans and Northern Europeans enjoyed.

The interaction of the contradictory Irish policy framework and American neo-liberal individualised work practices reproduces the economic market dominance over the social in contemporary Irish society. In the long term, these new forms of market individualisation could significantly alter Irish values, beliefs and practices against, for example, increased public expenditure for social services and socio-economic equality, undermining public and electoral support for, and organisational capacity to mobilise in support of, these collective social issues. In this case, the supposedly virtuous circle of American neo-liberalism and European-style partnership could instead, through a feedback loop process, gradually reduce public support for European-style social democratic partnership, while steadily increasing support for American economic neo-liberalism. In the end, contradictions between neo-liberal economic policy and social democratic partnership could be solved by quietly dropping the social goals.

Four chapters in the book empirically examine the national and firm level contradictions in the neo-liberal economic dominance over the social in the Irish workplace. Collings et al.'s chapter sets the scene for the influence of American FDI in Ireland, detailing the level and extent of US FDI in Ireland and its effects on the individualisation of the employment relationship in US MNC (multinational) subsidiaries (Chapter 7). Doherty's chapter looks at the challenge to trade union renewal in a unionised private sector firm and public sector organisation, focusing on unionised resistance to threats of deregulation, privatisation and work individualisation (Chapter 8). O'Connor's chapter looks at differences in the orientation to working time by management and employees in the IT sector, highlighting individual and collective strategies of resistance that employees have devised to control their working time (Chapter 9). Cunningham's chapter revisits the labour process perspective of work, critically analysing the struggles of workers in department stores in the retail sector to resist changes to their work identity and the fragmentation and deskilling of their work (Chapter 10).

5. LIFE-WORK IMBALANCES FOR IMMIGRANTS IN A DUAL LABOUR MARKET

Irish immigration policy during the Celtic Tiger has further contributed to the neo-liberal economic dominance of society in contemporary Ireland. Since the mid-1990s, Irish immigration policy has developed in a largely ad hoc and piecemeal manner based on attracting temporary legal workers, granting them restricted citizenship rights in order to cover skill shortages in the higher and lower skilled sectors of the labour market (Loyal, 2003). At the same time the state has tried to repulse and exclude asylum-seekers from the labour market. There has been very little policy learning in terms of the comparative successes and failures of immigration and integration policies from other countries of immigration, other than doing Ireland's part to build Fortress Europe against asylum seekers and unwanted immigrants. For example, since April 2000 Ireland has copied the UK's dispersal and direct provision policy for asylum-seekers. Further, the treatment of asylum-seekers as a "law and order" criminal and policing issue follows from the EU's Treaty of Amsterdam. Asylum-seekers are not officially allowed to work in Ireland while their claims are being processed, no matter their level of education and skill, although it is unofficially understood that many who abandon their state-imposed accommodation work in the informal economy (*ibid*).

The legal but temporary worker part of this immigration regime is claimed by the state to be market-driven and employer-led. In practice, however, the Irish immigration regime is highly regulated by the state. Thus, the state issues work permits to employers for lower skilled workers prepared to fill jobs that Irish or EU workers no longer want and to employees within high skill areas such as nursing, IT and construction. In this layer of the regime, the state's role is mainly administrative and regulatory, balancing employers' labour market demands with the smallest possible number of non-EU immigrants. For example, in 2002, of the 47,000 immigrants into Ireland, half were on work permits and five per cent on work visas and authorisations (Ruhs, 2003).

In both cases, the social rights of the legal immigrants are restricted by, for example, denying them the right to free medical care, social welfare entitlements and free education except for dependent children under 18 (Mac Éinri, 2001). In terms of their employment rights as workers, immigrants in both categories are legally entitled to be treated like Irish or EU workers with regard to labour market regulations such as the minimum wage, working time and conditions and employee relations. Yet, these employment rights cannot be systematically monitored by the Labour Inspectorate of the Department of Enterprise, Trade & Employment (DETE) with its 17 inspectors for the whole of the country. This leaves the reporting of employer abuses largely to immigrant workers, trade unions or immigrant organisations.

Currently, citizenship rights are also stratified with respect to those on work visas and permits. Work visas are granted to the individual immigrant for a period of two years and visa holders are allowed to switch employers, and bring in family members after three months, if supported by the visa holder (Ruhs, 2003). As of February 2004, they may bring in their marriage partner who is allowed to work in Ireland. This latter change in policy was primarily adopted for labour market reasons because too many immigrant nurses, especially from the Philippines, were leaving the country for higher salaries, better career prospects and more citizenship rights in other countries. On the other hand, employers apply and pay for work permits of up to one year that are renewable but tie the permit holder to the employer (*ibid*) except in exceptional cases approved by the Work Permits section of the DETE (Department of Enterprise, Trade & Employment). Those who hold work permits are only allowed to bring in family members after residing for one year in Ireland.

The Irish state's building of a Fortress Free Market has been accompanied by a racialisation of immigrants that mirrors the different policies for legal and unwanted immigrants. Loyal argues, "most of the countries of origin of the holders of work permits contained white populations, in contrast to the countries of origin of asylum seekers" with the former being "generally populated by white Christians who are, from the state's point of view, more easily 'assimilatable' into Irish society" (2003: 80). This racial division is less clear-cut with respect to the stratification of work visa and permit holders. Thus, work visa holders include nurses from the Philippines who are predominantly Catholic and IT specialists from largely Hindu regions of India while (prior to the accession of the new member states in May 2004) the highest proportion of work permit holders were Latvians.

Neo-liberalism and the free-market ethos is based on the free movement of both capital and labour. Therefore the response by the Irish Government to limit immigration runs counter to these ideals. While the United States, the neo-liberal ideal type, has annual national quotas of legal immigrants, Ireland has been very cautious to open the doors. Rather the Irish stance is much more in line with other EU countries that seek to protect national privileges from being diluted. Complicit in this stance is the Irish public who, while not voting for anti-immigration political parties, have expressed deep concerns about immigrants getting unfair advantages, particularly when it comes to sharing the already over-stretched welfare state. Hence, the electorate's overwhelming support to further restrict citizenship rights to immigrants and their children in the June 2004 referendum. The Irish now follow *"céad míle fáilte"* (one hundred thousand welcomes) with "when are you leaving?"

This attitude of both Government and people is the background for the last two substantive chapters in the book. Cunnigham et al.'s chapter looks at the tensions between multi-culturalism and neo-liberalism in Ireland (Chapter 11). Finally, Conlon et al. explore the many barriers refugees, often highly skilled, have in accessing employment in Ireland (Chapter 11).

Together the chapters in this book highlight that "development" is more than economic growth, and unmanaged economic growth can cause negative consequences for individuals, families and communities. Left unchallenged, these negative consequences may disrupt society and eventually the economy. For too long, we have concentrated on the economy and left society to look after itself. This book is a first attempt to look at how this unfettered economic growth has affected individuals, families, employees and migrants.

Chapter 2

WORK-LIFE BALANCE OF IRISH PARENTS: A CROSS-NATIONAL COMPARATIVE STUDY

Margret Fine-Davis

1. BACKGROUND

Demographic changes throughout Europe have led to a changing social situation requiring new social policies. The increasing labour force participation of women, particularly of women in the child-bearing years, has been accompanied by increasing needs for child care, flexible working arrangements and greater demands for equality in the workplace. The challenge that faces even the most advanced of the EU member states is how to relieve women of the double burden of employment and domestic duties, while encouraging men to take an active part in family and domestic life.

McKeown et al. in a review of research concerning fathering in an international context found that:

> . . . the more extensive a father's involvement with his children the more beneficial it is for them in terms of cognitive competence and performance at school as well as for empathy, self-esteem, self-control, life-skills and social competence; these children also have less sex-stereotyped beliefs and a more internal locus of control (1998: 423).

The international evidence on fathers' involvement suggests that while there has been some increase in participation in child care and domestic activities, fathers' behaviour has not kept pace with changing attitudes and cultural expectations in this area (*ibid*.: 425). These authors state that the implication of this analysis is that:

> . . . public policy should seek to create family-friendly measures, especially in the workplace, which maximise the choices men and women have to negotiate roles and responsibilities and will allow fathers as well as mothers the time and space for child care (*ibid*.: 427).

The purpose of the study reported here was to explore people's attitudes and experiences in coping with balancing work and family, with particular reference to the different perspectives of men and women. The complete results of the study are contained in Fine-Davis et al., 2004 (preliminary results are also contained in Fine-Davis et al., 2002 and Fine-Davis and Clarke, 2002). One of the main goals of this research was to identify the barriers to optimally combining work and family. In particular, we explored attitudinal barriers that make it more difficult for people to achieve work-life balance and whether or not these barriers impinge more on men than on women.

A second goal was to develop new social indicators to measure issues of work-life balance which could be utilised in studies with larger more representative samples in Ireland and Europe. The study was commissioned by the European Commission and the Irish Department of Justice, Equality and Law Reform.

This study brought together an interdisciplinary team of social scientists working in countries with different experiences. Denmark is an example of a Scandinavian country with advanced policies in the child care area, yet it still struggles with the question of how to involve men in greater sharing of roles. France is also advanced in terms of provision of child care, but it has experimented with different forms of child care policy than Denmark (Fagnani, 1998). Italy has traditionally had lower rates of female participation, yet this has been changing, particularly in Northern Italy. Ireland has also had a relatively traditional pattern; however, in the last 30 years the labour force participation of married women has increased geometrically from 7.5 per cent in 1971 to 46.4 per cent in 2001, with 64.7 per cent in the prime child-bearing age group 25–34 (CSO, various years). The economy has recently experienced a boom with an even greater demand for female labour. This in part has helped to stimulate new policies in the area of child care and flexible working.

2. METHOD

A cross-national study was carried out in Ireland, France, Italy and Denmark on comparative samples of 100 men and women in each country, for a total of 400 respondents. Each respondent was employed, living in a couple with a partner or spouse who was also employed, and had at least one child under six. The sample was stratified by sex, socio-economic status and employment in the public versus the private sector. These sampling parameters applied to all four countries and hence the samples are comparable. The Irish respondents were from Dublin and the samples from the other three countries were also from major cities: Paris, Copenhagen and Bologna. The design for the four-country sample is illustrated below:

Table 2.1: Sample Design: Four Countries (N=400)

		Public Sector	**Private Sector**		
Male	Low SES	50	50	100	200
	High SES	50	50	100	
Female	Low SES	50	50	100	200
	High SES	50	50	100	
	Total	200	200	400	

The overall design for the individual country samples was identical to this, except that the number of respondents totalled one quarter in each cell and overall. The samples, while systematically stratified and comparable from country to country, were nevertheless small. Furthermore, they were of city populations. Thus, while we are confident of the differences and relationships found in our sample where these were statistically significant, we cannot generalise to the larger population. Thus, the results hold for our sample and are suggestive of trends which are likely to occur in larger samples. Data would need to be collected on larger representative samples in order to generalise to whole countries.

3. THE IRISH SOCIAL CONTEXT: CHANGING GENDER ROLES AND SOCIAL POLICIES IN IRELAND

This chapter presents some of the major findings from the study, focusing on the Irish data in relation to the comparative data from the other three countries. Before presenting these results, it may be useful to highlight some key factors relevant to the Irish historical and social context. Ireland is a society which has undergone rapid social change over the last several decades. Concurrent with changing legislation, increased labour force participation and decreasing fertility, there has been a significant change in attitudes towards gender roles. In a study carried out in 1986 comparing attitudes in a Dublin sample with those studied in 1975, a significant shift was found for all groups — male and female — concerning gender-roles. "Most people no longer believed that a woman's role should be that of wife and mother, with the male playing the dominant role both inside and outside the home" (Fine-Davis 1988: 91).

In the context of changing social attitudes and increased labour force participation of married women, people have expressed consistent support for family-friendly policies. In the early 1980s a national survey of mothers (half employed and half non-employed) found a high degree of support for various changes in the workplace and the community including: flexible hours (88.3 per cent); greater availability of part-time jobs (96.4 per cent); extended leave for childbirth and child-rearing (73.9 per cent); parental leave for child's illness (90.9 per cent); flexibility for breastfeeding mothers (67.7 per cent); and work-sharing (89.2 per cent). Both paternity leave and parental leave were strongly favoured. Mothers reported that they commonly had to use their own annual leave, sick leave, or unpaid leave in case of a child's illness (Fine-Davis, 1983a).

In a nationwide representative survey carried out around the same time (1978), attitudes of men and women were also elicited concerning potential social policies to assist employed married women and women working in the home (Fine-Davis, 1983b: 160). It found that 71.7 per cent favoured provision of tax relief to people who employed child care workers and cleaners or home-helps in their homes. This was also supported by mothers of dependent children (both employed and non-employed) in the previous study referred to (Fine-Davis, 1983a). The Working Party on Child care Facilities for Working Parents (1983), taking cognisance of these views, recommended that "Fees and other related expenses incurred by working parents to have their children cared for at home, or otherwise, should be reckonable for income tax purposes" (*ibid.*: 9). Public policy has still failed to act on these and subsequent similar recommendations, including the widespread support for the provision of child care centres.

Public policy is only beginning to come to terms with public preferences evident over two decades ago. No doubt the changing economic situation in Ireland with decreased unemployment, increasing labour force participation of married women, and the need to recruit female labour to the workforce contributed to this policy response. It is also undoubtedly the result of changing gender role attitudes in Ireland (Fine-Davis, 1988; Whelan and Fahey, 1994) and the greater importance placed on reconciling work and family.

Economic barriers to providing child care were highlighted in a 1985 Government report, *Irish Women: Agenda for Practical Action* (Working Party on Women's Affairs and Family Law Reform, 1985). However, this argument no longer holds. Ireland is a thriving buoyant economy and women's labour force participation, including that of married women, contributed significantly to the Celtic Tiger, as pointed out in the ESRI's *Medium Term Review* (Fahey and FitzGerald, 1997).

While child care budget measures from 1999 to 2005 have been reasonably positive, the lack of a comprehensive, integrated long-term child care strategy still remains. The funding allocated in the last few budgets is going towards local child care initiatives and community-based groups, private sector child care and workplace child care. This mainly consists of subsidies for costs like capital expenditure and staff training. It does not provide for direct provision of child care, except in limited cases. The crucial question remains: how consistent can the quality be of such a diversity of child care provision? Moreover, the vast sums put into increased child benefit do not address the child care problem, as it can be spent on many other things. It could be argued that had this money gone into provision of high quality child care facilities across the board, it may have been more beneficial.

Given the benefits of quality early childhood education, the provision of a centralised high quality programme is essential for the young, for working parents with children, and for society to develop its citizens and prevent later social problems (Report on the National Forum for Early Childhood Education, 1998; Goodbody Economic Consultants, 1998; Department of Education and Science, 1999; Expert Working Group on Child Care, 1999).

In addition to a lack of consistent quality through a vast array of child care facilities, the issue of cost still remains. Child care costs in Ireland consume a higher proportion of working parents' earnings than in any other EU member state (Langford, 1999; *Irish Times*, 17 May 2001). Even though child benefit has been increased and taxes have been reduced, people have to spend an enormous portion of their take-home pay on child care costs, especially those on lower wages. Data from the Central Statistics Office National Household Survey indicates that the average weekly cost of child care for families with pre-school children was €105.36 nationally in 2002, and over €131 in Dublin (CSO, 2003).

Yet, child care is no longer seen as the major political issue it was during the height of the Celtic Tiger. It is both highly telling and unfortunate that the economic buoyancy of the market was the major impetus to highlighting the child care issue.

Clearly, child care is only one of many policy issues relevant to work-life balance. Other issues include flexible working, gender role attitudes and transportation. However, child care policy is an interesting example of how resistant government can be in a central policy area, and how responsive it can be when there are economic pressures to force policy change.

4. RESULTS FOR IRELAND IN COMPARATIVE PERSPECTIVE

Commuting and Working Time

Respondents were asked how long it took, on average, for them to get to work and also how long it took their partner to get to work. The average for all countries was just over half an hour (32 minutes). Average commuting times were longest for Irish respondents (39 minutes: 42 for men and 36 for women) and for French respondents (37 minutes). Italian respondents had significantly shorter commuting times (24 minutes), as did Danes (26 minutes) (see Tables 2.2 and 2.3).

Table 2.2: Average Commuting Time to Work (in Minutes) by Country

France	Italy	Denmark	Ireland
37	24	26	39

p<.000

Table 2.3: Average Commuting Time to Work (in Minutes): Ireland vs. All Countries by Sex

	Ireland (N=100)				All Countries (N=400)		
	Male	*Female*	*Total*		*Male*	*Female*	*Total*
Minutes	42	36	39		32	32	32

Respondents in the four countries spent, on average, 38 hours per week at work; however, men had a significantly longer working week than women (41 hours for men and 33 for women). Irish men had the longest working week (45 hours) and Irish women the shortest (32 hours) (see Table 2.4).

Table 2.4: Average Length of Work Week by Country and Sex (in hours)

	France	Italy	Denmark	Ireland
Males	41	41	40	45
Females	35	33	35	32

p =.002

In Ireland, the car was the most common form of transport — 70 per cent of respondents used it to get to work. This compared with only 57.5 per cent of car use for the four countries as a whole. Cycling to work was more common in the other countries (13 per cent for the total sample) as compared with only 2.4 per cent in Ireland. However, walking to work was more common in Ireland (12.8 per cent) than in the total sample (7.6 per cent). Irish women were more likely than men to walk to work (19 per cent of women versus 6.7 per cent of men) (Table 2.5).

Table 2.5: Mode of Transport Usually Used to Work: Ireland vs. All Countries

	Ireland (N=100)			All Countries (N=400)		
	Male%	*Female%*	*Total%*	*Male%*	*Female%*	*Total%*
Car	77.0	63.2	70.1	60.5	54.6	57.5
Train	6.6	7.5	7.0	14.9	19.2	17.1
Bus	16.3	10.4	13.4	5.7	13.7	9.7
Bicycle	1.7	3.1	2.4	12.3	14.1	13.2
Motorcycle	1.6	0.0	0.8	9.0	2.4	5.7
Walking	6.7	19.0	12.8	4.3	10.9	7.6
Other	0.0	0.0	0.0	1.1	0.0	.5
	100.0	100.0	100.0	100.0	100.0	100.0

The greater reliance on the car in Ireland relative to the other countries may be partly responsible for the longer commuting times due to traffic congestion. Those countries that relied more on trains and cycling and less on cars had shorter commuting times. As commuting time was a key predictor of successfully combining work and family, increased provision of effective public transport would be likely to assist in this area, together with staggered commuting hours.

Sharing of Domestic Chores and Child Care in the Home

A series of questions was asked to see who did what around the house: "Me" "My Partner" "Both of Us" or "Other". It was found that women carried out significantly more of the domestic and child care tasks in the home than men did in all four countries. There were also large discrepancies between male and female perceptions of who did what. Men were more likely to think both of the partners carried out tasks than women did. Women were more likely to report that they carried out the tasks (see Table 2.6).

Where men excelled was in taking care of the children. This was true in the case of feeding, bathing, taking to school and crèche, and changing nappies. But most of all, it was true in the case of playing with the children. Ninety per cent of Irish men said that both they and their partner played with the children. A similar proportion of women agreed that this was a shared activity.

These results corroborate those discussed by Giovannini for Italy and the other countries (2002) and it appears to be a cross-cultural trend (see also Fine-Davis, et al 2004).

Table 2.6: Who Usually Carries out Household and Child care Tasks: Percentage Responses of Irish Fathers and Mothers (N=100)

Shopping For Food

	Male %	Female %
Me	16	60
My partner	36	12
Both of us	48	28
Other	0	0
Total	100	100

$\chi^2 = 21.3$ df = 2 p≤0.001

Preparing Meals

	Male %	Female %
Me	18	52
My partner	38	8
Both of us	44	36
Other	0	4
Total	100	100

χ^2= 18.41 df = 2 p≤0.001

Washing Up

	Male %	Female %
Me	28	32
My partner	10	16
Both of us	58	50
Other	4	2
Total	100	100

χ^2=1.11 df = 2 n.s.

Managing Home Life

	Male %	Female %
Me	10	60
My partner	30	6
Both of us	60	34
Other	0	0
Total	100	100

χ^2=29.45 df = 2 p≤0.001

Washing and Ironing

	Male %	Female %
Me	6	70
My partner	60	2
Both of us	34	24
Other	0	4
Total	100	100

χ^2=56.94 df = 2 p≤0.001

Cleaning

	Male %	Female %
Me	10	42
My partner	22	8
Both of us	64	42
Other	4	8
Total	100	100

χ^2=16.06 df = 2 p≤0.001

Playing with the Children

	Male %	Female %
Me	6	2
My partner	4	6
Both of us	90	92
Other	0	0
Total	100	100

χ^2= 1.23 df = 2 n.s.

Time with the Family and for Oneself

Most people said they would like to spend more time with their families. This was true of 82 per cent of the Irish fathers in the sample, 58 per cent of whom said they'd like to spend more time, and 24 per cent of whom said they'd like to spend much more time. Sixty-two per cent of the mothers felt this way. While 58 per cent of the men said they would like their partners to spend more time with the family, this was true of 72 per cent of the women. Women in other countries were even keener than Irish women that their partners should spend more time with the family — 81 per cent felt this way.

Time for oneself was also an issue. Seventy-two per cent of Irish men said they would like to have more personal time (48 per cent more time; 24 per cent much more). This was even truer of Irish women, 80 per cent of whom would like more personal time.

Child Care Arrangements

The most common form of child care in Ireland for the young child was a crèche or child care centre (see Table 2.7). This was true in the case of 28 per cent of the children. However, this mode of child care was much more common in the other countries, cited in 45 per cent of cases in the total sample. Indeed, in Denmark 88 per cent of children are cared for in public day care, where child care is considered a public task (Hojgaard, 2002). The second most common mode of child care for the young child was grandparents, cited by 17 per cent of the Irish and 11 per cent of the all country sample. Unregistered child minders were cited by 12 per cent of the Irish sample, whereas this was less common in the other countries (5.8 per cent).

Grandparents were also very important in Ireland as the mode of child care used second or third most often. A full 58 per cent of the working parents in the sample relied on grandparents to some extent in meeting their child care needs. In view of the increasing labour force participation of women, this form of child care will soon be less available than it was in the past.

Respondents who used child care centres or crèches for their children were asked why they chose this option. The reason "to stimulate the child" was mentioned by only 28.5 per cent of Irish parents in contrast to 45 per cent of parents in the total sample. This suggests less of an awareness in Ireland of the benefits of an educational child care programme. This may help explain the lack of emphasis in government policy on the educational aspects of child care and the greater emphasis on simply providing places and cash in the form of child benefit payments.

People with two or more children had complex child care arrangements. Even with the best of arrangements, these can break down. When this happens the respondents reported a range of coping mechanisms. Using one's own annual leave was reported by 55 per cent of the women as the mode used sometimes (30.6 per cent), often (12 per cent) or always (12 per cent). Men also reported using their annual leave, although they did so less often than women (42 per cent of men reported using their own annual leave, 20 per cent sometimes, 18 often and 4 always) (see Table 2.8).

Table 2.7: Who Cares for Youngest Child the Most Often When You are at Work: Ireland vs. All Countries

	Ireland (N=100)	All Countries (N=400)
	Total %	Total %
Self	0.0	0.5
Partner	15.2	8.0
Grandparent	17.2	11.5
Other relative	1.0	1.3
Work creche/child care centre/nursery	11.1	5.3
Other creche/child care centre/nursery	28.3	45.0
School	12.1	14.8
Child minder (registered)	3.0	6.5
Child minder (unregistered)/ babysitter/neighbour	12.1	5.8
Other	0.0	1.6
Total	100.0	100.0

Table 2.8: Percentage of Respondents Using Own Annual Leave When Child Care Arrangements Break Down: Ireland vs. All Countries

	Ireland (N=100)			All Countries (N=400)		
	Male %	Female %	Total %	Male %	Female %	Total %
Never	34.0	22.4	28.0	43.8	35.9	39.8
Rarely	24.0	22.4	23.0	18.9	16.7	17.8
Sometimes	20.0	30.6	25.0	23.9	24.7	24.3
Often	18.0	12.2	15.0	10.0	15.2	12.5
Always	4.0	12.2	9.0	3.5	7.6	5.5
Total	100.0	100.0	100.0	100.0	100.0	100.0

Respondents were less likely to use their own sick leave when child care arrangements broke down, but women were more likely to do so than men. Thus, 14 per cent of the mothers in the sample said they used their own sick leave either "sometimes", "often" or "always", whereas only 6 per cent of the fathers said they did this "sometimes". Further, 78 per cent of the fathers said they "never" did this, whereas only 60 per cent of the mothers said they never did.

Parental leave would seem to be the ideal mechanism in this situation. Yet, because it is unpaid and moreover because it must be taken on a pre-planned basis — a three-month block, one week on, one week off, or one day a week — it cannot be used flexibly to meet child care emergencies.

Attitudes in the Workplace to Child Care Responsibilities

The study showed that there is most acceptance of flexibility in the workplace in Denmark. However, Ireland came second to Denmark in acceptance by colleagues of arriving late or leaving early for child care reasons (see Table 2.9). Yet, this flexibility was more available to higher occupational status workers than to lower in all countries.

Table 2.9: Acceptability of Leaving Earlier and/or Arriving Later Due to Problems Regarding Child Care: Cross-National Comparisons

	France	Italy	Denmark	Ireland	Sig.
By colleagues	4.6	4.6	5.1	4.8	P<0.05
By managers	4.0	3.9	4.9	4.7	p<0.001

(1 = very unacceptable, 6 = very acceptable)

Irish women were more likely than men to think their colleagues took account of their child care responsibilities pretty well. This pattern held in Denmark and France. In Ireland, one's immediate supervisor was also seen as quite accepting of the respondent's child care responsibilities, whereas French supervisors were seen as least receptive. However, supervisors of higher SES (socio-economic status) employees were more accepting than supervisors of lower SES employees in all countries.

Respondents were asked whether or not they agreed with the statement, "Many employees are resentful when men take extended leaves to care for newborn or adopted children." It was found that working parents in all of the four countries perceived more resentment if they worked in the private sector and less if they worked in the public sector.

There was less perceived resentment when women took extended leaves for child care reasons than if men did. In Ireland, there was also less perceived resentment among higher SES respondents. There were also sector by class differences in all countries. Those who perceived the most resentment were low SES parents working in the private sector, whereas the least resentment was on the part of low SES respondents in the public sector. This suggests that the public sector may engender a greater sense of entitlement to family friendly arrangements than the private sector. In the private sector, issues of competitiveness and profit may provide barriers.

Attitudes towards working fathers who availed of work-family programmes, such as job-sharing and part-time work were also explored. Were these men perceived as less serious about their careers than those who did not participate in such programmes?

Irish and French people were more likely to agree that this was so; men were more likely to agree; and workers in higher socio-economic occupations were more likely to think it was true.

Table 2.10: Perception that Men Who Participate in Work-Family Programmes are Viewed as Less Serious about Their Careers than Those Who Do Not

France	Italy	Denmark	Ireland
5.1	2.1	3.2	5.1

P<0.001

Male	Female
4.2	3.7

P<0. 05

SES	
Low	3.4
High	4.5

P< 0.01   (1 = strongly disagree; 7 = strongly agree)

The same question was asked in relation to women who partici-pate in work family programmes, and again there were significant country differences and socio-economic status effects (Table 2.11). Irish working parents perceived more prejudice toward women who participate in family friendly programmes than did working parents in the other three countries (although this prejudice held more strongly *vis-à-vis* men than women). There was a general feeling that people who worked part-time or job shared were seen as less serious about their career. In this climate, it will be more difficult to promote family friendly working arrangements and a greater sharing of gender roles unless there is attitude change.

Table 2.11: Perception that Women Who Participate in Work-Family Programmes are Viewed as Less Serious about Their Careers than Those Who Do Not

France	Italy	Denmark	Ireland
3.9	2.0	2.5	4.7

P <0.001

SES	
Low	2.7
High	3.8

P <0.001   (1 = strongly disagree; 7 = strongly agree)

Two further questions were asked concerning work pressure and demands. The first was: "To get ahead employees are expected to work over and above the normal hours whether at the workplace or at home". In Ireland and in France, there was a greater sense of pressure on employees to work over and above the normal hours in order to get ahead. This clearly is an added pressure when people are already trying to balance work and family. There was also a significant effect of socio-economic status in all countries that this sense of pressure is greater on those higher up the occupational ladder. The pressure is also greater in the private sector in all countries (see Table 2.12).

Table 2.12: Perception that "To Get Ahead, Employees Are Expected to Work Over and Above the Normal Hours, Whether at the Workplace or at Home"

France	Italy	Denmark	Ireland
4.9	2.9	3.3	5.2

$P < 0.001$

	SES	France	Italy	Denmark	Ireland
Male	Low	4.6	2.1	2.7	5.2
	High	5.6	3.3	3.8	6.2
Female	Low	3.6	3.3	2.2	3.7
	High	5.7	3.0	4.4	5.8

$P < 0.05$ (1 = strongly disagree; 7 = strongly agree)

Combining Work and Family Life: Predictors of Ease vs. Difficulty

There were significant differences between the four countries in terms of the ease or difficulty in combining work and family life. This was much easier in Denmark than in the other three countries (see Table 2.13). It was also more difficult for those in higher occupational status jobs, which may be related to the greater pressure which was found to exist for people in these jobs. The greater ease in Denmark of combining work and family life reflects the relatively even distribution of working hours between the sexes (and a more equal distribution of household labour between women and men); a high level of relatively affordable public day-care provision and generous provision of paid maternity and parental leave; and a workplace culture with a relatively relaxed and permissive attitude towards reconciling work and family life (Hojgaard, 2002).

Table 2.13: Ease vs. Difficulty in Combining Job and Family Life: Cross-national Comparisons

France	Italy	Denmark	Ireland
3.5	3.6	2.9	3.4

p<0.001   (1= very easy, 6 = very difficult)

Factors Determining Combination of Work and Family Life

When looking at the most important factors determining the ease or difficulty in combining work and family life, many of the things we would expect to be significant are not — like age, education and number of children. Instead, time was one of the most important factors (see Table 2.14). The length of one's partner's commuting time was particularly important. The longer the commuting time, the less time they would be around to help with the family. The importance of time was also expressed in the item "Do the hours you work create problems in your child care arrangements?" The more this was true for people, the more difficulty they had in combining work and family life. Not surprisingly, the more hours a person worked per week, the more difficulty they had combining work and family.

Table 2.14: Predictors of Ease/Difficulty in Combining Work and Family Life: All Countries — Males and Females (N=400)

Age	N.S.
Education	N.S.
Occupational status	N.S.
Partner's Commuting Time	★ ★ ★
Hours Worked per Week	★ ★
Number of Children	N.S.
Help Index	★ ★ ★
Colleagues' Acceptance of Your Child Care Responsibilities	★ ★ ★
Manager's Acceptance of Your Child Care Responsibilities	★
Hours You Work Create Problems in Child Care Arrangements	★ ★ ★

★ $p<0.05$; ★ ★ $p<0.01$; ★ ★ ★ $p<0.001$

Another very significant predictor was the amount of help a person received with domestic responsibilities. The more help one got, the easier it was to combine work and family. Attitudes in the workplace were also very important. Most important was a feeling that one's colleagues accepted one's child care responsibilities. A feeling that one's manager accepted one's child care responsibilities also helped a lot and was significantly related to ease in combining work and family.

All Countries — Males Only

Looking at the data for males only in the four countries, it was found that the longer the working week, the greater the difficulty combining work and family life (Table 2.15). Also important was colleagues' acceptance of one's child care responsibilities, manifested in the item about the acceptability of bringing a child to work, say for an hour if one had difficulty in child care arrangements. This was generally disapproved of in Ireland, much more so than in Denmark. This attitudinally "sensitive" item is a good predictor, as it is clearly tapping into the acceptance in the work-place culture.

Table 2.15: Predictors of Ease/Difficulty in Combining Work and Family Life: All Countries — Males only (N=200)

Age	N.S.
Education	N.S.
Occupational status	N.S.
Own Commuting Time	N.S.
Partner's Commuting Time	★
Hours Worked per Week	★★
Number of Children	N.S.
Help Index	N.S.
Colleagues' Acceptance of Bringing Child to Work	★★
Hours You Work Create Problems in Child Care Arrangements	★★★

★ p<0.05; ★ ★ p<0.01; ★ ★ ★ p<0.001

All Countries — Females Only

Time again was a key predictor of successfully combining work and family for women. One's own commuting time was significant as was one's partner's. The shorter the commuting time, the easier it was to combine work and family. Women whose hours created problems with their child care arrangements also had more difficulty reconciling work and family life. The amount of help women received was also significantly related to successfully combining work and family. The less help they received from their partner, the more difficulty they experienced combining work and family life. Finally, colleagues' attitudes were also important, as were those of the woman's immediate supervisor. The more accepting the attitudes concerning the woman's child care responsibilities, the easier she found it to combine work and family (Table 2.16).

Ireland Only

The factors that were significant in the all-country data were also significant for Ireland, and in most cases even more significant (Table 2.17). The most significant factors for Irish parents were: partner's commuting time; the number of hours worked per week; the amount of help received with domestic chores and child care at home; the extent to which one's hours create problems with child care arrangements; colleagues and employer's attitudes concerning one's child care responsibilities.

Table 2.16: Predictors of Ease/Difficulty in Combining Work and Family Life: All Countries —Females Only (N=200)

Age	N.S.
Education	N.S.
Occupational status	N.S.
Commuting Time	★
Partner's Commuting Time	★ ★
Hours Worked per Week	N.S.
Number of Children	N.S.
Help Index	★
Colleagues' Acceptance of Bringing Child to Work	★
How Well Immediate Supervisor Takes into Account Child Care Responsibilities	★
Hours You Work Create Problems in Child Care Arrangements	★ ★

★ p<0.05; ★ ★ p<0.01; ★ ★ ★ p<0.001

Table 2.17: Predictors of Ease/Difficulty in Combining Work and Family Life: Ireland Only (N = 100)

1. Age	N.S.
2. Education	N.S.
3. Occupational status	N.S.
4. Own Commuting Time	N.S.
5. Partner's Commuting Time	★ ★ ★
6. Hours Worked per Week	★ ★ ★
7. Help Index	★ ★ ★
8. Number of Children	N.S.
9. Colleagues' Acceptance of Bringing Child to Work	★
10. How Well Employer Takes into Account Child Care Responsibilities	★
11. Hours You Work Create Problems in Child Care Arrangements	★ ★ ★

★ $p<0.05$; ★ ★ $p<0.01$; ★ ★ ★ $p<0.001$

5. CONCLUSION

The findings clearly illustrate the pressure that working parents are under, particularly in relation to time. Ways need to be found to reduce this pressure, so that people can have more satisfying private and work lives. Time flexibility in the workplace appears to be particularly important. Equally, the attitudes in the workplace were found to be very important. Supportive attitudes on the part of colleagues, supervisors and employers appear to make a great deal of difference to the success of working parents in balancing work and family. Long working hours and long commuting times add to the difficulties. Policies needed in this regard include greater availability of flexible working hours and improved transportation policies to reduce these stresses on working parents.

Women are still bearing the major responsibility for child care and domestic chores. While men think they are sharing these, women often do not perceive it like that. This unequal division of labour in the household adds additional stress to women in balancing work and family, and often dealing with unsupportive attitudes in the workplace. In particular, attitudes towards flexible working patterns, including part-time work and job-sharing, need to be given more status so they are not seen as hindering men's and women's career development.

Further, there needs to be a more concerted effort at Government level to address the child care problem in a more comprehensive way. Were better child care arrangements available, open at hours convenient to working parents, the stresses on parents in relation to synchronising child care and work could in part be alleviated. This is, of course, apart from other important issues of cost and quality of child care. It is important to note that Danish parents were significantly more likely to find it easier to balance work and family life than were the parents in the other three countries. This is in no small part due to Danish public social supports including child care.

In its recent report *A Business Vision for Ireland: The New Decade*, IBEC refers to six drivers of competitiveness. One of these is quality of life. The report points out that:

> For the Irish economy to continue to develop, business needs to make the best use of the talents of as many people as possible. Therefore, employers should recognise the changing social structure in which a modern workforce operates, and the social and personal benefits of balancing work with other dimensions of people's lives. To be successful, business must embrace the approach of family-friendly and work/life balance policies, while understanding that such policies need to reflect business requirements (IBEC, 2003: 24).

While this is to be welcomed, the last caveat is, of course, often a stumbling block. However, increasingly, businesses are realising that family friendly policies in fact have positive effects on the "bottom line", since they produce committed and loyal workers, who more than pay back the company in productivity, reduced absenteeism, reduced turnover, etc. (Drew et al., 2002).

The time has come for these aspirations to become realities so that working parents are not squeezed by pressures of work and domestic responsibilities; that the economy does not lose the talent of women workers leaving the workforce for lack of sufficient social supports; and that men are enabled to participate in their children's development and not made to feel less manly or threatened in their careers by doing so.

Chapter 3

THE DIVISION OF UNPAID AND PAID WORK BETWEEN MEN AND WOMEN IN IRELAND

Valerie Richardson

1. INTRODUCTION

This chapter presents the findings of a study on the evaluation of policies in relation to the division of unpaid and paid work between men and women in Ireland. It was undertaken as part of a European study co-ordinated by the European Network on Policies and the Division of Unpaid and Paid Work based in the University of Tilburg, Netherlands. The aim of the study was to examine to what extent recent policies in the fields of employment, family friendly work initiatives, equality and child care influence the division of paid and unpaid work between men and women in Ireland. Analysis of secondary sources and national statistics together with empirical research surveying the opinion of key policy makers and observers in the relevant fields were used to undertake the study.

2. THEORETICAL FRAMEWORK

Willemsen and Frinking (1995) have argued that within the social sciences there have been basically three theoretical approaches to explain the division of paid and unpaid work among men and women on the micro-level of families: new home economics (Becker, 1981); exchange theory (Cook, 1987); and role theory (Parsons and Bales, 1955; Eagly, 1987). The first two have rational choice theory as their starting points which make the basic assumption that individuals and households make their decisions according to their preferences and based on a balance of positive and negative elements within the available choices. Role theory assumes that behaviour is influenced by norms and values and assumes a strong relationship between gender role attitudes and behaviour. All of these approaches have been used to explain aspects of the division of paid and unpaid work within households.

However, they do not explain time allocation patterns of women and men. In order to develop the theoretical underpinning of the European study, Willemsen and Frinking (1995) proposed an adaptation of Bourdieu's theory of practices. Bourdieu (1984: 101) proposed that all practices result from a relationship between habitus and capital within a given field. Habitus refers to a system of dispositions that function as schemes of perception, evaluation and action in which the basics of culture are laid down in childhood in the form of ways of behaving. It can also include gendered customs that are taken for granted resulting in, for example, an apparently "normal" division of tasks between the genders. Within Bourdieu's theory, capital refers to both material and symbolic goods that have value in a certain situation. These are: economic capital (e.g. income, assets); cultural capital (e.g. knowledge, values); and social capital (e.g. networks). Practices refer to frequently repeated actions, customs or duties which are usually accomplished without conscious deliberation. The male breadwinner, female homemaker and carer which is still predominant in Irish society can be seen as part of this routine of practices.

Thus, Willemsen and Frinking (1995) argue that the interaction of habitus, capital and practices can be used not only at an individual or micro level but also at the macro level where they can be used to describe a country's approach to welfare and the division of work. On the other hand, at the macro level, Bourdieu (1977) argues that social reality consists of a number of fields or networks such as politics, paid labour and family relations. By combining the micro and the macro levels, it is possible to study the influence of policy measures on the actual behaviour of men and women especially with regard to paid work, child care and household work and also whether people make use of the relevant available social policies. The hypothesis then is that habitus and capital influence the use of policies and that the use of policies influences practices. For example, capital operationalised as educational attainments allows one to earn well on the labour market; and the more one can earn on the labour market, the more attractive paid work is in comparison to unpaid work; while if one considers habitus, it is expected that the more egalitarian the attitude, or the greater level of equality within the culture, the more equal and egalitarian will be the division of work.[1] The European study, including the Irish contribution, was grounded in this theoretical framework.

3. THE IRISH CONTEXT TO THE STUDY

Labour Force Participation

Women's participation in the labour force remained fairly constant between 1961 and 1993 rising from 29 per cent to 34 per cent, but rising to 50.8 per cent by the fourth quarter of 2004 (Quarterly National Household Survey Fourth Quarter [QNHS], March 2005). While the participation rate has increased there has also been a dramatic change in its composition. The most significant feature has been the increased participation rate of married women and of women with children. The vast bulk of the increase occurred after 1971 when the participation rate rose from 7.5 per cent in 1971 to 30.9 per cent in 1989. By the fourth quarter of 2004

---

[1] For further discussion of Bourdieu's theoretical contribution to the sociology of welfare and the use of his theoretical approach to evaluation of policies see Chapter 2 in Peillon, M. (2001) *Welfare in Ireland: Actors, Resources and Strategies*, London: Praeger.

the participation rate of married women in paid employment had reached 50.9 per cent. In addition, 43.4 per cent of lone mothers were in employment at the end of 2004 (QNHS, March 2005). Despite the shortage of child care places for working parents and the lack of State provision, it is interesting to note that the highest participation rate of married women in the workforce (75.5 per cent) is for women between the age of 25 and 34 years, coinciding with the age when women are most likely to have young children. The increase has been linked to higher educational levels, a declining birth rate, a rising level of individualisation, the demand for a cheap labour force and women's willingness to provide that kind of labour (O'Connor, 1998: 37).

A study by the Employment Equality Agency *Women in the Labour Force* showed that men's earnings outstripped women's by an average of 15.5 per cent across the sectors; a gap attributed to discrimination, career choices and career interruption for caring responsibilities (Blackwell, 1989). After an eight-year period a similar gap was identified by an Economic and Social Research Institute study which found that in 1997 women earned 84.5 per cent of men's salaries (Barrett et al., 2000). The same study showed that a woman who has two children by the age of 29 by the end of her career will have spent nine years less in the labour force than a man with the equivalent qualifications. They comment that "about three quarters of the gap between men's and women's hourly wages can be attributed to the fact that women, under current social and economic structures, typically spend less time in the labour market than men and more time as carers in the home" (Barrett et al., 2000). Thus, the QNHS (March 2005) showed that the average working week is 37.1 hours with men showing an average of 41.3 hours and women 32.0 hours. Nearly four in ten females work for less than 35 hours a week compared to fewer than one in ten males. In addition part-time employment continues to be dominated by women with 15 per cent of women in employment being in part time employment compared to 4 per cent of men who are employed (QNHS, March 2005).

Child care responsibilities are one contributory factor to the lower working hours and part-time activity of women in the labour force. The Irish Congress of Trade Unions (ICTU) report *Identifying Members' Childcare Needs* published in March 2002 clearly demonstrated that child care responsibilities had an effect on the type of labour force participation, and that this was gender-specific. Child care responsibilities were generally shared with spouse or partner but very few men handled the responsibilities on their own. Just over 60 per cent of respondents felt that their childminding responsibilities had a bearing on their decision to avail of flexible work arrangements, but this was twice as likely to be the case for women than men. One quarter of all women in the survey stated that they had not applied for promotional opportunities because of child minding responsibilities, and of all the respondents who had not applied for promotional opportunities because of child minding responsibilities 90 per cent were female. Other impacts of these responsibilities included leaving the labour force altogether for a period of time. Some 30 per cent of male respondents compared to 3 per cent of female respondents stated that their partner had left work in order to look after children on a full time basis (ICTU, 2002: 10–13).

Women Working Full Time in the Home

The QNHS (2005) numbers the persons who describe themselves as engaged on home duties at 558,500. Of this total 553,300 (99 per cent) were women. As Kiely (1995(a): 100) points out, while much of the disparity between men and women is related to the fact that women who are not in the paid workforce usually do not register as unemployed, the main issue is that "it is an inescapable fact that it is women who do the housework". In addition, unpaid work in the home is seen as work of low status and of no monetary value when compared with paid work outside the home.

However, the number of women working full time in the home in Ireland is decreasing. In 1996 women who were full time in the home and whose husbands were in paid employment constituted 39 per cent of all married or cohabiting couples, whereas in 1986 they constituted 53 per cent of such couples. While these women constitute a fairly substantial number, very little attention has been paid to them by researchers or policy makers and they receive minimal reward and status for their work (O'Connor, 1998).

Women as Carers

Ireland has traditionally been a society of male breadwinners and female homemakers with women being responsible for child care and elder care. Even when they participate on an equal basis with husband or partner in the paid workforce, the primary responsibility for child care, the organisation of the home and the responsibilities for elder care has primarily remained with them (Kiely, 1995b; McKeown et al., 1998). Very little research evidence is available in Ireland on unpaid work or household tasks. A Euro-barometer study (Malpas and Lambert, 1993) showed that in Ireland as many as 84 per cent of men said that they did not have primary responsibility for even one of a selection of household tasks. Kiely (1995b) in a study of Irish urban families confirmed the general lack of participation by fathers in household duties and child care tasks. Kiely's study (1995b) found that apart from household repairs, mothers carried most responsibility for household tasks and child care duties. In addition mothers also made most of the decisions. Mothers emerged as the managers of the internal affairs of the family; this was in spite of over 80 per cent of the mothers expressing the view that husbands should share housework equally (Kiely, 1995b).

Malpas and Lambert (1993) showed that Ireland was similar to other European countries in the tasks undertaken by fathers and mothers. A study carried out for the Commission on the Family examined the role of fathers in contemporary Irish society (McKeown et al., 1998). They argued that fathers in Irish society are reinforced in their traditional roles by the existing system of work patterns where men work longer hours than women and by the social attitudes that care work is women's work. Further, state intervention in families — by health care, family care and child care professionals and legal decisions on custody of children — has a significant impact on fathers by shaping and reinforcing the existing parenting roles of mothers and fathers.

Inadequate child care provision has been consistently identified over the last number of years as the major inhibitor to women's participation in the labour market. Ireland traditionally subscribed to a child care model of maximum private responsibility, in which the state intervened only to provide a safety net of minimal child care support for the poor or children at risk with no state involvement in provision of child care services for working parents.

The beginning of a proactive approach on the part of the State to child care facilities began to emerge in government blueprints for action through the partnership agreements which all highlighted the necessity for developing concrete measures to bring about greater provision of child care facilities.[2] This movement was linked to the growing emphasis on equality and the development of an equality agenda, a policy Ireland was forced to adopt through EU directives rather than on its own initiative. Arising out of Partnership 2000 for Inclusion, Employment and Competitiveness, an Expert Working Group on Childcare prepared a *National Childcare Strategy* which was published in 1999. This document provided a basis on which Government began to develop child care policies to deal with the growing crisis in the sector. The Equal Opportunities Childcare Programme 2000–2006 has been the key policy document steering the increase in the supply of child care in Ireland. The initial monies set aside by Government for the programme was €318 million but is now estimated to reach €499.3 million by 2007. So far the money has pro-

---

[2] The Programme for Economic and Social Progress, The Programme for Partnership Government, Partnership 2000 for Inclusion, Employment and Competitiveness, The National Development Plan, The Report of the Commission on the Family, The Programme for Prosperity and Fairness.

vided 20,500 new centre-based child care places (Department of Justice, Equality and Law Reform, March 2005).

The Changing Labour Market

Since the mid-1990s until 2002, Ireland enjoyed unprecedented economic development together with a rapidly falling rate of unemployment and a developing shortage of labour. In order to deal with the employment crisis the Government and employers have attempted to address the issue of labour shortage by introducing measures to attract women back into the labour market together with measures to retain them. In addition to child care initiatives the Government has been proactive with the social partners in putting forward a family friendly workplace agenda arising out of the social partnership agreements. In particular the *Programme for Prosperity and Fairness* (Department of the Taoiseach, 2000: Framework 1 Annex IV) set out measures to assist in reconciling work and family life in order to underpin economic, social and equality objectives. ICTU in their fourth Equality Programme *Delivering Gender Equality 1999–2000* (1999) had as its main platform the need to ensure that there was an adequate supply of good quality, affordable child care in order to assist workers to reconcile work and family life and to strongly support and encourage the introduction of family friendly policies and practices. Child care continued as a major theme in an ICTU report on child care services which stated "child care must be seen as vital to ensuring women's participation in the labour force and is critical in respect of eliminating the gender pay gap" (2002: 3).

When the issue of women's participation in the labour market was first mooted, the EU agenda was based on an equality platform. However, the underlying incentive in the Irish situation seems to have shifted from one of equality of opportunity to one of an economic basis. Thus, one of the issues to be addressed in the European study was how far the equality or the economic agenda was driving policy development. That is, was policy following or leading the agenda?

4. METHODOLOGY OF THE STUDY

The European study used a dual approach methodology: at the micro level, a large quantitative study was undertaken by a number of participant countries; and at the macro level, a policy oriented study was used (Dunn, 1994). It was this latter method that was used in the Irish study and which is reported here. This method was used to obtain information from a panel of experts in the field of child care, employment, equal opportunities, family policy and academia. Fifteen questionnaires were sent out to representatives of the main actors in family policy in Ireland (of which eleven were returned). The panel included:

- Senior policy makers in the Department of Justice, Equality and Law Reform

- Department of Social, Community and Family Affairs

- IBEC

- ICTU

- Members of the Oireachtas with particular interest in family affairs

- The Equality Authority

- The National Women's Council of Ireland

- Six academics whose research has been in the area of women's issues, equality and family policy; and

- One independent researcher in the area of employment and family friendly workplace policies.

Participants were asked to complete the questionnaire based on their own expertise and knowledge of the field, placing emphasis on their evaluation of the impact of the policies on the division of paid and unpaid work between men and women. In particular, the questionnaire addressed the impact of policies in the area of equality, employment legislation, family friendly work/life and child care.

5. RESULTS OF STUDY

The overriding view of the experts was that the main impact of current policies lies in the increase in the number of women remaining in or re-entering the labour market. Thus, the impact is very firmly entrenched in the area of influencing the division of paid work rather than in the area of unpaid work. However, the panel expressed the view that the increase in the number of women in the work force cannot be attributed entirely to these areas of legislation and policy. The rapid economic growth experienced by Ireland from the middle of the 1990s had an enormous influence not only on the level of unemployment but also on the division of paid work between men and women. The Celtic Tiger produced an acute labour shortage, particularly within the services sector — traditionally a female dominated area — which necessitated the rapid recruitment of women into the labour force.

Impact of Policies on Paid Work

Where it was judged that policies had influenced the division of paid and unpaid work, it is very clear that legislation and policies have had the most significant effect in the area of paid work. On the issue of equal pay legislation, just over a quarter of the experts expressed the view that legislation on equal pay had been successful in equalising wages for women and men. Yet, there are difficulties in comparing men and women's wages in Ireland since the only data systematically collected focuses on industrial and manufacturing industries and women are predominantly employed in the service sector.

As O'Connor (1998: 196–197) has shown, women's low pay is related to their concentration in occupational groups which are predominantly female, defined as low skilled and poorly paid. Despite the existence of equal pay legislation, a study undertaken by the ESRI (Barrett et al., 2000) has shown that there remains a pay differential between men and women. They found that 17 per cent of women compared to 11 per cent of men were paid below the minimum wage level prior to the introduction of the minimum wage, and they estimate that the legislation will reduce the average wage gap by almost 1 per cent. Thus, while the introduction of equal pay legislation has gone some way to equalising pay between men and women, the impact of such policies has been limited.

The experts confirmed that the policies and legislation in the area of equal pay, employment equality, minimum wage and protection of part-time workers had increased the number of women at work. However, they agreed that the policies and legislation had not affected gender segregation in the workplace, and certainly had not impacted on the gender division of unpaid work.

In terms of maternity protection, all the experts agreed that the legislation had been successful in retaining women at work and had gone some way to changing attitudes towards women, and particularly mothers', participation in the paid workforce. They argued that the legislation had been successful in protecting the rights of women in the workforce but that it was inadequate in length and should be balanced with paid parental leave. Similarly almost half of the experts agreed that the Parental Leave Act should have an impact on retaining women in the workforce as should the provision of Carer's Leave; but, to have the greatest effect, both of these should be paid.

In contrast to the employment legislation, the experts' view relating to child care policy was that it was a deterrent to women remaining in paid work. Given that the Government is currently implementing a child care policy aimed at increasing the number of child care places available, the experts were of the opinion that — once this policy becomes effective with increased places becoming available and the possibility of increased workplace crèche facilities — it should have an impact on increasing the number of women in the paid workforce. However, they also argued that unless some tax incentives were made available the existing policies would be less effective. The majority view was that the child care crisis is not just one of supply but also one of cost. In fact, the Report of the National Strategy on Childcare (1999: 57–69) made six recommendations on supply measures and five de-

mand side measures which were aimed at improving the availability and affordability of child care in Ireland. Yet, policies are
presently concentrated on the supply measures.

The cost of housing was also seen as having an impact on
women's participation in the labour force. This was related to the
necessity for both partners to have an income to provide sufficient
resources to pay a mortgage.

Overall, the majority of the experts agreed that the current legislation and policies have had some impact on the number of
women in the workforce. They were emphatic, though, that the
present policies were emanating from an economic agenda rather
than an equality agenda. They believed that the cost of housing
and labour shortages were the main factors leading to policies to
develop family friendly work environments together with action
to increase the supplies of child care provision. A majority of the
experts agreed that the National Framework for the Development
of Family Friendly Policies at the level of the enterprise would
have an impact on the distribution of paid and unpaid work; but
again, that it was the economic factors leading this development
rather than consideration of equality factors, and that the impact
would be confined to the area of paid work.

Impact of Policies on Unpaid Work

The experts were clear that much of the legislation and policy had
failed to impact on the area of unpaid work. All the respondents
commented on the fact that it was easy to develop policies to encourage women to remain in or return to paid employment, but far
more difficult to have any impact on the division of unpaid work
within the domestic setting. This view was confirmed in the responses to the questions relating to maternity and parental leave.
While all of the respondents believed that the maternity protection
legislation had been successful in retaining women at work, only
half of them felt that it had had an impact on the division of child
care between couples. Similarly, while half of the respondents felt
that the Parental Leave Act would have an impact on retaining

women in the workforce, only a quarter of them thought it would impact on arrangements for child care between couples. Specifically, the unpaid nature of parental leave made it more likely that only women would avail of the provision. In contrast, three quarters of the experts believed that if parental leave was paid, it would have a positive impact on the child care arrangements between couples. The experts who expressed the view that policies had had an impact on the division of child care responsibilities between couples argued that where mothers were working outside the home the likelihood was that fathers were playing a greater part in the care of the children. However, none of the experts could offer Irish research evidence to support this view.

A similar pattern of responses was evident in relation to Carer's Leave. Almost three quarters of the respondents believed that this policy could have an impact on retaining women at work but only a quarter thought it would impact on the care arrangements between couples. These opinions were based on the argument that it would be women who would avail of Carer's Leave mainly because it is unpaid.

The overriding opinion of the experts was very clearly that the current policies had failed to impact to any great degree on the involvement of men in unpaid work. While they were positive about the increasing emphasis on developing family friendly work/life policies, they were sceptical regarding the impact these would have on the division of paid and unpaid work between men and women. This scepticism was clearly related to the fact that they believed that women would be in the majority of those availing of such arrangements. This view would be consistent with the current Irish research evidence suggesting that there is an over-representation of women, and under-representation of men, in the take-up of various employment options such as job sharing and term working (Fynes et al., 1996; Humphreys et al., 1999; Humphreys et al., 2000; IBEC, 2000a).

In relation to the actors in family policy and their impact on policies in Ireland, it was very clear that the experts endorsed the important role of the EU in this area. Irish Governments have tended to respond to EU directives, at least at the minimum level, particularly in the areas of equality and leave arrangements — and in several instances only after EU pressure. The experts were almost unanimous in their views of the importance of the role played by the social partners in initiating family work/life balance measures.

Overall, the panel's view was that, until there was a change in attitude to men and women sharing equally the unpaid work within the home, policies would have little impact on the division of paid and unpaid work between men and women.

Ireland in Comparison to Results of the European Partners in the Study

Similar results were obtained across the other European countries: Portugal, Spain, Greece, UK, Germany, Finland, France and the Netherlands. That is, the results showed that policies and legislation had been similar in affecting the participation of women in the paid labour force and very limited, if at all, in the participation of men in unpaid work. Across Europe, therefore, the concept of the New Man seems to be rather elusive in reality and it appears that while there are a wide variety of policies in place they are not necessarily achieving their aim in terms of equality and the division of paid and unpaid work.

International Social Survey Programme: Family Data Fielded in Ireland in 2002

Since the completion of this research, the International Social Survey Programme (ISSP) family data 2002 became available. It gives some indication of the division of household responsibilities and attitudes to working mothers. Irish attitudes to married women working and having children are still to some extent within the male breadwinner, female carer stereotype. The ISSP data shows that the general attitude of both sexes is that women should work full time after marriage, and before they have children; but that this should change once the children are born — they should remain in the home or work part time until the youngest child has started school, when the amount of paid work outside the home should increase. At the same time, just over 60 per cent of women and men agreed or strongly agreed that parents should receive financial benefits for child care where both of them work.

With the increasing numbers of women in the workforce over the past ten years it is difficult to assess how individual families have begun to organise their private family lives. There have been no time budget surveys carried out in Ireland from which conclusions can be drawn. However, the ISSP data gives some indication of the current situation. Just over 60 per cent of Irish female respondents believed that they did more than their fair share of household tasks compared to 6 per cent of men, while 44 per cent of the total respondents felt they did roughly their fair share. In analysing the type of tasks, 90 per cent of the women always or usually did the laundry, whereas 80 per cent of the men undertook small repairs around the house. One third of the women usually or always carried out caring functions within the family compared with 5 per cent of the men. Finally, three quarters of the women always or usually did the grocery shopping and always or usually did the household cleaning and preparation of meals.

This data clearly gives only a "snapshot" of the division of work within the home. It would be of more significance to obtain longitudinal data giving a picture of changes over time in order to monitor more clearly the influence of policies.

6. CONCLUSION

This research has shown that the impact of current policies and legislation is very clearly in the domain of paid work. The reasons for the increase in the numbers of women in the workforce are not just related to the legislation and policies relating to equality and employment. The impact is also related to the economic situation of rapid economic growth leading to shortages of labour, with female labour being used to fill the gaps. In addition, the increasing participation of women in higher secondary and third level education has provided an increasingly skilled female workforce who want to take up paid employment.

At the same time, it is difficult to separate cause and effect when considering the impact of policies on the division of paid and unpaid work. Thus, once there is an increase in the numbers of women in the work force, together with their increased participation in trade unions as social partners, the demand for better child care policies and family friendly work policies leads to policy development in these areas. It could be argued, then, that it is the increase in paid work itself which impacts on policy rather than vice versa. However, it is clear that caring and household responsibilities are affecting the type of participation for women within the workforce, their length of time at work, their promotional opportunities and the number of hours they work.

Further, while women's economic progress may increase their status at home and strengthen their bargaining power, it does not affect the gender division of unpaid work in the home. Where women receive a high level of pay, they tend to use other women to do the household duties which does not increase the level of men's household work. Deep rooted gender stereotypes still persist in the division of housework, and the "second shift" for women in housework, parental responsibilities and domestic management continues. The findings do not support the hypothesis that increasing policies of work/life balance affect unpaid work in the home. The actual behaviour of men and women in households is not influenced to any meaningful degree by policies designed for that purpose.

With regard to habitus, the co-ordinating team in Tilburg (Willemsen et al., 1998) argue that positive attitudes towards compatibility of job and family, stronger participation of men in families, and strong orientations towards paid work, play the dominant role with regard to the influence of habitus on the division of paid and unpaid work. A positive attitude towards working women and a negative attitude towards a traditional division of tasks are purely ideological and detached from the daily reality we have measured. A strong orientation towards the family, and the opinion that not only mothers themselves can look after their children, has only weak effects on the sharing of tasks. The important aspects of the habitus, that is those that may actually influence the division of paid and unpaid work, are those attitudes directed towards reconciling work and family interests. This means that men are expected to take a daily active role in the unpaid work and that women are expected to do more paid work and to be more work or career orientated. A belief in combining work and family, while doing no harm to the relationship or to parenthood, may have a strong effect.

In terms of capital, the results show that higher educated people make more use of policies. Higher educated men do more child care, while higher educated women do less housework and higher educated couples share more of the unpaid work. The data do not provide support for the hypothesis that policies may cause more egalitarianism. However, this does not mean that family policies such as child care and parental leave are useless or unnecessary. Policies can facilitate combining work and care, helping women to realise their working aspirations and men to fulfil their wish to care for their children. However, steps towards equality are more likely to be made by women.

The crucial issue to be addressed in Ireland is how can traditional attitudes to caring responsibilities be overcome so that men are encouraged to share equally in these tasks? This might be accomplished with an emphasis on education at secondary level, together with policies that provide men with the security of knowing that involvement in caring responsibilities and home duties will not affect their future work development or their income and will not undermine their masculinity. The current situation of women undertaking both paid work and the bulk of unpaid work is likely to continue until there is significant change in social attitudes and the pattern of male breadwinner/female homemaker roles in Irish society. Finally, there is a real need for further research to be undertaken in Ireland, particularly in the area of family values and for time budget surveys to assess the real impact of policies on the gender division of paid and unpaid work.

Chapter 4

TAKING FATHERS SERIOUSLY: FLEXIBLE WORKING IN AN IRISH COMPANY

Gráinne Collins and *Josephine Browne*

1. INTRODUCTION

This chapter explores the negotiation of changing gender roles in an Irish workplace. In particular it explores the reluctance of men to avail of family friendly working — even in an equal opportunities company. The data comes from data gathered during an equality audit of a large Irish company referred to throughout as UtilityCo.

As other chapters in this book show, there has been a rapid replacement of the male breadwinner model with the dual-earner model in Ireland. Following the large growth in female employment, a central issue has become how to accommodate children and family into this social reality (Mahon, 2002). There has been much work looking at these changes on women, especially on how women have to juggle the dual roles of worker and mother, balancing non-economic and economic issues (Groot and Van den Brink, 2000; Wunderink van Veen et al., 1997; Collins and Wickham, 2001). However, there has been little work examining how fathers are coping with the changing support mechanisms available to them in the home. The assumption that men have a full-time homemaker to support them, prepared to be geographically flexible if the job required, no longer holds. So while women have embraced the labour market, fathers with working partners might have to pull back from the labour market relative to fathers who have stay-at-home partners. Men are now challenged to combine breadwinning and care-giving (McKeown et al., 1998). There is little public acknowledgement that fathers of young children experience difficulties in balancing their working lives with home responsibilities. The majority of the rhetoric is solely on the difficulties of mothers, yet true and full equality cannot be achieved until men move to share family responsibilities.

To explore these issues and examine how family friendly policies are promoted, implemented and utilised, we draw on an equality audit of an Irish Company. UtilityCo has a good track record on promoting equality stretching back decades, and it has a large range of measures to promote flexible working. These measures are well used by mothers in the company and there is no stigma attached for the women — indeed some women have moved into high profile positions after returning to full-time working. Far less common is the use of family-friendly policies by fathers working in the company. There are a variety of reasons for this, which we explore below. However, the failure of family friendly working in this company is a good indicator of the possible success of equality policies in other companies. If within companies with a good track record on equality, fathers still think they will be discriminated against if they balance care-giving and breadwinning, the possibility of true gender equality in Ireland is far off.

This chapter is divided into four parts. First, we discuss the changing gender roles in Ireland. Second, we discuss the family friendly policies available to fathers and mothers in Ireland. Third, we look at family friendly working in one Irish company to shed light on issues. Fourth, we draw some conclusions.

2. CHANGING GENDER ROLES

Mothers have special protection under the Irish constitution. The constitution holds that mothers should not be forced to work outside the home to the neglect of their family responsibilities. No such clause protects fathers nor outlines their roles; the assumption is that they will dutifully fall into line to support mothers at home. That is, fathers should be good breadwinners but caring for children is strictly unnecessary since the Irish mother provides this function. This separation of roles between care and work was held up as the ideal for Irish men and women to follow and, in the decades after the founding of the state, by and large, they did so. Women left the labour force, voluntarily or otherwise, when they had children and fathers worked on. In 1987 only 27 per cent of all mothers worked; ten years later this figure was 42 per cent. The reasons for this change are varied but reflect shifting legal frameworks, expectations and increased financial dependence on two salaries (Collins and Wickham, 2004). However, allowing or forcing Irish mothers to work, encouraging Irish mothers to work and supporting Irish mothers to work are all very different things. The Irish Government has changed the legal framework and cajoled women to work (Department of the Taoiseach, 2000; Expert Group on Future Skill Needs, 2000); but only recently — prompted by the EU — has the Irish Government started to encourage Irish companies to adopt work-life balance policies. Direct provision of child care by the Government seems even further off (see Fine-Davis's chapter in this book).

Often this rhetoric of work-life balance, or family friendly working, is couched in instrumental terms: a flexible worker is a good and productive worker. That is, they'll be loyal and not take unnecessary leave if they have some control over their work schedules (see www.ibec.ie). Even with this coaxing, implementation and uptake of these policies are still at a very low level. Ireland is experiencing a cultural lag in moving from a male breadwinner model to a dual earner society (O'Dwyer, 2003). Thus, more women than men take up flexible working options — which in turn reinforces the gender division in the family and therefore in society as a whole. Specifically, uptake of these policies by men and fathers is very low and Irish men spend some of the longest hours away from their children compared to other EU fathers (see Fine-Davis in this book).

A routine assumption in much of the literature on the barriers women face to equality is that men are united in opposition to women. Studies that actually focus on men in organisations are however limited (Bird, 2001). Those studies that do exist reveal a myth of a unified masculine social identity (Collinson and Hearn, 1996). There are divisions among men based on hierarchy, race, age and — most importantly for this chapter — parental status (Kerfoot and Knights, 1996; 1998). Thus, Bird (2001: 1) argues that men "are subject to structural forces that make competition, control and conflict pervasive features of their every work lives . . . but not all men respond to those forces in the same way".

In particular a male long-hours culture is seen as a constraint on the transformation of the household division of labour held out by the feminist project (Green, 2001). A further factor in the low uptake of family friendly working by fathers is workplace culture. Many workplaces do not expect men who are fathers to behave any differently from men who are not fathers (McKeown et al., 1998). This means if we are to handle changes in the Irish gender contract we have to look to changes at the firm level. Before exploring these issues in one company, it is worth reminding ourselves of policies and law at the Irish national level.

3. POLICIES AVAILABLE IN IRELAND

On joining the then EEC in 1973, Ireland had to comply with European equality policies. From 1974 onwards a series of laws and policies have been introduced to promote equality including the Equal Pay Act 1974, the Employment Equality Act 1977 and the Maternity Act 1981. A consolidating act was passed in 1998 and covers equal pay, equality and harassment. Paternity leave is not recognised in law in Ireland and employers are not obliged to grant male employees special paternity leave (either paid or unpaid) following the birth of their child. Annual leave taken following the birth of a child is treated in employment law in the same way as leave taken at any other time of the year, and it is at the discretion of the employer when an employee can take annual leave. Some employers in Ireland (for example the civil services and some of the banks), however, do provide a period of paid leave from work for fathers but these are very much the exception. While male employees are not entitled under Irish law to either paid or unpaid paternity leave, they are entitled to parental leave. Parental leave entitles both parents who qualify to take a period of up to 14 weeks unpaid leave from employment in respect of a child who normally must be under five years of age.

4. POLICIES AVAILABLE IN UTILITYCO

This section details the efforts UtilityCo has made to achieve gender equality. UtilityCo's workforce is 80 per cent male. Female employment tends to be concentrated in traditional areas such as clerical, administrative, cleaning and canteen work. Very few women are employed in senior management positions or in blue-collar positions where women comprise less than five per cent of staff. Despite this gender segregation, UtilityCo was one of the first companies in Ireland to recognise the need to develop policies on equal opportunities. Action in this area began in the mid-1970s arising from proactive trade union representatives, with a strong gender equality agenda and an equally proactive Director of Personnel. From the 1980s episodic equality audits were conducted. There is an equality manager and an equality forum between unions and managers in the company. The findings of a 1990 audit found that too often managers made assumptions about career objectives of mothers and the company moved to counteract such impressions, but no equivalent change was done for fathers.

In 1999 the Equal Opportunities Office, in consultation with the unions and management, produced a guide for UtilityCo staff on how best to combine career with other responsibilities. The guide sets out company policy on: flexitime, maternity leave and company maternity benefits, adoption leave, foreign adoption, paternity leave, parental leave, *force majeure* leave and domestic leave. This was designed to help staff cope with these sudden crises so that excessive demands on annual leave were reduced. Domestic leave may be granted with or without pay depending on circumstances and length of time involved. There is an arrangement whereby an individual works 50 per cent of their normal working time in a variety of patterns. The initial change in contract is for a period of two years but, subject to management approval and local working arrangements, full-time employment can be resumed by giving three months' notice. Further clauses ensure job-sharers have access to promotion. In addition, career breaks of up to five years are available and automatically granted for child-rearing purposes.

Therefore the UtilityCo has extensive policies on work-life balance that are available for men and women and mothers and fathers in the company, and many of these go beyond the remit of national policies, with some measures being over a decade old. This makes UtilityCo an ideal place to examine gender and equality issues.

5. THE RESEARCH DATA

The equality audit consisted of an analysis of the company's anonymised personnel data and policy documents; a questionnaire to a random sample of the employees; interviews; and focus groups with employees.[1] All these sources of data are used in this chapter to explore the issue of men's attitudes to flexible working.

---

[1] The sample of questionnaire recipients was selected by a random sample of all UtilityCo employees with women and parents (where identifiable) over-sampled for. Thus, 721 men were sent the questionnaire (approximately 10 per cent of all male employees) and 383 women (approximately 20 per cent of all female employees). Four hundred and twenty-six useable questionnaires were returned (38.7 per cent).

The women who work for UtilityCo (Table 4.1) are slightly younger than their male counterparts and they have worked for UtilityCo, on average, a much shorter length of time: just under 14.5 years as opposed to men who on average have worked just over 21 years for the company. This reflects the historic legacy of gendered work practices in Ireland and in the company. Recent recruitment is much more gender balanced.

Table 4.1 Average Time Worked and Age by Gender

Sex	Age	Years in Company
Male	43.6	21.2
Female	39.3	14.5
Total	42.7	19.9

Source: Personnel data

Looking at full-time working, 99.8 per cent of the men working in UtilityCo are on full-time contracts compared to 87.1 per cent of women. Of those women on shortened hours, the majority work a 50 per cent contract but there are also variations around a four-day week. Therefore in UtilityCo men do not utilise reduced hours even though they are available. We explored the reasons for flexible working with some of the focus groups. A typical female response was:

> . . . when push comes to shove, it falls back on the woman to be at home really. If you are working seven days a week, when are you going to spend times with your family? For kids it's not fair either (female technician #1).

For females flexible working is seen as a necessity; men on the other hand saw it as an impossibility: "No job share — no flexi-time — we can't get it" (male technician #1). Or as another technician put it:

> There are facilities for women in this company and in the State and there's none for men, if you are an unmarried fa-

ther, you are on your own, you are an unmarried father.
. . . there's no such thing as an unmarried father's allowance (male technician #2).

Indeed some men saw reductions in working time as a threat:

We [even] had to stop coming in an additional hour, because the government decided this and we were deducted
pay (male technician #1).

Yet, at the same time, there was a recognition that their working
hours stopped them doing other activities:

I can't go for a swim at lunch time. I can't do that because I
haven't got time, because I don't have an hour for lunch
(male technician #1).

Reducing working hours is one thing but overtime is the other
side of the coin.

Male employees are also far more likely to work overtime than
female employees (Table 4.2). While men had accumulated an average of 115.9 hours of overtime two-thirds of the way through
the year, women had done twelve hours. Thus men in UtilityCo
are far less likely to opt for reduced hours contracts, and far more
likely to work overtime than women.

Table 4.2: Average Overtime by Gender

	Male	Female
Over time hours Year to Date	115.9	12.1
Overtime hours last payroll	4.0	0.4

Source: Personnel data

Figure 4.1: Hours Worked on the Previous Working Day by Gender

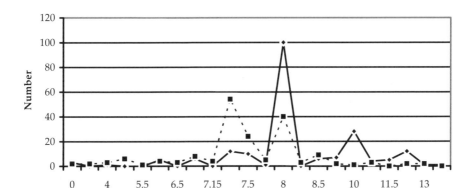

The ability of fathers to spend time with their children is thus constrained. Overall, however, UtilityCo does not have a culture of long hours. Only five employees reported working longer than 12 hours the previous day, and four of those reported that as unusual. The average hours worked in UtilityCo overall on the previous day were 8.6 hours, with over half of respondents working an eight-hour day, and 90 per cent working less than 10 hours. The pattern for men and women is slightly different because of a bi-modal pattern for women: they have two peaks — one at 7.25 and another at 8 hours (see Figure 4.1). For men, though, there is a single peak at 8 hours.

While male employees have a longer average working day, they are also less likely to be on reduced hours contracts and more likely to work overtime. However, as Table 4.1 highlighted, men in UtilityCo are older and have worked for longer in the company than women. This difference may bias the findings that men work longer hours than their female counterparts (see Table 4.3 which breaks down overtime by age category and gender).

Table 4.3: Average Overtime by Gender and Age

Age Category	Overtime Calculated Year to Date	
	Male	*Female*
Less than 30	87.7	9.0
30–39	129.1	11.5
40–49	126.7	16.1
Age 50+	112.7	10.1
Total	115.9	12.1

Source: Personnel data

Even when age is controlled for, men in the company are usually ten times more likely to work overtime than females. Men are also much less likely to be working a reduced hours contract (see Table 4.4) than women in the same age group. For instance, of all men in their thirties only 0.1 per cent work less than full time, but 19 per cent of women do.

Table 4.4: Per Cent Working Less than Full Time Hours by Gender and Age

Age Category	Male	Female
Less than 30	0.1	0.7
30-39	0.1	19.2
40-49	0.2	17.8
Age 50+	0.2	4.6

Source: Personnel data

This could reflect that men are concentrated in areas of the company where part-time working is seemingly more difficult to accommodate. Table 4.5 looks at one category of workers — clerical — that could shed light on this question. Yet, even when this category is controlled for, men are far less likely than women to work reduced hours contracts. Table 4.5 could be repeated for other categories of workers, but the conclusion would remain the same:

given age and category, women are always more likely to be on reduced hours contracts than men are; women are less likely to have worked overtime in the previous day; and women have, on average, a shorter working day.

Table 4.5: Per Cent Working Less than Full Time Hours by Gender and Age, Clerical Workers Only

Age Category	Male	Female
Less than 30	0	0
30-39	2.5	27.6
40-49	0	21.1
Age 50+	0	5.1

Source: Personnel data

This discrepancy in working time is translated into less take home pay for women. The average basic salary of men is €36,813, but women earn on average less than 80 per cent of this figure at €30,631. Men also received a third more permanent allowances than women in the company and 50 per cent more temporary allowances. Given the differences in overtime hours between men and women, a difference in overtime pay is not surprising but the extent of the gulf is: on average women took home €3,218 less in overtime than men did. This means that the average woman in UtilityCo took home only two thirds of what the average man took home (Table 4.6).

Table 4.6: Income by Gender % Female Earning of Male Earnings

	%
Salary	80
Cumulative earnings	75
Permanent allowances	34
Temp allowances	63
Overtime calculated	8

Source: Personnel data

The gender pay gap can be seen in all categories of income. Female employees have 80 per cent of the salary of male employees, 34 per cent of permanent allowances, 63 per cent of temporary allowances and only 8 per cent of the overtime of male employees. Part of the difference in pay between men and women is due to different average working hours. If only full-time employees are considered, the pay gap is 82.8 per cent for salary and 78.2 per cent for cumulative earnings years to date. So we have a situation where women work less, get paid less and therefore are less likely to get big income rises in the future — the disadvantage is cumulative.

While these breakdowns are interesting they do not allow us to examine parental status. We therefore conducted a questionnaire. There was a reasonable correspondence between questionnaire and personnel data on type of contract worked, age of respondent and length of service. A breakdown of employment status by gender reveals that men are much more likely to be employed in regular full time positions than women, and women are much likely than men to be on non-standard contracts such as part time or temporary contracts (Table 4.7). Nearly 23 per cent of women who answered the questionnaire are on non-standard contracts as opposed to just one per cent of men. Of the men on reduced hours contracts, none of them are fathers of school-aged children; however, 59 per cent of equivalent mothers are.

Table 4.7: Employment Status (%, rounded)

	Male %	Female %
Regular full time	95	70
Regular part time	1	13
Job sharer		5
Temporary Full Time (including contract)	4	5
Temporary Part Time (including contract)		7
Other	1	1
Total Number	218	195

Source: Questionnaire data

Overall the questionnaire revealed that older workers are more likely to be married, younger workers are more likely to be single or, if in a relationship, more likely to be cohabitating. As men are older than women in the company, on average, this means that men are more likely to be married. Thus, 80 per cent of men compared to 59 per cent of women are married. Only looking at the married or cohabitating employees (181 men and 133 women), we find that 62 per cent of men and 91 per cent of women had working partners. Of those with working partners (112 men and 119 women), 45 per cent of men's working partners worked part time as opposed to 4 per cent of women's working partners. Men whose partner was a full-time homemaker were aged on average 48.5, while those whose partner worked part-time were aged 45.5 and those whose partner worked full-time were aged 41.3.

As such, UtilityCo has a very traditional workforce — the modal pattern is men who work full time and have stay-at-home partners. But the situation is changing and younger men are much less likely to have a stay-at-home wife or partner (see Table 4.8 which looks at working hours by marital and parental status).

Overall, the average man worked 8.6 hours on the previous day. The average for men with children was 8.5 hours and 8.7 for men without children. However, an interesting pattern emerges when hours worked by marital status is looked at. All fathers work less hours than the equivalent non-fathers; the exception to this group are fathers whose partner is not in the labour force — this group of men work on average longer than the equivalent non-fathers.

The differences in working hours are interesting but do not tell us if men are able to combine their dual roles without working flexibly. Thus, a question was asked concerning whether flexible hours, if adopted, would help the employee. Four in ten men without children thought flexible hours would be no use whatsoever compared to only a quarter of men with children. The questionnaire respondents were also asked how flexibility would help them. The reasons given were: help manage child care (36 per cent), and spend time with their families (71 per cent). Yet only 10 per cent of fathers had taken parental leave; 20 per cent had taken paternity leave; and less than one per cent had taken a career break for child care purposes.

Table 4.8: Average Hours Worked the Previous Day by Gender and Marital Status

Marital Status		Male	Female
Single/widowed/divorced			
	No children	8.8	7.8
	Children	8.4	7.2
	Total	8.8	7.7
Partner not in paid employment			
	No children	8.4	7.8
	Children	8.5	8.0
	Total	8.5	8.0
Partner working part-time			
	No children	8.7	7.3
	Children	8.5	8.6
	Total	8.5	8.4
Partner working full-time			
	No children	8.9	7.5
	Children	8.7	7.0
	Total	8.8	7.2
Total			
	No children	8.7	7.6
	Children	8.5	7.2
	Total	8.6	7.4

Source: Questionnaire data

Four questions in the questionnaire sought to explore this issue further (see Tables 4.9 and 4.10). Overall, most workers do not think their working hours in UtilityCo are a problem, and there is very little variation in this belief between men and women. However, there is a difference between how parents and non-parents view working hours in UtilityCo. Fathers do not think the working times in UtilityCo are a problem, whereas mothers do. However, this generally positive view of fathers towards working hours hides differences between fathers.

Table 4.9: If You Have a Family, the Working Hours in UtilityCo are a Problem (%)

		Male	Female
Non-Parent			
	Strongly agree	10.5	5.3
	Agree	18.1	16.7
	Do not agree nor disagree	15.8	25.0
	Disagree	47.4	43.9
	Strongly disagree	8.3	9.1
Total		100.0	100.0
Parent			
	Strongly agree	7.2	13.2
	Agree	19.3	20.8
	Do not agree nor disagree	19.3	15.1
	Disagree	45.8	41.5
	Strongly disagree	8.4	9.4
Total		100	100

Source: Questionnaire data

The percentage of fathers agreeing that "If you have a family the working hours are a problem" increases with attachment of the father's partner to the labour force. If the father's partner is in the home full-time, 26.1 per cent think working hours are a problem, compared to 28.6 per cent of fathers who partners work part-time, and 36.6 per cent of men whose partners work full-time. Thus, if a man's partner is attached to the workforce, he is more likely to have problems with the hours.

Table 4.10: If You Have a Family, the Working Hours in UtilityCo are a Problem, Parents Only (%)

Marital Status		Male	Female
Single/widowed/divorced			
	Agree	66.7	83.3
	Do not agree or disagree		16.7
	Disagree	33.3	
		100.0	100.0
Partner not in paid employment			
	Agree	26.1	37.5
	Do not agree nor disagree	13.0	25.0
	Disagree	60.9	37.5
		100.0	100.0
Partner working part time			
	Agree	28.6	
	Do not agree nor disagree	19.0	25.0
	Disagree	52.4	75.0
		100.0	100.0
Partner working full time			
	Agree	36.6	30.9
	Do not agree nor disagree	14.6	11.8
	Disagree	48.8	57.4

Source: Questionnaire data

A clue to where the constraints for mothers and fathers might lie is found by looking at the answer to the question, "My family situation is taken into account by UtilityCo" (see Table 4.11). Again, there is little difference between the answers of men and women *per se*, but mothers are much more likely to agree with this question than fathers are. In other words, mothers feel that UtilityCo takes into account the family circumstances, but fathers do not feel that UtilityCo takes their family circumstances into account. Again, looking at marital status sheds light onto this distinction (see Table 4.11).

Table 4.11: My Family Situation is Taken into Account by UtilityCo, Parents Only (%)

Marital Status		Male	Female
Single/widowed/divorced			
	Agree	33.3	
	Do not agree nor disagree	66.7	16.7
	Disagree		83.3
		100.0	100.0
Partner not in paid employment			
	Agree	27.7	33.3
	Do not agree nor disagree	31.9	22.2
	Disagree	40.4	44.4
		100.0	100.0
Partner working part time			
	Agree	19.5	25.0
	Do not agree nor disagree	26.8	50.0
	Disagree	53.7	25.0
		100.0	100.0
Partner working full time			
	Agree	29.3	36.8
	Do not agree nor disagree	24.4	30.9
	Disagree	46.3	32.4

Source: Questionnaire data

Here an interesting difference emerges: while fathers with working partners think that UtilityCo does not take their family situation into account, it is fathers with partners working part-time who express most dissatisfaction with the situation. In contrast, women who are sole-breadwinners in their family do not think the company looks after their needs (but this figure needs to be treated with caution given the small sample size).

A further question was asked about promotion. Fathers with full-time or part-time working partners are likely to view promotion as a problem (26.3 and 21.4 per cent respectively). The group least likely to see it as a problem is fathers with a stay-at-home partner (14.9 per cent).

Thus, men who have wives and partners who work outside the home are more likely to be time pressured, and think the company does not take into account their circumstances. Yet they are not inclined to take reduced hours contracts. Why not? Is it that they are not aware of family friendly working policies? Do they think they would be discriminated against? Or that it would damage their career prospects?

Approximately 85 per cent of men and women say they are aware of UtilityCo's policies on equal opportunities, and two out of three respondents felt that UtilityCo did practise equal opportunities. Yet, when respondents looked at their manager they had a more jaundiced view. For instance, whereas 67 per cent of male respondents think UtilityCo takes equal opportunities seriously, only 50.2 per cent think that their manager does. The drop for women is less severe: 57 per cent of female respondents think UtilityCo takes equal opportunities seriously compared to 51.5 per cent who think their manager does.

According to one male worker, UtilityCo is just paying lip service to flexible working:

> When you go to look for it, they may not give it to you. . . .
> A lot depends on the local manager and who is asking. I
> have looked for it twice and have been turned down.

Thus, the attitudes of local management are implicated in fathers not viewing flexible working as a viable option. This is reflected in the attitude of one manager who stated that career breaks and job sharing were "really" for women: "One man applied for job share and we were aghast". The manager's reason for this attitude was the necessity of managers to be present: "Senior management could not job share. The role is important in the organisation; it requires your individual attention." This attitude was confirmed by a senior manager in UtilityCo who claimed that, in order to progress in the company, it is essential to put in the hours.

Clearly, part of the problem with men accessing family friendly working is the attitudes of their male managers — managers who themselves are more likely to have a stay-at-home partner. Another part of the explanation lies with the perception of part-time working. Specifically, both men and women thought that part-timers got unfairly treated in the company (see Table 4.12).

Table 4.12: The Perception of Who is Treated Better in UtilityCo

	Male	Female
Women — single	1.9	2.0
Women — married	1.9	2.2
Men — married	2.0	1.8
Men — single	2.0	1.9
Disabled people	2.0	2.0
Older employees	2.0	2.1
Younger employees	2.1	2.0
Temporary/Part-time staff	2.4	2.4

Source: Questionnaire data. A figure close to one indicates treatment is perceived to be better than average and close to three treatment is perceived to be worse than average.

Table 4.12 ranks the perception of employees about whom gets better treatment in the company. Both men and women agree temporary or part-time workers get treated least favourably — even more so than other possible marginal groups such as disabled, older or younger workers. As such, both men and women perceive that taking a reduced hours contract would deteriorate their treatment in the company (a perception reinforced in the responses of the part-time workers).

6. CONCLUSION

For decades after the founding of the Irish state there was a separation between investment and involvement with children (McKeown et al., 1998). This has now changed and both parents are increasingly expected to provide for their children financially and emotionally. The change for mothers has been recognised and is part of the public discourse. This can only be a good thing since two parents involved emotionally with children must be better than only one, assuming there are no dysfunctional family circumstances involved; likewise, two incomes reduces the risk of financial hardship under normal circumstances. At the same time, the change for men has not yet been recognised and is much more hidden as an issue.

With respect to the company, UtilityCo is a good place to work and employees view it as having equal opportunities policies. They also enjoy working there. However, only women avail of reduced hours policies in a day-to-day capacity. Men in UtilityCo are more welded to the idea of working regular, full-time hours and working as much overtime as possible. Yet, not all men are happy with this situation: young fathers in particular are likely to say that the company doesn't take into account their family situation. As several tables illustrate, the difference between younger and older men in the company is the employment status of their partners. So while young men think of UtilityCo as an equal opportunities employer, they actually perceive the company as not recognising their particular situation.

This paradox is partly explained by the informal ethos of the company: it is explicitly committed to equal opportunities, but implicitly committed to an image of a male breadwinner with a stay-at-home wife. The men at the top of the company came up ranks by fitting in with the company work practices and expectations, and therefore have little understanding of the changes in the family situation of men further down the ranks. Eventually, as men and women move up the hierarchy, this bias should change; but without active policy to encourage fathers to work flexibly, it might take a generation or more. This fits with findings from other countries which suggests that the uptake of family friendly working by men is inhibited by considerations of loss of income, increased workload and adverse impact on their career (Brandth and Kvande, 2001; Crompton, 2002; Lee and Duxbury, 1998).

Thus, even in a company with an exemplary history of equality measures, fathers are still reluctant to take family friendly working because it might damage their career. Until attitudes change, and it is as acceptable for men as women to take leave, this situation will continue. One way to make leave acceptable for men is to introduce legislation. At present Ireland is one of the few European countries where fathers have no entitlement to paternity leave. The Parental Leave Act of 1998 went some way to re-balance this bias — as it is available on a non-transfer basis to both parents. Yet the fact that it is unpaid and we still have a male-breadwinner ideology means that the take-up of parental leave is likely to be modest. Without a root and branch change in thinking to recognise that two-parent families are overwhelmingly two-earner families, fathers will continue to be caught in the trap of earning and caring. In that sense, Ireland echoes research in other countries which highlights the importance of welfare state ideology for the structure of the family — if the state takes a strong egalitarian position then the outcome for both mothers and fathers will be more equal (Bennett, 2002; Crompton, 2002; Esping-Andersen, 1990; Esping-Andersen, 1996; Korpi, 2000; Lane, 1993; Shaver, 2002). And the lessons for gender equality from those studies is that if we really want gender equality then we have to take fathers seriously (Featherstone, 2003).

Chapter 5

WOMEN AND WORK IN THE IRISH ICT SECTOR

Lidia Greco

1. INTRODUCTION

It is often argued that modern societies allow the prevalence of meritocratic values and that workplaces hinge upon non-gender biased behaviours. Empirical investigation however continues to show much variation in the work lives of men and women. This variation concerns both "structural" elements, such as careers, wages and work conditions, and the "emotions" of work that deeply affect workplace dynamics. Nonetheless, the specific study of gender relations in post-Fordist bureaucratic organisations has been a neglected area of organisational studies. Consideration of a gender perspective allows us to analyse the practices that, in flexible work organisations, reproduce gender differences and, more importantly, highlight the hidden mechanisms that, encapsulated into cultural values, lie at the basis of organisations. This approach is also sensitive to contradictions and ambiguities in the social construction of gender relations in organisations, where discrimination or equal opportunities are generated. Finally, it allows us to consider the meaning and consequences of what are culturally defined as masculine and feminine ways of thinking, valuing and acting (Alvesson and Billing, 1997).

This chapter explores women's work in the Irish information and communication technology (ICT) companies on the basis of a series of biographical interviews. It aims to shed some light on the organisation of work and on the model of industrial relations in the Irish ICT companies and their implications for women's employment. It investigates women's presence at the workplace and their career paths as well as their strategies to balance the private and public sphere. It seeks therefore to provide an understanding of the opportunities, choices, limits, coping strategies and detours that organisations pose to women's work — as perceived by women.

In Ireland as in other countries, employment in the ICT sector is traditionally a male "preserve". Nonetheless, during the 1990s, the industry's rapid growth offered a series of unexpected opportunities to women willing to enter the industry. Companies hired a significant number of women with non-technical skills, alongside those with strong technical competences. In addition, the nature of the tasks involved at work and the organisation of the labour process guaranteed women the opportunity of doing challenging jobs that were relatively better paid than jobs in other sectors. Arguably, then, the sector underwent a process of feminisation in an expansionary phase of the country's economy. In addition, women entered ICT organisations following the Government's and other institutions' efforts to orient women towards more technical subjects at university and in the economy.

This chapter suggests that the prevailing configuration of work and employment relationships in the Irish ICT industry produce new and different forms of inequality through a variety of symbolic and material factors. At the same time, women's presence in the Irish ICT sector is shaped by the ways women develop their own biographies based on the paths available to them in gendered contexts.

2. FLEXIBLE WORK ORGANISATIONS AND WOMEN'S EMPLOYMENT

The new economy in the context of globalisation has transformed economic and social relations across the globe. Contemporary organisations require constant innovation to compete (Asheim, 2000); and knowledge has become the means to achieve competitive advantage (Drucker, 1969). The organisation of work and the model of employment relationships have radically changed too (Drucker, 1988; Gibbons et al., 1994; Castells, 2000; Newell et al., 2002) (see Table 5.1)). Yet, all work processes and workplaces have not undergone the same transformations. Traditional forms of organisation continue to survive along with their job structures and employment relations.

Table 5.1: Comparing Bureaucratic and Flexible Work Organisations

Bureaucratic Organisation	Flexible Organisation
Hierarchy	Autonomy
Specialisation	Multi-skilling
Internal career and opportunities based on qualification and skill	External career path based on achievements and subject to market appraisal
Internal generalised training	Individualised training
Pay related to rank and seniority	Performance-related pay
Command and control supervision	Micro-level job control
Job security	Employability security
Collective bargaining	Individual claims

At organisational level, flexibility, multi-skilling, job autonomy and self-responsibility have displaced rigid divisions of labour and the fragmentation of tasks. Such features are especially crucial managing knowledge workers (Newell et al., 2002). Because of the intangible nature of knowledge-based services, relations of command and control are inadequate to manage the information and analysis that "symbolic analysts" provide (Reich, 1991; Newell et al., 2002). Instead, managing knowledge workers requires flexibility and individualisation. Consequently, wages, career progression and benefits have become increasingly individualised, linked to the market through performance; while the system of industrial relations has been displaced by a human resources management framework.

Further, bridging barriers between company areas and between sectors and occupations is recognised as an added value. Cooperation may occur in two ways: workplace teamwork that encourages group interaction and shared activities (Prahalad and Hamel, 1994); and devolution of responsibilities from management to the employee based on trust (Osterman, 2000). Thus, decision-making becomes more dispersed; organisations undergo delayering; and learning and knowledge are increasingly conceptualised as social activities rather than individual endeavours (Brown and Druguid, 1991; Wenger, 1998).

The demise of bureaucratic organisations seemed to open up new opportunities for women at work. For some feminists, bureaucracies are inherently masculine (Ferguson, 1984) because bureaucratic features are typically associated with masculinity or acting in masculine ways (Wajcman, 1996). In addition, bureaucratic arrangements such as full-time work and long-term employment relationship work against women (Stone, 2001). For others, organisations are not gendered but become biased in favour of men through organisational structures of power and the social composition of jobs (Kanter, 1977). More cultural explanations suggest that patriarchal processes of gender and identity construction influence women's perceptions of their role both at work and in the family (Acker, 1990; 1998). By prising the public from the private sphere, bureaucracies influence decisions concerning future work options and construction of career paths.

The re-configuration of work towards less rigid practices and reduced hierarchies is supposed to make organisations less prone to gendered practices and values. Work is typically project-based and carried out by teams; teamwork fosters porous gender roles, allowing individuals to reconfigure their expected social positions; individualisation of career paths allows employees to shape their careers; the focus on knowledge blurs the contours of gender identities; and the workplace become gender neutral, promoting equality between male and female employees. The remaining sections of the paper explore these contentions in the context of the Irish software industry.

3. WOMEN ENTER THE IRISH ICT INDUSTRY: OVERVIEW AND RESEARCH METHODS

For the Irish economy, the 1990s was a decade of sustained growth. Thus, the labour market expanded by 38,000 units per annum between 1991 and 1999. A substantial contribution came from women: their participation rate grew from 35 per cent in 1991 to 56 per cent in 2000 (European Commission, 2002). Female employment expanded under socio-institutional factors such as modified fertility patterns, higher educational achievements, the removal of legislative constraints on female employment and the introduction of the employment equality legislation.

The feminisation of the labour market affected all sectors of the Irish economy. A significant number of women seized the opportunities offered by fast growing sectors such as ICT including software. Its revenues grew from €2,189 million in 1991 to €10,150 million in 2000,[1] contributing nearly 10 per cent of national GDP despite employing only around 2 per cent of the total workforce. During the 1990s, employment in the software industry grew by 15 per cent annually compared to 6 per cent for the rest of the economy (Arora et al., 2001: 5). In addition, employment in the software sector grew faster than in all other manufacturing sectors (McIver Consulting, 1998: 12) and growth in the second half of the decade was almost twice the first: 20.6 per cent and 10.9 per cent

[1] Data from the National Informatics Directorate, previously known as the National Software Directorate. This is a subsection within Enterprise Ireland, an Irish governmental organisation. Data can be found on the following webpage http://www.nsd.ie/htm/ssii/stat.htm

respectively (Crone, 2002: 5). By the end of 2002, 30 per cent of those employed in the industry were women (CSO, 2003). Yet, women in software were more likely to have lower levels of education and to enter the sector with non-technical or "soft" technical skills, holding degrees in Arts or Languages.

Women's presence in the ICT industry was therefore a novel phenomenon for both companies and women entering them. The next sections of the chapter use qualitative material to explore some of the issues around women and work in the industry. The data come from a European funded project called "Widening Women's Work in Information and Communication Technology" that involved Ireland and six other European countries.[2] The project investigated the gender gap in ICT professions and proposed pathways to improve women's participation in the sectoral labour market. Biographical narratives and employment trajectories were the instruments used to investigate gender presence and relationships. The aim was to explore how women engage reflexively with opportunities and constraints and to highlight the resources they mobilise during transition periods.

This approach is complementary to an analysis of organisational structures and cultures. Twenty biographical interviews were conducted in the period between October 2002 and February 2003. The women interviewed belong to different ages and professional categories; married women and women with children were interviewed along with single women. Some men were also interviewed to compare and contrast experiences (see Table 5.2).

---

[2] These countries were: Italy, the UK, Austria, Belgium, France and Portugal.

Table 5.2: Respondents' Basic Information

Inter-viewee	Sex	Age	Marital Status	Chil-dren	Job Title
1	M	31	Cohabiting	None	Senior software engineer
2	F	32	Married	None	Senior software engineer
3	F	30	Cohabiting	None	Technical writer
4	F	24	Single	None	Localisation engineer
5	F	26	Single	None	IT manager
6	F	27	Cohabiting	None	Data mining manager
7	F	28	Married	None	Project manager
8	M	31	Cohabiting	None	Developer
9	M	32	Cohabiting	None	Developer
10	F	39	Married	One	Programme manager
11	F	32	Married	One	Software developer
12	F	-	Married	Two	Senior engineer
13	F	32	Cohabiting	None	Tech writer (left industry)
14	F	33	Cohabiting	None	Technical writer
15	F	35	Married	One	Senior software engineer
16	F	31	Cohabiting	None	Unix sys administrator
17	M	34	Married	One	Programme manager
18	M	31	Cohabiting	None	Marketing manager
19	F	41	Cohabiting	Two	Engineering manager
20	F	25	Single	None	Software Eng (left industry)

4. WOMEN AND ICT WORK ORGANISATION AND EMPLOYMENT RELATIONSHIPS

Two key aspects characterise work in the Irish ICT companies studied. First, work is based on projects consisting of the manufacture and development of a product, a specific part of a product or the development of an intermediate or final service. The duration of a project, from weeks to years, defines the flow and quantity of work. Typically, the project manager defines a series of deadlines that will allow the achievement of the final deadline. This defines the date on which the product is to be released and is often dictated by market expectations linked to sales.

Working by projects undermines traditional work organisation and unleashes new potentialities. One of the dimensions that undergoes a radical change is the notion of time (O'Carroll, 2003). Freed from fixed working hours, ICT workers have become increasingly task-oriented: what is important is the completion of work (symbolised by a deadline) and not the way in which work is organised or achieved. This means that employees enjoy a relatively wide space of manoeuvre with regard to working times and the amount of daily work. Overall, long working hours is not a characteristic of the Irish ICT sector. Nonetheless, long working hours are potential and unpredictable, a matter of fact when the project deadline approaches. From a wider perspective, this notion of time and the flexibility deriving from it would seem to allow employees the combination of public and private spheres. In addition, without heavy formal control, individuals are supposed to be able to manage themselves. A company's emphasis is on self-management and responsibility towards the project and colleagues and friends who are in the team. Work contracts in the Irish industry are full-time reflecting the industry's young and mainly male dominated workforce. Thus, the industry's practice of flexible working time does not include contractual alternatives to full-time work.

Second, the workforce in the Irish ICT companies is organised in teams. Teams are of various sizes but typically include a team leader and a number of engineers. Each team contributes to the development of a specific aspect of the project. In turn, individuals in each team are in charge of a specific job; in some cases, people may work simultaneously on different projects. Being part of a team requires cooperation and alignment with others' work; it implies the distribution of tasks, the discussion of issues and the production and control of reports. Teamwork, as a genuine work practice, synthesises therefore parcelisation and a global vision. It offers the opportunity of enjoying close personal relationships with colleagues; in addition, it is a widespread belief in the industry that a good team influences the qualitative outcome at work. A team has a limited internal hierarchy: managers are visible and close. Teamwork relationships are in other words nurtured by a great deal of informality. This is reflected in work practices and organisational culture. Social events often take place with the aim of team building. Further, employment relations are individualised: career paths, wages and work conditions are negotiated individually and are performance-driven. Trade unions are absent in nearly all companies.

Several strands of sociological and management literature have stressed the positive implications that the work practices highlighted above have on both employees and company's performances (Arthur and Rousseau, 1996). Whilst not denying the overall positive nature of these work arrangements, I suggest that the main qualifying features of the work organisation in the Irish ICT companies poses great challenges to the women working in the industry and to other groups in the workforce, such as male parents. Such challenges need to be highlighted as they affect not only the quality of women's presence in the industry but also their chances of remaining in it. The evidence given below is organised according to the issues highlighted in this section.

Working Time Arrangements and the Blurring of "Private-Public" Borders

The flexibility of working hours is something that employees in the Irish ICT companies greatly appreciate. As employees work on individualised schedules, they are able to modulate their daily work. As suggested below:

> With concern to working time, the standard would be 9.00 to half past 5.00, I suppose traditionally; but in our teamwork we are actually quite flexible and so particularly it depends on where people live or if they have activities in the evening. It is ok to start earlier and finish earlier or to

start late and finish late, provided that the work is done (interviewee 7).

However, time self-management and task orientation are often prone to erode the private sphere and to collide with private interests; ultimately, they become a source of disadvantage at work for those categories of workers, primarily women, that have family commitments. The unpredictability of working hours, especially when deadlines approach, blurs the borders between work and private life and the incursions of the first in the second become very common. The achievement of a deadline becomes the main priority: it is not uncommon therefore that employees are requested to stretch their working days or be available during the weekends. The flexibility of working times are bartered with potential long working hours and the unpredictability of work in some circumstances, according to "tacit" or "unspoken agreements" existing in the industry. In some cases, the invasion of work into the private sphere is formalised. As indicated below:

> . . . in your contract, it says, if you have to work overtime to get your work done it is expected of you. It is actually in the contract when you sign, you cannot say you didn't know (interviewee 7).

Potential long working hours and work unpredictability become serious issues for working mothers and in particular those who do not have a supporting partner or cannot rely on child care provision. Further, in contrast to the rhetoric, time spent at work and the full availability when conditions require it symbolise commitment to the organisation, responsibility and productivity. Commitment in these organisations is often constructed as finite and non-expandable, implying that somebody with commitments outside work is less reliable and productive. Women with children are the most penalised for two reasons: since they still carry the main burden of family duties, women often fail to meet these expectations; and many internalise this discourse, accepting penalties deriving from it. In most cases, women's inability to ensure the commitment requested by the organisation implies give up further responsibility in it:

> The fact that I have to leave at 5.30 every day I think would make it difficult for me to have more responsibilities. I think I could do more. . . . It is not limiting me and my current job and I am not looking for anything else at the moment. I made a choice (interviewee 11).

Any Flexibility but No "Non-Standard" Contracts

Contracts in the Irish ICT industry are typically full-time. If requested specific arrangements are worked out individually, through individual negotiations, and often at great cost for the single worker. Out of the four women with children interviewed during this research, three were on a full-time job. Furthermore, individual preferences become much more difficult to arrange if they needed to be reconciled with management responsibilities, as indicated below from a woman manager:

> I have two engineers in my team who do that [work from home] but it is easier for an engineer than for a manager, because an engineer would be in touch all day by e-mail and it does work pretty well, but I think for a manager you cannot do telework, you need to be in the office, going around, talking to people and seeing what's happening, getting updated (interviewee 12).

Such individual, unsystematic, arrangements can be said to produce neither a change in the organisational culture nor do they alter individual perceptions. In other words, the narratives of these women show how organisations' dominant values remain intact when it comes to the social construction of the "ideal worker". Such values affect also how workers who make use of non-standard contracts perceive themselves and are perceived within organisations. The same manager explains:

> It's more difficult for women to reduce working hours in
> the company . . . if you want to reduce your working hours,
> there is a kind of feeling that they could get someone else
> who could do the job and do more (interviewee 12).

Maternity is another meaningful example of a cultural constraint
that is difficult to overcome. A well-established (although illegal)
practice in these companies consists of not replacing women who
are going to take maternity leave. A process of work reorganisation occurs within the team whose members take charge
of the functions exercised by the person who is leaving or is away.
Therefore, while team self-organisation is an example of adaptation to changing conditions, it is also true that women's sense of
entitlement is interpreted more as a perk rather than as a basic
human need and right. Since organisational responses to employees' family needs are often constructed as benefits rather than
rights, their entitlement creates anxiety as the sense of equity and
responsibility towards colleagues is also considered important.

The "Flat" Organisation from Another Perspective:
The Personalisation of Work Relationships

Teamwork in Irish ICT companies is said to contribute positively
to individual achievements and, indirectly, to corporate performances. Less attention has been paid to the implications for women
employees of the tendency for teamwork to "personalise" work
relationships. The blurring of borders between personal and professional dimensions is conceptualised and treated as unproblem-
atic. By contrast, the empirical evidence suggests that the actual
possibility of balancing work and domestic responsibilities lie in
the capacity of establishing "friendly" work relationships with
one's own manager. Conversely, it would seem that pure professional relationships are not sufficient. This aspect differentiates
women's and men's experiences. In many of women's narratives
and in none of the ones told by men, a negative personal relationship with the manager rather than the actual content or nature of
the job has been a source of negative work performance and emo-

tional strain that — in the most serious cases — led to the decision to quit. As interviewee 10 remembers:

> The guy I reported to, I never really got on well with him, I never really thought he listened to me or wanted my input, so I left. I never tried to make a deal with him. I think it was more about the fact I couldn't really get on with him (interviewee 10).

Situations in which women had to manage difficult relationships with their bosses are also more common. As interviewee 3 explained:

> I know one girl . . . she is very able and she had a lot of difficulties related to the project she worked on. She got very frustrated because her immediate boss, he was very dismissive of her problems . . . she was always treated by her superior like she wasn't able, and generally speaking the women in the department did not particularly like that manager they found him quite patronising (interviewee 3).

Conversely, when friendly relationships between managers and employees are established, the manager acts as a facilitator in circumstances when work and family life needs to be balanced and in cases of career advancements. For example, interviewee 12 noted that:

> The first time I went to maternity leave, [the name of a woman colleague] was actually my manger at that time, so she was very understanding about the issue. Then, when I was away she kept my job open for me and it was still available for me when I came back (interviewee 12).

Informality: Women, Networks and Power Relations

The informality of work relationships and practices was regarded as a major source of attraction by the vast majority of respondents. However, it was simultaneously seen as problematic by many of the same workers, particularly by women. Informality was said to be the perfect environment for the production and reproduction of power relations. Through social practices such as playing football together or going out for beer, the actors involved retain, select and pass knowledge and job opportunities within the company's internal labour market. If power is conceptualised as relational (Foucault, 1971), it follows that insiders have better chances of hearing about job opportunities and gaining a reputation among managers. Informality caused problems for women across a range of experiences such as the absence of clear criteria for promotions:

> Often people would become promoted without anybody else knowing there was a vacancy available. Suddenly you would hear this person got this job, but in the public sector if any vacancy comes up it is published inside, outside, that is very clear and open, process of applications and interview and selections. In the private sector suddenly somebody has got this job and you go "I would have been interested been in that job", but you would never have known (interviewee 16).

Informality also fuelled the laddish culture, leading to marginality for women:

> . . . there were about 40 people in the IT department, maybe 3 or 4 women out of 40 and I found I hated it at the beginning. There was a very bullying atmosphere and I don't know if it is in all workplaces, and people were just not nice to each other . . . maybe I felt it because I was a woman, but to be honest, there were women who were in that group of people as well (interviewee 16).

5. WOMEN'S CAREER PATHS

Most of the themes illustrated in the previous sections are present in the two exemplary career narratives presented below. They have been chosen as they symbolise the mix of strategies and accidental detours that women in Irish ICT companies have adopted at work.

Planning a Career: Playing with Men's Rules, Adaptive Behaviour and Survival Strategies

Interviewee 10 works as a programme manager in a medium size Irish company. She worked as an engineer first and then as a project leader — at one time leading up to 40 people. On the verge of 40, she has achieved one of the highest managerial levels in her company.

After her first job of three years, interviewee 10 entered a company that marked her consequent career moves. In a dynamic and technically advanced environment, interviewee 10 discovered a passion for her work. The company was the first one in Ireland to develop C++ (a computer language) and interviewee 10 was one of its developers. Despite the disorganisation, interviewee 10 found that life in the company was extremely fascinating. The company was eventually taken over, but that did not worry interviewee 10. As she recalls:

> We weren't concerned really about the job at that stage, we were all young, no mortgage, no children, no worries. We were just happy to be kept together as a group. . . . We were quite cocky about it: we were skilled, we were good, we had no problem in getting a new job, and in fact a lot of people didn't have any problem to get a new job when they started to drop off.

Around the same time, interviewee 10 started to realise the gendered nature of her workplace. Although not hostile, workplace relations occurred in a male-dominated context, embedding male cultural values. Realising this, she began to assume men's behaviours convinced that the survival in a male environment implied "to be like men". As she recalls:

> You need to compete. When you go in somewhere you have to have your first success before they start taking you

seriously and your first success is always you being right and the others being wrong. It is an element to prove yourself, you arrive in a company and you start working on the project and until you get to a position where — there is always a dominant guy on the team — and until he's wrong and you are right, you'll never be respected. Once you have done that once, you will be asked again.

This choice affected how she planned her career. The interviewee changed job and joined another company. However, disagreement about a project led to her early departure. Interviewee 10 was also put off by the lack of competitive atmosphere that she had come to love in her previous job. In her next job, she again found what she was looking for:

When I went to [IT company] I went in with the attitude that I was going to make it work, it was a very successful project. The head of the technical direction . . . would be responsible for looking at new technologies and to investigate this or that. He had what I called "the hobby group". He was great and the people around were great, and we worked on things that nobody had worked on before.

As the work environment hinged upon masculine values in this company too, interviewee 10 had to prove her competence; yet, it was not acknowledged precisely because of her gender:

I worked with an engineer who wasn't . . . very kind and he knew it all and we had many fights. I guess he was ok, he was a funny guy, but he was a bit mean, nobody really liked him because he was very ambitious, so he came in to make his mark. . . . I think, after 6-8 months he learnt how to respect me because I did more than him, I was more experienced and there was a huge amount of stuff that he could learn from me. . . . It didn't work out like that because I worked very hard, because I stayed there long hours, I liked the work and I was never leaving before 8.00 o'clock in the evening, from 10.00 o'clock in the morning, every day.

Clearly, work had become very much a lifestyle for interviewee 10. When she joined her present company, interviewee 10 assumed a managerial role. Soon after, though, her decision to have a child put interviewee 10 in a new situation. The male environment with which she had learnt to come to terms showed its lack of support. During her pregnancy, she carried on working the same amount of hours conscious that it would not be accepted if she slowed down. She went on maternity leave at the time in which the new product on which her team had worked was about to be released. By this time, the value of her private life was as great as the interviewee's care for her job:

> When I went to maternity leave, I was paranoid: I had built the product from nothing and it was my baby as well. I organised the manager that I knew and I said I wanted to go back to it [the job] after the maternity leave, rather than come back and do other stuff. The one who worked for me, he didn't really want to do it, but he did it. He said that he was taking the job for the period when I was in maternity leave and then I would take over once back. I set him up and I told him what to do when I was gone.

Interviewee 10 entered the Irish software industry with a strong technical background before the boom period of the mid-1990s. At that time, women's presence in the sector was scarce: the first company in which she worked had around 30 employees and only two of them were women. This "structural" condition had a significant impact on the way interviewee 10 approached her career. Yet, her work story, moving from one job or company to another, shows conscious personal choices activating different resources and strategies. The most important detour of her career occurred because of her child's birth; more precisely, when she found out that her child was ill and needed therapy.

A Broken Career in the ICT Sector: Accidental Entry and Conscious Exit

Interviewee 13 is an Irish woman who entered the IT sector nearly 10 years ago. Hers is a story of a woman who did not choose to enter the industry. Her educational background and personal attitudes were ones that would be incompatible with the IT sector. Due to a series of accidental events, she got her first job in the industry and then moved twice. In the course of her professional path, interviewee 13 realised the cost of being in an environment to which she was not attracted and, ultimately, disliked. Recently, she decided to leave the sector. Interviewee 13 has a degree in English and History. While participating in computer classes, she never had an interest in them. After college, she did a computer course for a year but:

> I was put down that I wasn't very good at maths, because you have to have functions and all this sort of things to be able to program . . . at that time people were only interested in teaching how to program, and I had no interest in how to program.

Like many graduates she looked for her first job and encountered difficulties. However, her brother worked for a small company that had a contract with an Irish bank and it offered her a job. In this sense, her first encounter with the ICT sector was accidental. The job was not a technical job as it consisted of replacing old back-office hardware with new computers: her brother and another man were in charge of fixing and testing the system. Although interviewee 13 eventually became a project administrator, her work consisted of dealing with clients. By this time, she felt the shadow of segregation, especially in relation to learning opportunities:

> I wasn't actually dealing with the tech side of it, which I did complain about. I thought it was sexist because they would send the guys to a course in IBM and I got really pissed off about that and they knew more about that than

me. But part of the reason was that they could train me up to do the job that the other guys were doing, they couldn't train them how to talk to people on the phone or schedule meetings.

With no future prospects and without codified technical knowledge, interviewee 13 accepted a friend's suggestion to apply to another company as a technical writer. In that period, the industry was booming and the company was expanding. As she recalls, the company was "hiring people continuously and they had three or four new people starting every week for the first three months". This circumstance favoured interviewee 13 who got the job in the company as a technical writer but "no other jobs because I didn't know anything about computers at all when I left college, no experience at all". Her initial confidence about her abilities in this new work context clashed with the structure of power hinging on technical knowledge:

> Once I got into the company if you were looking for promotion, you had to pretend you knew more than you really did. At the beginning I was not faking. At the beginning it's normal to ask questions, but after six months you are supposed to know what you are talking about, so you stop asking. When people asked me to do something I used to say, "ok, no problem" even though I had no clue about what they were talking about. So that was difficult. If you are a woman in a woman environment and you talk about computers it's easier to admit, "I don't know what you are talking about", but if you are a woman and you are around men you have to pretend you know everything otherwise they make fun of you.

Further, the production process was informed by gender-biased rules in that all scripts had to go through an editorial phase and then be sent to an IT consultant to be verified. The IT consultants were mostly men in the programming area. As interviewee 13 explains:

Writers are less important than the IT consultants, despite the fact that many of the writers knew as much on the subject as the IT consultants did, and they certainly in a lot of cases worked a lot harder than the IT consultants. I think there was this fear in the company that if they gave writers a greater sense of importance, and if they were given the same sort of responsibilities as IT consultants have, they would want to be paid the same.

Alongside the difficulty of coping with her work environment and rules, interviewee 13 felt uncomfortable with some specific aspects of jobs in the ICT industry. As she indicates:

In the IT business, you have to keep updated about your subject all the time, re-train constantly and keep informed of what is happening and I think you can really do that if you have some interest. There are only two ways you can do that: one is to be really interested and the other one is if you have a real financial incentive. I had neither of these so I had no idea of what's going on in the IT world. That is why I left at the end.

Favoured by positive circumstances, interviewee 13's story epitomises the story of many Irish women who entered the industry with "soft" competences and low personal inclination and soon faced the difficulty of coping with the structure of priorities where "heavy" technical skills were considered central for climbing the career ladder.

6. CONCLUSIONS

In the last decade or so, discourses on the new knowledge economy have overwhelmingly taken the stage and quickly found a crowd of enthusiastic followers. Driven primarily by ICTs, the focus on knowledge as the main source of wealth creation and the role attributed to knowledge workers suggested that the traditional bureaucratic command and control structures were being jettisoned in favour of more flexible team- and project-based organisations. Hierarchies and role separation gave way to trust, coordination and informality. In this context, what matters is workers' contribution to knowledge creation. An obvious implication of such discourses is that a gender analysis of knowledge intensive work organisations would prove their gender neutrality and, consequently, their less iniquitous nature towards women's employment.

This chapter has used empirical evidence to investigate if such theoretical claims are justified in the specific reality of the Irish ICT industry. It has explored the existence of some gender inequalities within companies. On the basis of biographical interviews, the chapter indicates that the growth of the industry in Ireland has supplied many Irish women the opportunity to enter innovative organisations and to do challenging jobs. However, it has also shown that the nature of the ICT industry conceals a number of problematic aspects for the women working in it. Potential and unpredictable long working hours are a problem for working mothers who, in addition, have no possibility to access non-standard employment contracts.

In many Irish ICT organisations, human resources management and labour relations have little in common with long established industries. When companies (the majority in the Irish case) do not have more structured internal systems and established criteria, career progressions and wage negotiations are individualised and, therefore, heavily dependent on managers' appraisals. Coupled with the individualisation of employment relationships, the prevailing context of informality negatively affects women's employment. "Presenteeism", expressed both at work with long working hours and total availability, and in social events, seems to be a typical male habit playing against women with family responsibilities.

The chapter does not suggest that Irish ICT companies produce clear discriminatory practices. Nonetheless, the generalised claim that they are gender-neutral neglects the gendered nature of organisations and the hidden barriers that — under the heading of company's cultural values and practices — prevent women from

the achievement of a full professional development. It is in this respect that new and different forms of inequality have come to the
surface in the industry.

Chapter 6

A "CHILLY CULTURE" FOR WOMEN? GENDERED EXCLUSIONS IN ICT WORK

Paschal Preston **and** *Carol MacKeogh*

The new knowledge-based society must be an inclusive society . . . [and] in emphasising digital inclusion, the European Commission aims to distinguish the European approach to the information society from other regions of the
world (EC 2002: 4).

1. POST-FEMINISM AND "MAINSTREAMING GENDER"

The "knowledge society" of the early twenty-first century seems
to be marked by very insecure, if not contradictory, understandings of the relations between women, technology and work. On
the one hand, some have defined the advent of a new century as
an important "moment for rethinking" the prevailing concepts
and images of women and men's roles and status in the workplace and in the wider society (Hughes and Kerfoot, 2002: 473).
Many of the established concepts, concerns and values which had
animated feminist thinking over the latter third of the twentieth
century now seem to be subject to major challenges, even if only
in the form of benign neglect.

These challenges are manifest both in terms of the academic
literature and especially at the level of the everyday experience.

Popular discourses assume or assert that women have "made it". Commentators declare that we have reached a truly "post-feminist" era and they frequently "cite evidence of widening opportunities, choices and potential in women's lives" to back up such claims (Hughes and Kerfoot, 2002: 474).

Indeed, the idea that we have arrived at a "post-feminist era" has become a popular theme in the mass media in recent years. This idea is usually centred round a number of overlapping claims to the effect that: support for the women's movement has dramatically eroded and many young women are increasingly anti-feminist, often suggesting that the movement is irrelevant to contemporary society or adopting a "no, but . . ." version of feminism (Hall and Rodrigues, 2003). Such claims have filtered through the contemporary popular culture even if some academic researchers find that the underlying assumptions are unsubstantiated and emphasise that there is little empirical support for such post-feminist claims (Hall and Rodrigues, 2003).

Of course, during the 1960s and 1970s, the academy proved to be an influential site for the revival of feminist politics. It operated as an important resource for the articulation of powerful critiques of gender inequalities in the workplace and other social arenas. Indeed, gender studies has been one of the major growth areas of the social science and humanities fields since the 1970s. This included research focused on women's changing if unequal position in the economy and the arena of paid work, a significant portion of which addressed the role of new IT and other technology issues (Bowlby and Preston, 1985). But even as regards academic research and theoretical concerns, some researchers now worry as to whether such feminist concerns are becoming merely "the province of old (or middle-aged) women" (Rupp, 2001: 165).

On the other hand, in recent years there has been a significant increase in official, state-sponsored policy initiatives to reduce gender exclusions or inequalities, especially those related to economic and employment domains. Here, in particular, we may note the growth of a distinctive "state-sponsored feminism", much of it with a focus on gender aspects of participation in new

ICT and other "high-technology", research or knowledge-intensive sectors. Indeed, Ireland and many other EU member countries have witnessed a spate of both EU-level and national government initiatives explicitly focused on "mainstreaming gender" issues in recent years. Such policy strategies are manifestly concerned to increase women's participation in the technology or knowledge-intensive industries and occupations that are deemed central to an increasingly "knowledge-based" economy or "information society". In addition, concerns about gender inequalities (women's "exclusion") have been at the heart of many "digital divide" initiatives launched by governmental and industrial agencies in recent years. Such "inclusion initiatives" have been explicitly framed to eliminate or reduce what are perceived as significant inequalities in the levels of women's participation with respect to the design, production and use of new digital technologies as well as their access to or use of the Internet.

This chapter addresses empirical aspects of women's changing roles and participation in the production and use of new information and communication technologies (ICTs) with particular emphasis on the Irish context where this sector is especially important. As leading-edge or pervasive new technologies in the contemporary economy, new ICTs may be treated as strategic sites for analysing the evolving role and forms of gendered inequalities (Bowlby and Preston, 1985). As regards the current debates and the apparent uncertainties or antimonies surrounding women's participation and roles, our research suggests that declarations of the demise or irrelevance of feminist concerns about gender equality in the workplace are somewhat premature. Indeed, we will indicate how this applies with particular force to the modes and levels of women's participation in the new ICT production sector.

The chapter draws on selective aspects of Ireland-based research conducted as part of an EU-funded, multi-country project: "Strategies for Inclusion: Gender and the Information Society" (SIGIS). In Section 2, we briefly describe the overall concerns and key findings emerging from this project concerning women's engagement with new ICTs. In Section 3, we summarise our findings related to women's roles and participation in the new ICT supplying sector and in the wider information economy. In Section 4 we draw on some case studies to address some of the key features and factors impacting on women's relative "exclusion" in the new ICT sector. Finally in Section 5 we flag some conclusions and implications arising from this study.

2. WOMEN AND ICT VERSUS WOMEN IN ICT

This chapter draws on research conducted as part of the SIGIS project which was set up to "inquire into inclusion strategies to involve women in the development and use of ICTs". This project focused on "inclusion" efforts and initiatives related to women's engagement with new ICTs in the context of the EU's "information society" project and prevailing concerns about the "digital divide". SIGIS's aims centred on: analysis of a range of such inclusion strategies and processes; drawing lessons from the relative success and failure of such efforts; and providing a knowledge base to support new inclusion efforts.

The SIGIS work was undertaken by five research centres from Ireland, Italy, the Netherlands, Norway and the UK in 2001–2003. Funded by the EU, SIGIS is probably one of the largest studies of gender and technology ever. The project partners undertook detailed reviews of the relevant statistics and literature in the five countries whilst they conducted and analysed 48 case studies over a two and a half year period. The SIGIS research included three clusters of case studies: private sector initiatives; public sector initiatives; and user-orientated case-studies. In total, SIGIS investigated 30 inclusion initiatives and 18 user studies in a diverse range of settings.[1]

One of the key findings from the SIGIS project's combination of ICT production and user orientated research concerns a significant distinction between the evolving status of *women in ICT* on

[1] All of the SIGIS research reports are available on-line: www.sigis-ist.org. The authors acknowledge the financial support of the EC's Fifth Framework (IST) programme which made this research possible.

the one hand and *women and ICT* on the other. Overall, we found that more women than men are excluded, both as users and as designers/producers of new information and communications technologies. But this research indicates that the levels and scope of women's relative exclusion are less marked when it comes to the use of new ICTs compared to the situation in the production and design of ICTs.

As regards the *use* of ICT products and services, the overall trend is one of reducing or closing the gender gap. Yet, this research concludes that diffusion alone is not sufficient to close the gap all together. Specific inclusion efforts are still warranted in this area. By contrast, there is a persistent and sizeable gender gap when it comes to the design and supply of new ICTs. In sum, the SIGIS research suggests that the overall picture across Europe is a contradictory one: optimistic with respect to what we call women *and* ICT but pessimistic with respect to women *in* ICT.

Our surveys indicate that there are now very few differences between men's and women's computer and Internet usage in Ireland; indeed, some data suggest that women's usage may now exceed that of male users. At the same time, we confirmed a continuing, if declining, gender gap in terms of ownership of some ICT products and, to a less extent, in terms of access and use. The research also confirms that gender *cuts across* other factors in the digital divide: income, occupation and age are generally more significant than gender in access to ICT and other factors such as being a member of an ethnic minority or lone parenthood also playing a role.

However, it must be recognised that not all cases of non-use are involuntary or dysfunctional. Mere quantitative barometers of the relative use and uptake of new ICTs tend to neglect the important dimension of new ICTs' *relevance* to the users and their specific socio-cultural contexts and so lead to mistaken assumptions about the forms and extent of "exclusion". The SIGIS studies of ICT products indicate that it is not always more effective to design for women specifically as opposed to designing "for everybody" including women. Ideally, the latter strategy embraces the interests and tastes of *heterogeneous* groups of girls/women and boys/men and thus to gender plurality.

Having briefly flagged the key distinction between *"women in ICTs"* and *"women and ICTs"*, and some findings related to gender aspects of the use of new ICTs, we now turn to focus on issues related to *women in ICTs* in the following sections.

3. A PARTICULARLY "CHILLY" SECTOR: WOMEN IN NEW ICT SUPPLYING INDUSTRIES

In this section, we summarise our findings related to women's roles and participation in the production of new ICT and in the wider information or knowledge-based sectors of the Irish economy.

The "information society" concept has played a central role across a spectrum of policy areas and discourses in the EU and most member states since the early 1990s. Following the publication of the Bangemann Report (EU, 1994), the information society became a key motif or mantra for the overall European integration project as well as for many specific policy fields such as research, communications, media, trade and competition. The parallel term, "knowledge-based economy", has become the more popular term since the Lisbon meeting of the European Council in 2000. The latter meeting adopted an ambitious strategy to make Europe "the most dynamic knowledge-based economy in the world, capable of sustainable economic growth, with more and better jobs and greater social cohesion" (EC, 2002: 7).

In such policy discourses, the key terms "information society" and "knowledge-based economy" tend to be rarely defined in explicit fashion; rather they tend to be invoked with very different meanings or implied definitions. Yet, we find at their core the common assumption that the current trajectory of economic development is marked by the expanding role of knowledge-based or information-intensive occupations and industries. They are closely bound up with images of the de-materialisation of economic activities and a relative expansion of certain "knowledge-based" services sectors. Furthermore, such "high-level, grey-matter" jobs and industries are deemed to be not only high-status and associated with high levels of value-added and employee remuneration, but also to comprise strategically important sectors of "comparative advantage" for the advanced capitalist economies in the face of increasing competition from other regions of the world. Yet, the notion of an information *society* may be taken as a somewhat chaotic concept, but it can be distinguished from that of an information or knowledge-based *sector*. In sum, there are aspects of this tradition of academic research and debate that help shed light on key aspects of contemporary socio-economic change (Preston, 2001). To this end, we developed an operational definition of a primary information sector (PIS) which embraces both new ICT supplying sectors as well as other "knowledge-based" and "information-intensive" sectors in line with earlier academic work indicated above (Preston, 2001).

Table 6.1: PIS Industries Share (%) of Total Employment in Ireland, 1986–2002

Industry	1986	1991	1996	2002
Total: All PIS Industries	15.28	16.88	19.85	22.71
PIS 1) New ICT sub-sector	2.39	2.59	3.16	6.08
PIS 2) I/K-I Services	12.89	14.29	16.68	16.63

Note: PIS refers to the primary information sector; PIS 1) refers to the industries supplying new ICT devices, systems, software and services ; PIS 2) refers to information/knowledge-intensive (I/K-I) service industries.

Source: Author's categories and analysis based on data from CSO, "Census of Population" datasets.

Applying this to Irish employment data, we find that the PIS accounts for a growing share of all jobs over the 1986–2002 period (Table 6.1). This trend applies to each of the two major component sub-sectors of the PIS indicated here: the industries supplying new ICT Device, System and Services; and all other information or knowledge-intensive services industries (Table 6.1).

In terms of the gender distribution of employment in 2002 women accounted for 41 per cent of total employment across all sectors of the economy whilst they accounted for a significantly higher share of the jobs in the primary information sectors (Figure 6.1). At almost 49 per cent of the total, women now occupy just about half of all the jobs in the "knowledge-based" or "information-intensive" sectors of the Irish economy. When we zoom in on the details for the two major component sub-sectors of the PIS, we find sharply contrasting situations. This shows that women occupy the majority (almost 54 per cent) of jobs in the largest component of the PIS — the knowledge-based or information-intensive services industries (Figure 6.1). But women occupy only one-third (33.7 per cent) of the jobs in the PIS sub-sector involved in the production of new ICT products and services. Although the total employment in the ICT device, system and services supplying industries grew significantly throughout the 1990s, women's shares of such employment actually declined over the period 1990–2002.

Figure 6.1: Gender Shares (%) of Jobs in Primary Info/Knowledge Sectors (PIS), Ireland, 2002

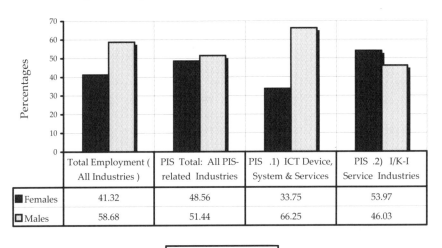

	Total Employment (All Industries)	PIS Total: All PIS-related Industries	PIS .1) ICT Device, System & Services	PIS .2) I/K-I Service Industries
■ Females	41.32	48.56	33.75	53.97
□ Males	58.68	51.44	66.25	46.03

■ Females □ Males

Source: Author's categories and analysis based on data from CSO, "Census of Population" datasets.

Very similar trends emerge from an occupational analysis of employment change in Ireland. Women's share of all information and knowledge intensive occupations has continued to increase, often at a rate exceeding their expanding share of total employment. But when it comes to key technical occupations related to the design, production and implementation of new ICT systems and networks, women's share of such jobs actually declined over the 1990–2002 period. Women's percentage share of jobs in the ICT sector also decreases in line with the seniority of posts and functions. In this respect at least, the new ICT sector is little different to other sectors.

This data refers to Ireland, but the SIGIS project's research indicates a significant under-representation of women in the ICT supply industries and related occupations can also be found in many other EU countries and in the USA. One challenge here is that the official statistical data often fails to provide robust measures of gender employment and there are variations in coverage across different national settings. Notwithstanding such difficulties, estimates of the general pattern for EU countries suggest that women accounted for between 25 per cent and 35 per cent of core ICT jobs in the 2000–2001 period. Furthermore, the project's research indicates that trends of women's under-representation and processes of exclusion differ significantly between the core ICT producing sectors and key application sectors (such as internet/web-based magazines and web design services). In quantitative and qualitative terms, the "inclusion" challenges appear to be much more prominent in the core ICT producing sectors compared to the digital content and other application sectors.

This research indicates that women have significantly increased their share of jobs within most knowledge-intensive industries and occupations over the past few decades. But a similar shift has not occurred in the core ICT supplying industries — indeed women's share of jobs in this area has declined over time in the case of some countries. The research points to very peculiar and significant challenges concerning women's role in the core ICT industries.

One other special and striking feature of the core ICT industries in recent years is that there has been a significant leakage of experienced, mid-career women workers in many EU states, particularly in the UK. This finding clearly indicates that the key challenges for gender inclusion in new ICT are not simply those of recruitment. The retention of experienced women workers appears to be a very significant and peculiar problem in the core ICT supply industries. Often this leakage of mid-career women is due to family reasons, but this reason or "choice" cannot be viewed as straightforward or inevitable in terms of contemporary gender identities and roles. Such decisions to leave work tend to be weighed against the advantages of continuing in a job where there are perceived impediments to promotion and self-development. In other words, there is still a lot that policy makers and employers can do to facilitate an increase in women in ICT supplying industries (as the some of the SIGIS case studies illustrate).

These findings are somewhat ironic given that the ICT supply industries are often defined as the core of an emergent knowledge-based or information society marked by pronounced decline in gender inequalities. Indeed, such claims have featured prominently in discourses surrounding new ICT and the "information revolution" ever since the 1970s, with one popular "theorist" proclaiming that such developments were rendering concerns about gender divides historically redundant (Bowlby and Preston, 1985).

One common myth has been the assertion that knowledge-based and other "high-tech" sectors would be more conducive to women succeeding because of the greater reliance on "brain not brawn". This research suggests that such predictions were not merely premature, but plain wrong-headed, and especially so when it comes to trends in the core ICT production sector.

4. WHY "GENDER (STILL) MATTERS" IN THE NEW ICT SECTOR

In this section, we draw on our Irish case studies to address some issues surrounding women's roles in the sector producing new

ICT products and services. The discussion mainly focuses on two relevant Irish cases: a study of women working in ICT industries (exploring how they view their status, positions and prospects in this sector) and an interview survey with human relations managers in European offices of six major ICT corporations. Whilst access to (especially, professional) workers in the new ICT industries for research purposes is notoriously difficult, in this case, the work reported here was facilitated by networking with members of the Irish branch of Women in IT International (WITI).

Women in ICT Case Study

The survey of women working in the ICT supply sector involved 61 respondents. The majority of these women were in middle to higher level management, and most worked for large companies with more than 1,000 employees. Of those women ICT workers living with a partner or spouse, most were the main wage-earner. In half of those cases, the woman also takes primary responsibility for child care.

The survey revealed that all but one were working on full-time contracts. This research indicated that, despite the much-hyped "flexibility" associated with new ICT, in practice the scope for part-time or other employee-centred modes of flexible working arrangements is almost non-existent in this sector. These findings are in line with those of other studies (e.g. see Greco this book).

When asked what they saw as the main barriers to promotion in the sector, the majority of the 54 respondents to this question believed that the sector tended to operate in particular ways which tended to discriminate against women.

The most common complaint was that the sector is especially male dominated; that it has traditionally appealed to men; and that their numerical strength makes the lack of a "critical mass" difficult for women.

A second set of respondents stated said that the work conditions, in particular the hours, were difficult for women in this sector; further, a culture of high commitment (made evident through long hours) made the sector less family-friendly; also, there was further time pressure in the sector due to the prevailing perceptions of a much greater need for continuous upskilling.

In a second open question, respondents were asked what they considered were the top barriers to women's advancement to senior management in general.

A high proportion of respondents (29 per cent) reported that clashes between family and work commitments formed the greatest barrier; some simply said "having children" or "child care", others referred to the long working hours; many pointed out that women opted for family life over work life though their comments indicated that they were not happy with the conditions under which such choices had to be made.

A strong sense of gender discrimination emerged from this general question; thus, 21 per cent reported a "jobs for the boys" syndrome; they also reported "male domination" and that they did not feel part of the "old boys' club".

In an earlier question relating to the reasons why women gained recognition, respondents reported a high degree of confidence in their work ability. However, many felt that in general, women's abilities are not recognised and that there is a tendency to assume that women are not up to the job. Respondents suggested that women were not "seen" to be as committed to work as to home and family, and/or while this may be so for some women, there is a perception that all others seem to be "tarred by the same brush".

This survey also asked of respondents, "what is the single thing that would make a big difference in you progressing your career?" The data was then coded into nine categories, and whilst no one factor scored extremely highly and thus cell numbers are very low, a hierarchy did emerge.

For example, 22 per cent of respondents felt that improved work conditions, particularly those that might impact on home life such as flexible and or shorter work hours, would impact most. This was closely followed by a category entitled "being taken seriously — being seen" (19 per cent); this category grouped together a number of comments that talked about the need for greater recognition of women's abilities and greater appreciation of their managerial skills; these women felt that actually doing the work was no problem but that they were not acknowledged for it; this feeling of a lack of visibility emerged from a number of questions.

Finally, 17 per cent of women reported that they felt they needed to develop further skills in order to progress their career and 13 per cent of women reported that more personal development such as confidence building, motivation or self-knowledge were keys to their progression.

In essence, these research findings tend to highlight barriers associated with the poor levels of access by women to flexible and employee-orientated or family friendly working arrangements within the ICT sector. The respondents in this survey are themselves already successfully working in the ICT sector (many at a fairly senior level). Yet their responses clearly indicate that issues around flexibility and work-life balance were key drawbacks for women in the sector. Whilst this is also an issue for other sectors, it is perceived to be more pointed and critical in the ICT sector.

Here, we have highlighted responses to a few questions that converge around the issues of flexible work arrangements and work-life balance. Yet, we should note that a more complex picture emerged from the overall study. The women respondents cited a range of issues — symbolic, personal and structural — that impacted on their working lives but clearly, discourses around work-life balance play a central role. This case study underlines how important work-life balance is perceived as a major problem by women successfully working in ICT and that such balance is more difficult to achieve in that sector.

Study of Human Resources Managers in Major ICT Firms

The second SIGIS Irish case study comprised interviews with human resources (HR) managers in ICT companies. These were all multinational corporations including Intel, Dell, IBM, Microsoft, Sun Microsystems and HP. According to the IDA, these are some of the leading companies in the sector who employ 55,000 people and whose annual exports exceed €28 billion.

One initial concern in this survey of human resources personnel was to enquire as to whether and how they considered that the ICT sector was a coherent sector and whether it was different or distinct from other sectors. Respondents generally reported perceptions that the sector was indeed distinct and that it was marked by specific characteristics which affected their approaches and practices as human relations professionals. The relatively rapid pace of change and the individualised nature of work were cited as reasons as to why particular HR models tended to dominate in the sector.

For example, one HR manager stated that:

> I suppose the whole individualised work pay determination performance management systems — all of that is very common in ICT sector and would be different to other areas — it is predominantly non-union, performance-based — a lot of profit share elements — pay, stock. . . . Because of the pace of change, you couldn't work with a union the way we operate. . . . There is a high performance culture here like a lot of other companies in the business.

A number of HR managers believed that unlike other sectors, the ICT industry operated as a meritocracy. Promotion through the ranks was based on reaching performance targets, and this tended to counter the importance of networks or croneyism. One HR manager put it as follows:

> The pace of development is much higher in ICT sector than in other sectors so people's ability to advance is much more linked to performance, much more so than it would be in other companies where tenure and experience can be important — so you can see people get promotion with relatively little experience in very senior positions.

However, some HR interviewees referred to this more as a "perception" of a performance-based system in the sector. In other words they referred to it as something others believed in. Not all HR personnel actually believe that the system works purely on merit, but nonetheless this is the perception that they are dealing with — possibly among their managers. One respondent stated:

> . . . the belief is that those issues are [found only] in traditional companies — that there is a glass ceiling and women are discriminated against. But in the ICT sector nobody is discriminated against — it's all performance-based. . . . . It's been seen as a kind of brave new world and golden opportunities for everyone.

Our HR respondents tended to argue that merit and performance were the key, or perceived to be key, to promotion in the sector. Yet, there was an acknowledgement that what was termed "presentism" was also a factor particularly in terms of achievements. "Presentism" entailed not simply doing the job but being seen to do the job whatever the time commitment, "a 12-hour day scenario" as one put it.

This factor was also identified in the study of women in ICT where there was a strong feeling that "presentism" was an important element in promotion — indeed, more important than delivering results. Visibility and being seen to be available for long hours were key criteria and clearly these have time implications.

Collective representation of workers by independent trade unions or professional associations is usually not tolerated by firms in the ICT supply sector. Yet these firms also tend to emphasise or assume a self-image of being highly attentive to their staff interests and needs. Most such firms in this study emphasised how they conducted their own in-house research to ascertain and address staff or personnel issues. The HR respondents also reported that their own staff research revealed that issues around work-life balance were top of the list whilst other key issues included "career progression and information and how you go about developing a career".

As with the women in the ICT study, several of our HR respondents acknowledged fundamental difficulties with respect to work-life balance issues. There is a recognition that these are particularly prominent in the ICT sector where the part-time jobs share of all jobs is approximately 6 per cent only. The responses of HR managers tended to emphasise the industry's specific features or structural pressures which lead to, or require, a full-time commitment on the part of staff. At the same time, these interviewees also indicated a certain awareness of a need to improve work-life balance conditions within the sector.

> . . . we have a high performance culture like a lot of other companies in the business and by its nature conflicts with the work life balance so it's a big struggle to get that right. . . . There were some initiatives — family friendly days — but in the end of the day only 6 per cent of the jobs in the ICT sector are part-time so it's a highly full-time orientated, permanent-contract sector . . .

These HR managers also suggested that the issues of work-life balance and job flexibility were more problematic in the case of certain functions compared to others within the sector. They argued that functions which relied on the greatest training input were the most difficult to operate on a flexible basis. Essentially, the less skilled the job is perceived to be, the greater the chance that it could be operated flexibly.

For example, one HR respondent suggested that:

> . . . It relates to the work you're doing and the links with customer be they internal or external — if it creates a difficulty — if there are problems with customers. . . . We've targeted women to work part time shifts in some areas — evening shifts to cover customer needs and so on but it's at the fringes — it's not in the core . . . it may not be possible for the person to go part time or maybe there are other roles outside of that department that they can look at – if you've got one person with a key skill you need that person full-time, the business needs that person full-time.

It is worth highlighting that the functions which relied on the greatest training input seem to be regarded within the industry as the most difficult to operate on a flexible basis. The less skilled the job the greater the chance that it could be operated flexibly.

It was also noted that flexible or part time working was closely related to promotion.

> I mean if you're a senior manager and you're out for half the week you really would have missed out on half the de-cisions — it would be almost impossible — you can do it at lower levels but it's virtually impossible at middle man-agement — it's all very snappy, very quick — so it wouldn't make sense to go after women to work part-time at senior level.

In sum, one of the main issues impacting on the inclusion of women in the ICT sector identified in the interviews with the HR personnel revolved around work-life balance. Flexible working arrangements were seen as a major initiative that could impact positively on work-life conflict, and by and large, were availed of primarily by women. Yet, such initiatives are seen by HR as par-ticularly difficult in the fast-moving ICT sector. Not only are they difficult in the sector, but are particularly problematic in certain more technical functions and at more senior levels of manage-ment. Clearly, flexibility is a double-edged sword as far as women are concerned. While it is viewed as a potential solution in terms of keeping women in the workplace, it is also potentially an in-strument that will reinforce segregation.

In one company, the solution was not to tackle the structures that were limiting flexibility in particular functions, but to "steer" women towards the functions that would provide them with the greatest flexibility.

> I understand the nature of your requirements for flexibility ... but in the current role I can't facilitate that and in some respects my hands are tied by this requirement. However, what we can do over time is look to steer you into here

> maybe and it may take some time but we can work it from
> a different route.

All of these companies had officially adopted some form of flexible working policies. However, moving from policy to practice was seen as especially challenging by those companies that were committed to such an initiative. To some extent, HR managers acknowledge that work-life balance is problematic in the ICT sector. But at the same time, they also advanced a number of specific arguments as to why, in their view, more employee-orientated and family friendly flexible working conditions may continue to be particularly difficult or inappropriate in the case of this sector.

The "flexibility" of working practices and processes has long been celebrated as a defining feature of the new ICT supply sector. But these and other SIGIS case studies indicate that the prevailing practice of "flexibility" in the working practices and culture of the ICT supply sector tend to be framed around a highly specific, partial and restrictive concept of "flexibility". In essence, the prevailing notions of "flexibility" are highly firm-centred or project/product-centred rather than employee or family-centred.

5. TOWARDS A "COOL" RATHER THAN "CHILLY" CULTURE FOR WOMEN IN ICT

Overall, the project's research reveals many encouraging signs of a closing gender gap or digital divide with respect to the use of ICT products — what we call women *and* ICT. In sharp contrast, however, the research reveals a pessimistic trend when it comes to the position of women in the ICT industries and occupations.

The evidence from this research suggests that women in the ICT sector are not finding the promised shangri-la, whether post-feminist or otherwise. It points to significant differences with respect to the role of women across different domains of the "high-tech" or knowledge-based sub-sectors of the contemporary Irish economy. It reveals very peculiar and significant challenges concerning women's role in the core ICT industries, which run counter to the overall trends. Indeed, the research indicates that the relative employment position of women in this "new" sector may be deteriorating compared to other sectors.

In particular, our findings clearly point to significant differences in women's roles and in the status of "gender matters" between the new ICT supply sector on the one hand and the wider information sector/economy on the other. The factors contributing to this outcome are multiple and complex, including some related to women's own preferences in response to deep seated features of the sector's work culture.

In this chapter, we have identified the key issues of work-life balance and flexibility, not least because these were identified by the women in our Irish surveys as a key factor with regard to promotion and professional success. When we investigated the HR perspective we found that while all the companies have formal policies in place to allow flexible working arrangements, in practice these are somewhat one-sided and restricted in scope. They are less likely to apply to core functions or to more senior levels of management.

Employers and policy makers concerned with "skill shortages" often assume that the "feeder pipe" is the key to understanding women's career paths, that women are not presenting with the skills and experience to occupy core functions and key management roles. This research suggests that this explanation is only half the story.

While skills may be an important factor in such "leading edge" industries, the unequal role of women must be considered also in relation to other factors. For example, it may sometimes represent an "informed" refusal to play the competitive game of upward mobility based on a calculus of the downside costs of promotion in terms of factors such as extended working hours and pressures on work-life balance. Such considerations apply to the "leaky pipe" syndrome whereby many women workers leave the ICT production sector despite many years of accumulated experience and skills.

Many current "inclusion" policies and initiatives tends to emphasise the need to change the public "image" of working life and practices in the ICT sector, as some of the SIGIS case studies indicate. Such initiatives often seek to represent work in new ICT supply industries as "cool", fashionable and consistent with contemporary self-images of women's identities and roles.

These strategies are clearly in line with the prevailing fashion for public relations techniques and "spin-doctoring" initiatives across all policy domains, and they may well have some limited effects. But unless these techniques are linked to more fundamental strategies of change in work-place practices, they are ultimately flawed and unlikely to prove very effective in the long or even short-term. The evidence from this research suggests that the key challenges are not primarily or simply those of "image" or the public representation of gender aspects of work culture and practices in the core ICT supply industries or in related higher education programmes.

This research suggests a serious lack of a comprehensive or "joined-up" policy in most companies and countries with respect to gender and ICT, whereby explicit support for women into ICT efforts sit alongside wider digital inclusion efforts which are "gender blind". The evidence from SIGIS research indicates that gender gaps in digital inclusion will not disappear without intervention, from board level of corporate decision-making and practices, not merely by external governmental or educational bodies. To be effective, change policies must be spear-headed by top executives, including senior men, as gender issues have, so far, been left to women, despite the strong economic rationale to take action. If companies and governments are serious about gender inclusion in this key sub-sector of an "information society", then a thorough and nuanced awareness of gender and other sources of exclusion must underpin digital inclusion strategies, be they industry-, education-, work- or community-based.

Chapter 7

American Multinational Subsidiaries in Ireland: Changing the Nature of Employment Relations?

David G. Collings, Patrick Gunnigle and *Michael J. Morley*

1. Introduction

The attraction of foreign direct investment (FDI) has been the cornerstone of Irish Government policy since the mid-1950s. The success of this policy has led O'Toole to describe Ireland as "the most globalised country on earth" (2003: 4). The economic significance of the FDI sector on the Irish economy is highlighted by employment in that sector, accounting for some 50 per cent of manufacturing employment compared to an average of 19 per cent of all sectors (Barry, 2002). Multinationals (MNCs) of US origin are by far the most significant in the Irish context, accounting for 70 per cent of total industrial exports (O'Higgins, 2002). Indeed *The Economist* (1997) highlighted the significance of US investment, emphasising the fact that approximately a quarter of all new American manufacturing investment in Europe located in Ireland in the period 1980-1997, while some 40 per cent of all new US inward investment in the electronics sector located there. In terms of employment in these firms, the impact is significant with 89,158 people employed in some 489 firms,[1] representing almost 7.6 per cent of the non-agricultural private sector labour force.[2]

This chapter examines the nature of human resource management (HRM) and industrial relations (IR) practice in US multinational subsidiaries in Ireland. We argue that US firms exhibit distinctive characteristics in the individualistic nature of the employment relationship in these increasingly non-union establishments, including performance related pay (Gunnigle, O'Sullivan and Kinsella, 2002; Gunnigle, Turner and D'Art, 1998; Roche, 2001). We also consider the potential impact of these practices on employees' work experience in these organisations. In illuminating the debate we draw on the national business system approach of Whitley (1999) and "varieties of capitalism" approach of Hall and Soskice (2001). We also draw on US economic history and outline the implications of the nature of US industry for the management of human resource management (HRM) and industrial relations (IR) in US subsidiaries (Edwards and Ferner, 2002). Further, we point to some potential societial impacts of these practices (Kochan and Osterman, 1994).

The chapter is structured in seven sections. Following this introduction, we firstly provide a summary outline of FDI in Ireland; we then consider the impact of country of origin on management practice; the nature of US management practice; the literature on IR and HRM practices in US multinational subsidiaries in Ireland; and, finally we examine some societal level outcomes.

2. FDI IN IRELAND

Much of the growth in the Irish economy over the past number of years (in particular 1987 to present) has been attributed FDI. There

---

[1] These figures are derived from data supplied by IDA Ireland based on the Forfas employment survey. The figure includes only those firms which are supported by IDA Ireland and thus may be understated.

[2] This figure is calculated using the employment figures referred to above and using a measure of private sector non-agricultural employment as 1,181,000. This figure also excludes those employed in their own right without employees (Forfás, 2003).

are now over 1,000 overseas firms employing almost 130,000 people operating in Ireland.[3] OECD data show a three-fold increase in FDI inflows to Ireland in the period 1990–1998. US industry accounted for 85 per cent of these inflows (OECD, 1999). While Ireland accounts for only 1 per cent of the European population, 27 per cent of all US greenfield investment in Europe is located there (Harney, 2000). One commentator even suggests that:

> It may now be more realistic to think of the Irish economy not as a region of Europe, but as an outpost of the United States attached to the edge of Europe (Haughton, 2000: 36).

The trends of recent years are in stark contrast to the economic and industrial climate in Ireland for much of the twentieth century. The country's economic success had been described as a tale of two economies:

> [A] still backward, unproductive and labour-intensive one owned by the Irish, and a modern exceptionally productive and capital-intensive one owned by foreigners (*The Economist*, 1997: 21).

The different phases of FDI in Ireland can be summarised thus: prior to the late 1950s, FDI focused on serving the home market; during the late 1950s and 1960s, FDI sectors were characterised by firms exporting mature, standardised and relatively labour intensive products such as clothing, textiles and light engineering; since the late 1960s, the focus has switched to more sophisticated products such as machinery, pharmaceuticals, instruments and electronics (Kirby, 2002); finally, in recent years, governmental agencies have shifted from attracting new greenfield start-ups towards the retention of existing MNCs (Gunnigle et al., 2003). Increasing attention has also been paid on moving Irish subsidiaries up the value

---

[3] This figure is again derived from data supplied from the IDA based on the Forfas Annual Employment Survey 2002. The figure can be broken down into 133,084 permanent jobs and 12,226 so called "other jobs".

chain by producing higher margin products or services and emphasising research and development (R&D) capabilities.

Multinationals operating in Ireland operate in a number of different sectors. Presently, Ireland is a particularly strong location in the pharmaceutical and healthcare, biotechnology and international services areas (IDA, 2001). Table 7.1 sets out the total employment figures for the various sectors.

Table 7.1: FDI by Sector 2003: IDA Supported Companies

Sector	Employment
Electronics and Engineering	56,894
Pharmaceutical and Healthcare	19,463
Miscellaneous Industry	9,242
International and Financial Services	43,394
Total	128,993

Source: Industrial Development Agency, Annual Report (2003).

When one examines the ownership patterns of multinational firms operating in Ireland, a clear trend emerges. There has been a shift in dependence from UK owned enterprises to US owned ones (See Tables 7.2 and 7.3). In fact the relevant percentages of US and UK firms have reversed.

Table 7.2: FDI by Ownership (per cent of firms) 1959–1967

UK	40%
Germany	20%
US	16%
Netherlands	5%
Other	19%
Total	100 n = 273

Source: Department of Foreign Affairs, Facts about Ireland (1969) (Adapted from Pattinson 2001).

There is little doubt that the foreign sector has had a significant impact on Ireland's economic performance. Any analysis of the influence of these firms should however be considered with one caveat — transfer pricing strategies of these firms may result in an overstating of their contribution to Ireland's output, exports and economic growth (Tansey, 1998).

Table 7.3: Country of Origin IDA Supported Companies 2003

Origin	No. of Companies	Total Employment
US	489	89,158
Germany	149	11,394
UK	118	8,086
Rest of Europe	214	15,602
Asia Pacific	44	2,937
Rest of the World	40	1,816
Total	1,054	128,993

Source: IDA (2003)

The move from protectionism in the early 1960s had a relatively immediate effect on the Irish economy. In the period 1960 to 1973, real GDP increased at a rate of 4.4 per cent per annum (Haughton, 2000). Many commentators have attributed this growth to the contribution of newly established MNCs to the Irish economy (Ó Gráda, 1997; Haughton, 2000). Other factors which were significant include increased labour productivity, reductions in trade barriers through the negotiation of the Anglo-Irish Free Trade Agreement and Ireland's subscription to the General Agreement on Trades and Tariffs (GATT) in 1967 (Haughton, 2000). By 1973 overseas firms accounted for approximately one-third of all employment in manufacturing.

Ireland joined the European Economic Community (EEC) in 1973. Following an initial GDP growth rate of 4.2 per cent in the period following accession, the economy began to stagnate in the early 1980s. Unemployment rose to 17.4 per cent by 1986, and national debt rose to 120 per cent of national income a year later, while GDP per capita fell to 63 per cent of the UK level (Haughton, 2000; *The Economist*, 1997). The country was in economic crisis.

In 1987, the Fianna Fáil Government of the day turned to a fiscal austerity policy in an attempt to rejuvenate the Irish economy (Kirby, 2002). It also enlisted the assistance of the social partners (most significantly trade unions and employers) through social partnership type agreements, which have become a dominant feature of collective bargaining in Ireland (D'Art and Turner, 2002).

Investment by foreign-owned enterprises continued at a substantial rate during the 1990s (see Table 7.4) and there is little doubt that this continued investment contributed significantly to the country's economic performance. US investment amounted to $4.6 billion in 1999 and $7.4 billion in 2000, highlighting the trend of rising US investment in Ireland (Forfás, 2002: 32). Even allowing for the post-9/11 slowdown in world FDI levels, US investment in Ireland reached $7.6 billion in 2002 (Forfás, 2004: 35).

A review of the levels of output and contributions to exports in the past decade is useful in evaluating the contribution of MNCs to the Irish economy. Gross manufacturing output from the foreign owned manufacturing sector increased at an annual average rate of 17.2 per cent per annum in the period 1992 to 1997. If measured as a percentage of manufacturing exports, the relevant shares of the sector are 50.7 per cent in 1992 and 61 per cent in 1997. This represents an annual average growth rate of 18.1 per cent in the same period (O'Sullivan, 2000: 264–5).

Table 7.4: FDI Inflows to Ireland 1990-1998 (IR£ Million)

	1990	1991	1992	1993	1994	1995	1996	1997	1998
Total Inflow	125	232	221	261	207	235	360	383	415
1990 (Base Year = 100)	100	186	177	209	166	188	288	306	332
U.S. Inflow	65	113	135	192	153	184	300	323	324
1990 (Base Year = 100)	100	174	208	295	235	283	461	497	498

Source: OECD *International Direct Investment Statistics Yearbook* (2000)

In summary, US investment in Ireland has been particularly significant and thus Ireland represents an interesting country in which to study the human resource practices of US multinational subsidiaries. We now consider how multinational firms manage HRM and IR issues in their foreign subsidiaries. Specifically we will focus on the extent to which these firms implement standardised practices in these subsidiaries *vis-à-vis* the extent to which management practice has to be localised to account for local institutional contexts.

3. THE COUNTRY OF ORIGIN EFFECT ON MANAGEMENT PRACTICE

The issue of how MNCs manage HRM and IR across borders, the influences of national business systems on this process and the implications for host country IR systems has been a source of considerable debate in recent years (Ferner, 2000). It has been argued that MNCs transfer policies from their home to host operations. This so-called "home country effect" has been attributed to the embeddedness of multinationals in their country of origin (Ferner, 2000). Indeed Gunnigle et al. (2002) postulate that in seeking to develop HRM practices and policies in their subsidiaries, organisations strive to seek a balance between implementing practices that conform to their host environment (localisation) and pursuing distinctive practices in the foreign operations based on those employed in their home environment (standardisation).

In exploring this debate we point to two broad streams of literature which inform the debate. Firstly, writers such as Harbison and Myers (1959) and Kerr et al. (1973) have argued that developments in technology and economics are creating a less differentiated world order. At organisation level this manifests itself in "a common logic of industrialism" or a common set of management requirements that are resulting in a convergence of managerial techniques, regardless of cultural or national differences. The logic of this argument is that the impact of national origin on management practices in MNCs will progressively decline as globalisation leads to the adoption of more generic, standardised practices. This implies a degree of disembeddedness of organisational practices and structures, which override nationally or regionally specific institutions or behavioural dispositions (Harzing and Sorge, 2003).

This convergence thesis has come under increasing scrutiny in recent years and a number of commentators have pointed to continued divergence in management practice. Earlier attempts to explain continued convergence tended to rely on Hofstedean notions of cultural difference, whereby variations in management practice are attributed to the embedded cultural characteristics of different nationalities on criterion such as individualism/collectivism, uncertainty avoidance and other such criteria used by Hofstede (1980) to explore differences in culture and management practice between nations. However, commentators such as Ferner (2000) note that such explanations fail to highlight the influence of the business system in an MNC's country of origin on management practices in the firm's foreign subsidiaries, and that one of the prime challenges to this convergence thesis has come from the emerging institutionalist approach.

Consequently, a number of recent studies have focused on the notion of national business systems and their distinctive impact on management practices in MNCs (Hall and Soskice, 2001; Whitley, 1999). These writers emphasise the cultural and institutional distinctiveness of different national business systems, and thus argue that globalisation may not lead to an increasing convergence of practices since many MNCs remain firmly rooted in the business systems in which they originate (Whitley, 1999). In contrast to the convergence thesis outlined above, divergence "is conterminous with the embeddedness of organisations and other actors in regionally or nationally different societies or in any other locally more idiosyncratic arrangements" (Harzing and Sorge, 2003: 188). The key implication emerging from this school is that although "competition between national systems at the international level leads to much borrowing and diffusion of practices, it does not necessarily promote convergence, since borrowings are integrated into pre-existing and nationally distinctive complexities of business practice" (Ferner, 2000: 2). Thus, as Djelic (1998) notes, although similarities have increased across national units, local peculiarities remain sufficiently meaningful and persistent such that it is still possible to identify and contrast distinct national models of industrial production and the like.

Empirical research has suggested that US multinationals are more likely than firms from other countries to implement standardised approaches across their foreign subsidiaries (Gooderham et al., 1999; Gunnigle et al., 2002). These studies indicate that although all MNCs localise their practices to some extent, the degree of localisation is less in US multinationals than in their European counterparts. A number of factors can be advanced to explain this finding, firstly the "economic dominance" thesis suggests that firms emanating from economically successful nations can more credibly impose practices on foreign subsidiaries (Smith and Meskins, 1995). Also significant is a tradition of US management having a universally accepted right to manage given the nature of the free market economic thesis advanced by American governments. This *laissez-faire* economic model resulted in US organisations developing in a context where they could manage in ways which they wanted with minimal governmental interference. As Hall and Soskice (2001) note, management in US firms generally have unilateral control over the firm and the implications of this for HRM and IR practice in their subsidiaries will now be discussed.

4. THE NATURE OF HUMAN RESOURCE MANAGEMENT AND INDUSTRIAL RELATIONS IN AMERICAN ORGANISATIONS

There is little doubt that the American system of industrial relations is significantly different to that of any other industrialised country. Indeed Jacoby (1985) argues that the subject of American exceptionalism has been of great interest to both historians and social scientists alike. Particularly prominent in the US context has been the dominance of non-union industrial relations. This anti-union ideology is generally attributed to the development of American industry. Most notable in this regard is, as Leidhner (2002) notes, the fact that the balance of power in the US workplace favours capital more than in most other countries. Arguably this is most apparent in terms of the doctrine of "Employment at Will" which underscores all aspects of the employment relationship in American industry. This widely accepted doctrine means that, in the absence of contracts or legislation, employment contracts are "at-will", and thus can be terminated by either party without explanation or cause; thus workers have no ongoing right to employment and no legal obligation for fairness is placed on employers (Leidner, 2002).

The evolution of the power relationship alluded to above can be traced to the development of US industry. The lack of legislative support of worker collectives prior to the 1930s resulted in non-union practices prevailing for the majority of US employees (Kochan et al., 1986). Guest (1990) posits that at this stage individualism became ingrained in US culture. This individualism is often characterised in terms of a meritocracy, where ambition predominates (*ibid.*). This is reflected in articulations of the "American Dream", which Guest (1990) argues was first formally articulated in the context of the New Deal in the 1930s. While different variations have been presented over the years, Guest (1990) postulates that a number of common themes emerge. Most significant, in terms of our consideration of the industrial relations context of US industry, is the view of America as a land of opportunity, where through self-improvement and hard work anyone can become a success. Thus the emphasis in US culture is on individuals grasping opportunities as they present themselves and making the most of them, with government and employers aiding simply in terms of providing a context (Guest, 1990). This is significant for a number of reasons: firstly, it intensified managements' perceived right to manage; and secondly it amplifies individualistic tendencies and notions of meritocracy ingrained in US culture.

Leidner (2002: 27), when examining the nature of employment relations in the US fast-food industry, highlights this cultural idiosyncrasy thus:

> The American values of individualism and meritocracy suggest that workers should improve their lot by moving out of fast-food jobs rather than by improving the compensation and working conditions of the jobs.

As such, the obligation is placed on the individual to improve their situation by exiting the unsatisfactory working situation and moving on to a more rewarding or satisfactory job.

Clearly reflective of this ideology is the welfare capitalist movement which developed during the late nineteenth century. This involved America's large corporations developing a uniquely American response to the "labour question" which was private and managerial as opposed to governmental and labourist (Jacoby, 1997). This movement viewed the industrial enterprise as the source of stability and security in modern society, as opposed to government or trade unions (Jacoby, 1997). These firms emphasised job security (achieved through an emphasis on internal labour markets), good rates of pay, a variety of welfare benefits and non-union forms of employment relations (*ibid.*).

However, non-union employment relations were never universal in the US context and indeed the co-existence of a union and non-union sector is striking. As was the case in most other industrialised countries, skilled craftsmen were in the vanguard in terms of establishing and joining labour collectives, and formed national unions in the 1860s. By the 1880s their unskilled colleagues had began to engage in union activity and the Knights of Labor came to prominence with some 700,000 mainly unskilled members. The Knights' prominence had come to an end by the turn of the century as the American Federation of Labor (AFL), a pragmatic business union, drove the Knights from the field. While the Knights had aimed to reform society as a whole, the AFL espoused pragmatic business unionism, with a focus on improving the wages and working conditions of members rather than the more utopian goals of the Knights (Wheeler and McClendon, 1998). Although it has been argued that the unionised sector in the US has been characterised by openly adversarial relations be-tween management and labour, Wheeler and McClendon (1998) posit that this conflict is circumscribed by the limited goals of America's pragmatic business unions.

Unionism never really took hold in US industry[4] and a num-ber of reasons are commonly advanced for this. Initially this was due to the fact that industrial income in US industry was compa-rable to American farm labour and generally higher than factory workers in Europe (Wheeler and McClendon, 1998). Other com-monly advanced reasons include: the absence of feudalism in the country; early mass enfranchisement; working class heterogene-ity; high rates of social mobility; and the dominant value system of individualism referred to earlier. As Jacoby (1985) astutely notes, however, these explanations overemphasise the role of la-bour in fashioning American unionism, whilst downplaying the obvious hostility of US management towards unions. Adams (2003) concurs with this criticism and notes that institutional fac-tors more accurately explain the differences. North American em-ployers can act on their interests, an option not available to their European counterparts due to the institutional constraints placed upon them (Adams, 2003).

Following the national business system approach discussed above we now argue that as US multinationals expanded abroad they carried some of their distinctive national baggage with them in establishing and managing their Irish operations.

5. HRM AND IR IN AMERICAN SUBSIDIARIES IN IRELAND

We turn next to the extant research evidence available on HRM and IR practice in US multinational subsidiaries in Ireland. Early research on the IR practices of incoming MNCs clearly indicated that there was little difference between industrial relations prac-

---

[4] The level of union density in the US is approximately 15 per cent, while in the private sector the level is only 10 per cent (Adams, 2003).

tice in these firms and indigenous companies. Specifically, Enderwick (1986) found no evidence that MNCs which set up subsidiaries in Ireland showed a strong preference for operating on a non-union basis. Also significant was a study by Kelly and Brannick (1985) indicating that "In general MNCs are regarded as no different than Irish firms and the trend seems to be one of conformity with the host country's institutions, values and practices" (1985: 109). These studies formed the basis for what became known as the conformance thesis, which suggested that the IR and HR practices of multinational subsidiaries operating in Ireland conform to traditional national practice (Geary and Roche, 2001; Turner, D'Art and Gunnigle, 2001).

More recent studies have criticised this thesis. While acknowledging that differences endure in terms of management practice in firms of different nationalities, Turner et al. (2001) posit that the host country effect is becoming less significant due to a decline in distinctions between management practice in different countries. Geary and Roche (2001) call this the new conformance thesis. Instead, they argue that HRM policies originating at the headquarters significantly impact on management practice in subsidiaries, and that Irish IR practice remains distinctive in terms of the country of origin effect. Whatever the case, both schools acknowledge that US organisations are distinctive in that they are far less likely to recognise trade unions.

Geary and Roche (1995) point to a number of significant waves of investment which have impacted on the nature of IR practice in Irish subsidiaries. In the first wave, companies clearly conformed to Irish IR practice. Differences began to emerge during the second wave of inward investment in the 1960s, becoming more pronounced in the 1970s and 1980s, and with the third wave of investment thereafter. We will examine the research evidence pertinent to third wave US companies.

Union Recognition and Avoidance

Employment density represents the cohort of a country's population that are union members expressed as a percentage of the employed workforce. Irish employment density rose consistently
from the 1930s (approximately 20 per cent) to 1980 when it peaked
at 61.93 per cent (Roche and Ashmore, 2001). Density levels have
decreased significantly since 1980 with the 1995 figure just above
53 per cent (Roche and Ashmore, 2001). One of the most significant explanations of the falling levels of unionisation in Ireland is
the impact of US multinationals (see Wallace, 2003). Recent studies have clearly indicated an accelerated and consistent trend of
union avoidance in US multinational subsidiaries, particularly in
the high tech sector (Gunnigle, MacCurtain and Morley, 2001;
Roche, 2001). More recent research by Gunnigle, Collings and
Morley (2005) has also identified a significant trend. Their research found that MNC subsidiaries with a tradition of union recognition and collective bargaining had recently established new
plants in Ireland on a non-union basis. This practice, whereby
companies that already recognise trade unions set up new plants
on a non-union basis, is termed "double breasting". They posit
that this trend indicates that host country effects are increasingly
being over-ridden by country of origin effects.

How can one account for the increasing propensity for US
multinational companies to impose their home country preferences and operate on a non-union basis? It is useful to consider
the institutional context which existed when the first significant
US MNCs located in Ireland (the 1950s and 1960s). At this time a
number of factors increased the likelihood of incoming firms recognising and negotiating with trade unions. Perhaps most important was that government agencies charged with attracting this
investment, and the employers' organisation at the time, recommended that they did so. Also significant were the negative consequences of EI Shannon's failed attempt to establish in Ireland on
a non-union basis. Both of these factors were confirmed as significant in the decision of the companies in Gunnigle, Collings and

Morley's (2005) study to recognise and negotiate with trade unions in their original establishments.

Over time, these institutional constraints have lessened. As Roche (2001: 184) notes "more intense competition in product markets and for foreign direct investment has meant that employers have gained increased scope to determine the character of employment relations regimes at enterprise and workplace level". Since the 1980s, governmental agencies attracting incoming FDI have taken a neutral stance on the issue of union recognition. Also significant has been the so-called "demonstration effect" whereby the successful establishment of multinational subsidiaries on a non-union basis and more significantly the maintenance of this non-union status over an extended period has challenged the conventional wisdom that unionisation was inevitable (Wallace, 2003). The following section will consider the impact of this non-union status on these employees' work experience.

Impacts of Non-unionism on Employees' Work Experience

Considerable debate exists on the extent to which the employment relationship has become more individualised (Gunnigle et al., 1998; Roche, 2001; Doherty in this book). Gunnigle et al. (1997) studied all "large" greenfield establishments which were set up in Ireland in the period 1987–92. Their study pointed to a greater emphasis on individualism which was characterised in terms of usage of performance related pay systems linked to appraisal and increased direct employee communication. Their data identify the country of origin as the most significant variable in explaining variations of collectivism and individualism, with US ownership most negatively impacting upon levels of union recognition and density. The later study (Gunnigle et al., 1998) pointed to a growing propensity of employers in Irish, non-union, greenfield sites to use individual performance related pay (IPRP) which they claim indicated a growing propensity of these employers to exclude trade unions and individualise the employment relationship. Again the use of individual PRP was most closely associated with country of ownership with US organisations most likely to utilise IPRP (Gunnigle et al., 1998: 571).

Thus, the use of IPRP and union non-recognition are consistent with marginalising trade unions and are essentially "an individualist management tool, with important implications for industrial relations" (Gunnigle et al., 1998: 574). By linking individual performance to incremental pay rewards, these companies challenged the tradition of pay increments based on collectively negotiated and applicable "across the board" to all relevant employees.

Roche (1998) is highly critical of these studies for methodological reasons. Specifically, he postulates that individual performance related pay may be a poor indicator of individualism and that of the 20 pair-wise correlations used as discrete indicators on individualism and collectivism only 8 were statistically significant. He argues that the data "point to weak or contingent relationships between individualism and collectivism in Greenfield plants" (Roche, 2001: 185). While Roche (2001: 201) argues that "we need to move beyond the individualization thesis and its associated argument concerning the secular trend in industrial relations systems", his research confirms Gunnigle et al.'s finding that recently established US enterprises are more likely to set up on a non-union basis and more likely to use IPRP systems. Thus the most significant implication of these studies is that more recently established US owned enterprises in Ireland are more likely to establish on a non-union basis and to use IPRP systems and other individualist practices designed to circumvent trade union influence.

Arguably the fact that the vast majority of greenfield US establishments set up in Ireland on a non-union basis has a significant impact on the nature of the employment relationship for those employed in these firms. For D'Art (2002), these impacts include: the utilisation of pay above the norm and gain or profit sharing schemes; an increasing emphasis on training, internal labour markets and non-union grievance procedures. The non-union enterprise can have positive implications for the employees concerned, particularly those in knowledge jobs, with high labour mobility. The negative connotations of non-union management relations for employees emerge in the lower value jobs. These employees are often subject to the "harsh realities" of non-union management–employee relations. Fluctuations in product and labour markets often result in reductions in employment tenure and security through the use of short-term contracts and sub-contracting (Legge, 1998). Legge (1998) argues that in contrast to management rhetoric which posits the virtues of flexibility in improving employees' work experience, the bulk of the empirical evidence suggests that the opposite is the case for those on the periphery of the labour market. This is consistent with Royle's research in the fast-food industry in the German and UK context (Royle and Towers, 2002). His findings indicate that employees were generally subjected to arbitrary management rule, with wages generally in line with minimum wage requirements, and relatively poor working conditions.

In terms of the overall impact of IPRP systems, Kessler (2001) points to a number of negative individual level outcomes. Most significant of these is a potential reduction in employee commitment where inequalities exist in the system. While IPRP is widely identified in the literature as positive from an organisational point of view, it can potentially impact on individual employees in a number of ways. It may be a manifestation of employer attempts to marginalise unions; and may lead to dissatisfaction resulting from perceived inequalities in the system for others. Whatever the effect, the extant literature clearly indicated that US multinational subsidiaries in Ireland (particularly newer, greenfield establishments) are more likely to use individual performance related pay systems.

6. SOCIETAL LEVEL IMPACTS

The final section of this chapter will outline potential impacts of the management practices of the US multinational subsidiaries on Irish society at large. Potentially the most significant macro level effect is the threat to pluralist IR traditions and the trade union movement in Ireland through establishment on a non-union basis. This includes "double breasting" by firms in the pharmaceutical and healthcare sectors, targeted by the IDA as a key target area for future investment (Gunnigle et al., 2005). One could reasonably expect further growth of the non-union sector, even allowing for the post-9/11 slowdown in US investment in Ireland.

This trend of union avoidance has been problematic for the Irish trade union movement. D'Art and Turner argue that trade union recognition is the key determinant of union growth. They point to two distinct but complementary steps to union recognition (2002: 13): an employee's right to join a union guaranteed under Art. 40.6.1.iii of the Irish Constitution; and the willingness of employers to recognise and negotiate with trade unions on behalf of their employees. In this regard there has been a historical reluctance of Irish governments to statutorily legislate for trade union recognition as this undermines the voluntaristic principles which underpin Irish industrial relations. Recent trends of union decline (and the high profile recognition dispute in Ryanair) have forced the issue of statutory union recognition to the fore of unions' agendas at national level.

Union claims for statutory union recognition highlight the potential societal level impact of US corporations in Ireland. These claims came to the fore in negotiating the national partnership agreements, Programme for Prosperity and Fairness and Sustaining Progress. The negotiation of the former resulted in the appointment of a high level commission on union recognition, culminating in the introduction of the Industrial Relations (Amendment) Act 2001. However, the act has been characterised as a dismal failure (D'Art and Turner, 2002: 33). The Irish Congress of Trade Unions unsuccessfully attempted to gain recognition legislation similar to that introduced in the UK during negotiations for Sustaining Progress.

The potential impact of union recognition on the FDI sector was arguably significant in drafting the act and the limited scope of the re-negotiation in Sustaining Progress. It is more likely that statutory union recognition will be achieved through the European Charter of Fundamental Rights rather than through Irish Government choice, given the influence of US multinationals in this sphere. As Wallace (2003: 21) notes:

> It appears that the unions, employers and government may be happy to have the matter addressed at European Union level, which would not single Ireland out and could limit any potential effect on US foreign direct investment.

A further significant impact of US subsidiaries in Ireland is on union and non-union wage differentials. Flood and Toner (1996) found that non-union companies in Ireland were forced to pay rates above those in unionised counterparts to reduce the propensity of employees to unionise. In the absence of trade union penetration in the wider context, how many of these firms would continue to follow these high wage practices? D'Art (2002: 44) posits "the ability to pay lower wages and manage without challenge is the very raison d'être of non-unionism". Thus, if trade union density levels were to continue to fall and reach levels close to those in the US, differentials between union and non-union companies could level out and reverse.

7. CONCLUSION

The impact of US multinationals on the work experience of employees of US subsidiaries in Ireland depends on the value added by individual employees to the company concerned. While employees at the higher end of the human capital value chain gain from IPRP and other HRM policies characteristic of management practice in US subsidiaries, it is those at the margins of the labour market who are most likely to lose out in the absence of collective representation, or a minimum threshold level of union density in the broader society. At a public policy level, O'Toole (2003) notes that while the Irish boom was driven by some centre-right policies such as low corporation taxes, wage moderation and fiscal responsibility, other policies were supplied by the left, namely an interventionist state, public spending on human capital, international solidarity from the EU, and an intelligent trade union movement. Thus while Ireland does not reflect fully the *laissez-faire*, market economic model of the US, it is also not as highly regulated as some other countries in mainland Europe. Irish policy makers must balance the trade off between the economic efficiency outcomes of courting further FDI investment while at the same time balancing social equity outcomes for Irish employees (Kleiner and Ham, 2003) by ensuring the Irish legislative framework remains sufficiently protective of employees rights in the workplace. Arguably a policy shift toward the free market model is unlikely given the countervailing influence of the European Union, combined with the prevalence of coalition governments promoting bias towards compromise (Hyman, 2004).

Chapter 8

INDIVIDUALS AT WORK? COLLECTIVISM AND NEW EMPLOYMENT IN THE IRISH WORKPLACE

Michael Doherty

1. INTRODUCTION

At the beginning of the twenty-first century Irish trade unions, like their counterparts across Europe and throughout the industrialised world, are facing an uncertain future. The trade unions of Ireland are among the oldest economic institutions of the modern world (Wallace et al., 2004). From beginnings as mere offshoots of UK-based unions, the period of sustained growth in Ireland from the late 1950s (after the abandonment of economic protectionism) catapulted trade unions into the heart of Irish social, economic and especially working life. The 1960s and 1970s were periods of sustained improvements in living standards, rapid wage growth and an approximation of full employment for many (if not all) categories of workers. A weak form of neo-corporatism in the form of National Wage Agreements negotiated by the social partners had given unions a direct role in influencing government economic policy (Hardiman, 1988). The union movement, too, had a close and complex relationship with Fianna Fáil, the dominant political party of post-Independence Ireland, which enabled it to gain ready access to influential policy-makers (Allen, 1997). A surge in economic confidence in this era brought about a "drift of power to the workplace union, with shop stewards dominating the collective bargaining scene at plant level" (Wallace et al., 2004: 11). This was frequently accompanied by rising levels of industrial action (D'Art and Turner, 2002). Thus, the experience of the workplace union was a very salient (if not always positive) one for the majority of Irish workers.

Trade union density in Ireland reached a high point of 62 per cent in 1980; by 2004 this figure would fall below 40 per cent. In between times the Irish economy had suffered severe depressions in the 1980s and early 1990s, with levels of unemployment approaching 20 per cent, before the onset of the "Celtic Tiger" era with its rapid growth, employment creation and social partnership process. In the light of the new, globalised economy, how is modern workplace trade unionism experienced by contemporary workers? Is workplace unionism still a prominent element of the everyday work experience?

Irish unions, like most others in the industrialised world, have faced a decade or more of hard times with frequent questioning of the commitment of the modern worker to collective aims and actions (Ferner and Hyman, 1998; Martin and Ross, 1999). First, unions that have traditionally acted on the national stage are being confronted by the dynamics of a global economy and the growth of transnational capital (Soskice, 1999), the implications of which are particularly profound for small open economies. In Ireland, almost 100,000 people are employed by US multinational companies (MNCs) alone (Roche and Geary, 2002; Gunnigle et al., 2002). The increasing power of capital to "take flight" (Streeck, 1999) has led many to argue that the power of capital relative to that of organised labour and the nation state has increased (Allen, 2000).

Second, there has been a continuation and acceleration of long-term transformations in economic and employment structure, in particular growth in private service sector employment (Castells, 1996; O'Connell, 2000). This growth has been associated in the literature with the dominant need for "flexibility" in employment relations (Adnett, 1996), including the growth of various forms of "atypical" work such as part-time, temporary and agency work (Beck, 2000). Third, and perhaps most importantly, unions have been accused of being antiquated and superfluous because they have not realised that collective organisational principles and forms of action are *passé* (Lind, 1996; Giddens, 1998). The decline in trade union membership is particularly relevant in the context of the ongoing debates around the undermining of worker collectivism and solidarity by the increasing atomisation of social and working life (Esping-Andersen, 1999).

This chapter explores the extent to which the impact of structural labour market changes and the discourse of "new individualism" are reflected in the attitudes, experiences and activities of Irish trade union members in the workplace. Drawing on case study data from two work sites in the public and private sectors respectively, the chapter argues that the "collective experience" based on membership of, and support for, the workplace union remains a salient part of working life in Ireland. In both cases the shifting nature of employment — privatisation and deregulation in public transport; flexibility and new management techniques in financial services — is questioning the commitment of workers to trade unions and presenting fresh challenges for the workplace union (Bacon and Storey 1993). Yet, the data suggests that the "individualisation thesis" (Beck, 1992; Giddens, 1998) is by no means an uncontested one.

2. THE INDIVIDUALISATION THESIS AND TRADE UNIONS

The literature of the last two decades has overwhelmingly identified trade unions as major victims of the increasing fragmentation and individualisation of social and working life (Beck, 2002; Waddington and Hoffman, 2002). The shift towards private sector services is associated with important labour market features that militate against trade union organisation, requiring unions to develop recruitment and representation strategies appropriate for the "new" constituencies of female workers, part-time workers and temporary workers (Dickens, 2004; Hyman, 1999). Arguably, this renders the notion of a standardised group of workers pursuing similar interests increasingly difficult to sustain (Bacon and Storey, 1996; Leijnse, 1996).

In the public sector, following the general rejection of Keynesianism and state ownership, there have been major moves towards economic deregulation, including the privatisation of state-owned industries (Crouch, 1999). As the public sector has traditionally been heavily unionised and characterised by bureaucratic structures that encouraged standardised work relations, this has clear implications for trade union membership (Carter, 2004; Conley, 2002).

These changes are associated with arguments around post-Fordism (Lash and Urry, 1987; Boyer, 1988). Post-Fordist changes are often said to involve more cooperative industrial relations at the workplace, where employers seek to enhance the status and well-being of their workers through, for example, participative decision-making and enhanced job security (Hirst and Zeitlin, 1990). However others, like Kelly, argue that

> the "skilled content" of new manufacturing jobs or service sector employment can be easily exaggerated . . . if anything the trend . . . is towards less security of employment, except for small groups of core workers (1998: 151).

Collective Failure?

These structural changes have been seen by many as signalling a break-up of a traditionally homogenous and collective experience of employment, fostering the diffusion of individual orientations at the expense of traditional forms of class-related solidarity (Lash and Urry, 1987; Zoll and Valkenburg, 1995).

Have these changes been accompanied by a general erosion of societal collectivism? Beck argues that the changes in the labour market — through its interlinked processes of education, mobility and competition — have become the driving force behind the individualisation of peoples' lives (1992; 2000); while in the USA,

Putnam has impressively documented a sea change in attitudes to collective engagement in all areas of social life, particularly amongst the young (2001). Equally, Madsen (1997) has pointed out that personal experience is increasingly shaped by multiplicity and that the basic security offered by the welfare state has increased individual orientation to non-material needs.

Not only is the workplace said to be changing but its significance in the economy and society is also said to be dwindling in comparison with the sphere of consumption (Kelly, 1998). Consumption, it is argued, has become more significant in the economy as a source of wealth, employment and, indeed, identity. Changing patterns of consumption allow people (and workers) more choice in the construction of a diverse range of lifestyles; choice that is less constrained than ever before by social or occupational ties (Harvey, 1990). One way in which the pre-eminence of the sovereign individual is demonstrated occurs through the decline of collective organisational principles and forms of action. This is shown in terms of employment relations through the decline in trade union densities, industrial action and rank-and-file trade union participation (Fosh and Cohen, 1990).

While the changes described above are argued to be universal, the economic boom of the last decade has led to a transformation in Irish social and working life. As an economy influenced by both the neo-liberal US and the European "social model", Ireland has combined a high dependence on foreign investment and MNCs, with a much admired model of neo-corporatist governance (Boucher and Collins, 2003). Thus trade unions have been systematically excluded in newer American MNCs and brought to the heart of partnership in Irish social and economic life. Further, there has been a strong focus on private service sector employment (IT, financial services), yet employment in the heavily unionised public sector has progressively expanded (O'Connell, 2000). Finally, we can clearly observe the prominence of many of the elements said to be required for an increase in the significance of consumption including higher average disposable income, increased range of available goods and services, and the easing of "traditional social constraints" like religion (Lash and Urry, 1987; O'Toole, 2003).

3. THE CASE STUDIES

The data presented here focuses on two worksites; one in the transport sector (a bus company) and one in the financial services sector (a bank).[1] I conducted 33 formal interviews with employers, union members, representatives and officials, and engaged in non-participant observation of daily work routines. As with any case study research, there are distinctive circumstances that apply to these workplaces and issues about the lack of generalisability do arise (Black et al., 1997). Both present a relatively benign atmosphere for trade union activity. Bus Company is a traditional, public sector employer with virtually universal unionisation levels. People's Bank is a foreign subsidiary, private sector service employer, but has a long tradition of union recognition and continues to support basic trade union institutions. Nevertheless, these features are not necessarily unique and many of the general industrial relations and union features equally apply to other large, unionised organisations. Crucially, both are and have been enduring a period of continuous change that is fundamentally altering employment practices; in particular privatisation and deregulation in public transport, and flexibility and new management techniques in financial services.

The Irish Bank Officials Association (IBOA) represents over 17,000 members in Ireland's banking and finance industry. My focus is on People's Bank branch in suburbia, which encompasses lending services, securities, corporate lending and the legal department. The People's Bank is located on a greenfield site on the outskirts of a major city. There are around 200 People's Bank employees based there, of whom 160 are full-time with a further 40 part-time or temporary. Exact figures for membership of the IBOA at the branch are unavailable but union informants estimate that

---

[1] As a guarantee of confidentiality was given to the respondents, all names of people, businesses and places have been changed.

about 50 to 60 per cent are members. The Services, Industrial, Professional and Technical Union (SIPTU) represents around 4,000 bus workers in Bus Company, a public transport company that operates citywide. The Bus Company garage in Cubtown was pinpointed as the second case study site. Essentially, this is the place where bus drivers begin and end their routes, and deal with any administrative issues. There is also a canteen and some social facilities there. As with all Bus Company garages, two unions co-exist side by side, SIPTU and the National Bus and Railworkers Union (NBRU). The SIPTU/NBRU membership split is about 40 per cent to 60 per cent in Cubtown respectively (with 232 SIPTU members).

The Salience of Collectivism[2]

Why do employees become members of trade unions and what do they expect their union to deliver? The rationale for union membership is often described along an ideological-instrumental continuum (Hartley, 1996). At one end workers join for predominantly collective motives, for example, ideological commitment to unionism and the protection of the vulnerable employee in the asymmetric employment relationship; at the other the motivation is more individualistic, for instance, access to employment insurance and legal services. If there has been a general decline in collectivist values and an erosion of occupational ties as outlined above, we would expect that union members would join for predominantly individualistic motives (Van der Veen, 1996). Equally, we might anticipate that they would expect their union to deliver more individualised benefits.

Unsurprisingly perhaps, given that they voluntarily donate their time to union activities, the five local representatives interviewed professed a strong ideological belief in the need for trade unions. However, several other respondents reported similar be-

---

[2] This section follows a similar structure to that of Black et al (1997). Interestingly, it also tends to corroborate their findings on the salience of collectivism in a British context.

liefs like, "I do really believe in them and I would encourage everyone to join them" (Irene, IBOA member). Overall, just under half the respondents professed some ideological preference for union membership (often in terms of the union as a guarantor of better working conditions);[3] and, in line with the findings of Waddington and Whitsun (1996) in the UK, who found that joining a union in principle was more likely among white collar employees, the majority of these were bank workers.

Perhaps, given the small sample size, what is significant is that in both cases the local representatives and union officials believed that if it were required they would have the ideological backing of the majority of members, "If you're not going to get the backing don't ask the question . . . but I'm lucky, very lucky" (David, IBOA official). Further, this ideological commitment demonstrated by the local representatives is to a large extent sustained by the ordinary members: "(the local representatives) are great and they think the same way we're thinking here" (Gearoid, SIPTU member).

The other most important reason for joining the union (and many respondents identified this in addition to their ideological preferences) was to gain a measure of protection against management: "make no mistake, upper management will screw you if they can, be certain of that" (Aidan, IBOA member). This may reflect arguments around the increased power of transnational capital *vis-à-vis* labour: "some of the stories I've heard out there about people who just kind of get screwed over and the union helped them get out of it" (Hector, IBOA member); or indeed the insecurity that accompanies modern employment relations: "Just the thought of [the union] being there for management limits them" (Jim, SIPTU member).

---

[3] It might be argued that viewing union membership as necessary for protecting working conditions is itself an individualistic motive; I would argue at the very least however it corresponds with Goldthorpe et al.'s (1968) "instrumental collectivism".

Union Potential: Membership Expectation

Having joined a union, what is it that members expect the union to provide for them? Three particular points emerge from the data on this issue. Firstly, again protection from unfair treatment by management was a key concern:

> . . . they look after you, you know. I mean, your rights. Things can go pear-shaped very easy in a job without a union (Kevin, SIPTU member).

In the case of Bus Company, protection for the individual was a significant factor. For example, several respondents had themselves experienced problems with management (suspension, problems with pension entitlements, even dismissal) and in each case the union had provided them with what they perceived as excellent support. This was less frequent in People's Bank, but several respondents referred to union membership as a type of "cover plan" in case of any possible future difficulties.

Secondly, in both companies there was significant use of the local union representatives as a "resource":

> . . . they nearly descend upon you as soon as you walk in the door, with various problems . . . you're needed for all sorts of things, you're like a go-between, really, between the people you're representing and their families nearly, as well as the company (Donal, SIPTU workplace representative).

Another representative in People's Bank referred to himself as a "contact point". This expectation of what the union can offer is a more constructive conception of unionism than the "defensive" nature of the unions' protection function. In this case, the representatives were seen as being able to offer reliable and professional advice on various work and non-work related issues.

Perhaps disturbing from a trade union perspective, however, was the fact that most members felt that the union either had diminished or insufficient influence over other areas of working life. In Bus Company the intention by the state to progressively franchise out the company's routes to private operators (what members perceived as privatisation) was the burning issue of the moment. There was deep frustration amongst members that the union had not gone ahead with threatened strike action, "we're not happy with the union because . . . they had to pull back. Just go out and stay out" (Gearoid, SIPTU member).

There were also some doubts expressed as to the viability of such action: "strikes nowadays don't do anybody any good" (Niall, SIPTU member). There was evidence in both cases of a general feeling that union power and influence, at least as measured in terms of industrial action, had declined:

> to be brutally honest, you'll never see a strike coming again in the foreseeable future . . . [with] the likes of the LRC and these intermediaries; I think there's more willingness now for guys to sort things out (Gary, IBOA workplace representative).

In terms of pay bargaining, the general view was that with the advent of social partnership, the union at the workplace was virtually redundant: "pay is less relevant now because of the partnership agreement" (Aidan, IBOA member). The interesting point here is that despite a general view that unions had insufficient influence in respect of two of the traditionally fundamental areas of union activity — capacity to take industrial action and pay bargaining — respondents generally reported high degrees of satisfaction with what their union achieves in the workplace. This may indicate a significant shift in union members' conception of the function of trade unions.

A final point in relation to members' expectations of what their union can provide relates to arguments around a US style "business unionism" model (Heery and Kelly, 1994). This model relies on trade union activities external to the workplace, particularly the provision of individual, consumer-type services (Waddington and Hoffman, 2000). Examples of the types of services unions provide are individual welfare benefits like sickness benefits; financial service packages such as insurance packages; legal services; and leisure-centred items like cinema ticket discount cards. This new focus on members as "customers" is claimed to represent an adjustment to a "new individualism" among members, whose identities are formed increasingly around their consumption patterns (Bacon and Storey, 1996). Both SIPTU and the IBOA offer services of this nature.

Among the Bus Company respondents, however, not one interviewee mentioned individual services of these types as being relevant to their union membership. In People's Bank, a more concerted effort is being made by union officials to promote these benefits:

> . . . we have a car insurance scheme; we have holiday insurance, squash court, cheap cinema tickets. But that's what a modern day trade union has to do (Frank, IBOA official).

Yet only one bank employee pointed to the availability of discounted car insurance as a significant factor in his decision to join. In general, while bank workers were more likely than their transport colleagues to avail of these services, the services were tangential to their expectations of what the union should provide for them.

Union Delivery: Instrumental Salience

Having looked at what union members expect from their union we now turn to the question of whether they felt their union was in fact successful in achieving these aims. As indicated above, in terms of pay many members did not see the workplace union as particularly relevant.[4] In both workplaces the union was seen as having a positive influence in some of the "newer, qualitative"

---

[4] As noted, many (primarily IBOA) members felt the advent of social partnership had removed this issue as a salient workplace one (although several also acknowledged the role of their union in those negotiations); others (primarily SIPTU) noted that unions, to an extent, were victims of their own success in that as pay levels were generally satisfactory, members were not looking to the union on this issue. Of course, were that situation to change a different response might well be forthcoming.

areas of representation (Hyman, 1999), for example, sexual harassment and gender equality. As noted above, respondents also
rated the unions very highly on being effective in representing
employees in individual disputes with management (on the basis
of either personal experience or word of mouth).

The two areas where unions were not felt to be delivering
were in Bus Company on the issue of job protection and in People's Bank on the issue of individual "consumer" services. On the
former there was deep frustration amongst all the lay union respondents that concerted industrial action had not been taken
against the planned deregulation of the bus market:

> . . . they've delayed the strike, which I think is stupid. They
> have the backing of the whole garage (Gearoid, SIPTU
> member).

On the latter, those limited number of members who had availed
of things like discounted car insurance were not satisfied with the
outcome. This illustrates the problem for unions of this type of
service provision: competing with specialist providers who may
be more adept at providing customer satisfaction (Klandermans,
1996).

Yet, in both of these areas the "individualisation" thesis (including the advocacy of "business unionism") is challenged. Thus,
workers were frustrated by their union's *failure* to take collective
action, while the value to unions of offering individualised, consumer services is questioned.

The Nature of Collective Action

Hyman (1999) has argued that many unions have traditionally
exhibited a view of worker solidarity that, following Durkheim,
can be termed "mechanical solidarity" in which standardised
rules and values are imposed on members whose circumstances
were relatively homogenous. Barling et al. (1992) point out most
of the time little is required of trade union members in the way of
participation in union affairs: voting in elections, authorising the

(automated) payment of membership subscriptions, and so on. Nevertheless, the decline in the incidence of industrial action and membership participation in "everyday" union business has been cited as further evidence of a general erosion of collectivism (Putnam, 2001).[5]

In terms of industrial action, it was noted above that many respondents (particularly amongst the bank employees) indicated a belief that this element of trade unionism may no longer be as relevant: "obviously . . . nobody wants conflict. Industrial stability is a good thing" (Eoghan, IBOA member). However, several writers have pointed to the role of grievances (and how they are used by union representatives) in stimulating membership participation in industrial action (Klandermans, 1992; Kelly and Heery, 1994). This was clear in both workplaces. In Bus Company the perceived threat to jobs, pay and working conditions from deregulation had created an environment in which there was a firm commitment at grass roots level to strike action:

> . . . it'll only take a spark, really I think, for some major disruption to take place. The situation on the ground is very volatile; the men are every angry, very frustrated when they see what's happening (Donal, SIPTU workplace representative).

The role of the workplace representative in such situations is crucial (Fosh, 1981; Fosh and Cohen, 1990). Here, the SIPTU representatives were clearly tapping into to the "latent workplace solidarity" (Fosh, 1993: 580) and the ideological basis of many of the members' union membership to arouse the required support for action, in this case action that would not be sanctioned by the union leadership:

---

[5] Although as Kelly (1998) rather sardonically notes, "in the literature on trade unionism . . . one of the most frequent complaints by writers and activists, from the Webbs onward, has been the lack of interest in branch affairs by the rank-and-file membership and the chronically low level of attendance at union meetings."

> . . . the men may well take [illegal] action. . . . I happen to
> agree with the men and I won't be doing anything to stop it
> (Donal, SIPTU workplace representative).

In People's Bank, action was also being taken to address a perceived injustice. Thus, in response to a refusal by management to
provide increased remuneration rates for lower grades of bank
staff, the union had instructed members not to cooperate with the
conducting of staff appraisals. Although all of the IBOA respondents were at higher levels of grade and pay and therefore not
personally affected by this issue, and some had, in principle, no
problems with the appraisal system, the following quote is typical:

> I definitely agree with the union on that. And I wouldn't
> sign off my appraisal as part of it. And I think that's the
> general mood of a lot of people in the bank, who I've come
> across. They're not going to do their appraisals until the
> union say, "green light, go ahead" (Hector, IBOA member).

In terms of other types of membership participation, the respondents were asked general questions about both formal (voting in
ballots, standing for election, attending meetings) and informal
(talking about the union, reading the newsletter/circulars, helping
the local representative) forms of participation (Hartley, 1996).
Levels of formal participation in both workplaces were low. All
union officials reported difficulties in getting people to adopt the
position of local representative. For example, in People's Bank one
of the workplace representatives described himself as an inactive
member!

In both cases, however, informal participation levels were relatively high, particularly in Bus Company. This most often related
to going to the local representative informally for help or advice
or reading union literature. Clearly, though, even this (limited)
level of membership participation can have implications. This is
suggested by Fosh who argues that:

during a surge of participation, a significant proportion of the members shift from an attitude of leaving it to others to one of assuming their share of the group action as their latent workplace solidarity emerges (1993: 580).

Possible explanations for low general levels of participation will be discussed below.

The New Employment Relationship

As outlined above, the shift to an economy dominated by private sector services, and often characterised by the privatisation of state enterprises has a number of implications for the employment relationship (Greco, 2002; Thompson, 2003). In Bus Company, we have already seen that the issue of impending deregulation (or as the drivers saw it, privatisation) was the key issue for many respondents. Almost without exception the drivers were prepared to strike to attempt to fend off this outcome. The general fear was that moving them to the status of private sector employees was a naked attempt to downgrade their pay and working conditions, and endanger their job security:[6]

> . . . working for a private operator we'd lose all our working conditions, and those guys hire and fire at will. . . . We can't live under those circumstances in this day and age . . . we shouldn't have to (Donal, SIPTU workplace representative).

The financial services industry has undergone significant change in recent decades and is viewed as being in the vanguard of new, post-Fordist employment (Hutton, 1996; Sassen, 2000, Regini et al., 2000). At People's Bank, a key issue for respondents was job security. Interestingly, again, this was not always an issue that affected the respondents personally, many were core personnel, but there was an awareness that the nature of financial services

---

[6] It should be noted, too, that most respondents made reference to their view of the job as a "public service", which they felt would be downgraded to the detriment of the general public if the plans went ahead.

employment had become more fluid. It was pointed out to IBOA members at a union meeting that the bank was quite happy with high levels of staff turnover at junior levels (IBOA members meeting, June 2003). In fact, three of the (middle grade) younger respondents were actively seeking other employment.

Several of the respondents had begun life at the bank as temporary workers. This was significant in that the union does not attempt to recruit such employees:

> I joined the union after I was made permanent. There wasn't much point I was told, in joining before I was made permanent (Jill, IBOA member).

So, on the one hand, the bank is pursuing a policy of high levels of staff turnover and increased numbers of temporary staff and, on the other, these staff are not encouraged (indeed are discouraged) to take up union membership. This has clear implications for workplace collectivism, given the increasing share of part-time and temporary Irish workers (O'Connell, 2000).

Consumption, Time and Non-Participation

Low levels of (at least formal) participation in union affairs were common in both workplaces. One explanation for low levels of rank-and-file participation is that such activity is now seen as largely irrelevant in comparison with the importance of consumption in the lives of working people (Harvey, 1990). However, the data suggest that an alternative explanation may be simply one related to time pressures. All of the bank respondents (including those only in their present jobs for up to a year) reported that workloads were constantly increasing:

> I think the way people are working isn't conducive to their own health . . . if you're having to do it week-in, week-out you're physically, mentally under a lot more strain all the time (Eoghan, IBOA member).

Frequently, time pressures and work stresses were accompanied by family and domestic responsibilities:

> I was actually offered a promotion here and I turned it down. One of the reasons was my wife works in a bank, she works in the IFSC, and we've two kids (Gary, IBOA workplace representative).

A big problem was that work levels were on the increase at the same time that the bank was increasingly adopting a policy of high staff turnover levels. This illustrates that employers may decide to make specific trade-offs in the type of "flexible" work practices they pursue. Attempts to pursue functional flexibility (which requires a skilled, well-trained workforce, implying a long-term commitment by the firm to the employment relationship) will make it difficult to implement numerical flexibility (which is not based on any training element, but fluid external labour markets and therefore a low commitment employer/employee relationship Lodovici, 1999; Regini, 1999). Clearly the latter, at least in terms of non-core workers, is the model preferred at People's Bank.

While participation levels at Bus Company were higher, and there was general satisfaction with working conditions, issues of stress and work intensification were raised by several respondents:

> . . . at the moment, the times that you're expected to do your journey as one man with the traffic conditions. . . . You don't even get time to get out and stretch your legs. It's crazy (Niall, SIPTU member).

Again, time pressure was linked frequently with domestic responsibilities. Thus, both union representatives and company officials noted that issues of "life/work" balance were increasingly surfacing, particularly for workers with long commutes. The significance of time and/or domestic responsibilities is significant for another aspect of the collective work experience as well. In both companies there were quite extensive sports and social facilities. However, many respondents complained that they simply did not have the time to avail of them. The data suggest, therefore that, in terms of non-participation in union (and indeed other non-job specific workplace activities), the rise of consumption is less relevant than issues of work intensification and time pressure.

4. CONCLUSIONS

This chapter has considered arguments around the demise of collectivism, the rise of consumption, and structural changes in the nature of employment in Ireland that impact on union members' participation in and relationship with their trade union. Far from a decline in the salience of trade unionism to working life, the importance of the union is clearly acknowledged. Indeed, in Bus Company union membership is central in the lives of workers under threat from macro-economic structural changes. This salience has persisted even though a majority of respondents feel that their union's role has diminished or that it has unsatisfactory influence over many key areas of working life. This has been demonstrated by the willingness in both workplaces of members to take industrial action over perceived injustices.

What is clear, however, is that most respondents feel under threat from ever more powerful employers. The salience of the union, then, as a protective mechanism has remained important. Finally, we have seen that many recent changes in the employment sphere are perceived as negative by employees. Most respondents reported work and stress intensification and greater job insecurity. This intensification has also resulted in severe time pressure that impedes the ability of members to participate fully in union and, indeed social, activities at the workplace, but has reinforced their belief in the necessity of union membership.

Chapter 9

THE LONG AND THE SHORT OF IT: WORKING TIME IN THE IRISH IT SECTOR

Aileen O'Carroll

1. INTRODUCTION

This chapter is based upon a research project that examined the working time of those employed in the Irish software industries. Twenty-one high-end IT workers participated. The group comprised both men and women and a variety of occupations (programmers, technical writers and marketing executives). Some worked in large companies, some in small. Some companies were Irish owned, some were not. The participants in the project were asked, over the course of a year (from October 1999 to September 2000), to fill in weekly time diaries that noted their starting and finishing times. They were also interviewed five times throughout the year, and material from those interviews illustrates the points made in this argument. In popular mythology, computer workers are supposed to work long hours. There are stories of the programmer who slept under his desk, or programmed nude late into the night, scaring the cleaners (Bronson, 1999). However, most of the respondents in this study did not report long working hours. How can this deviation from the popular myth of long hours in the IT sector be explained?

2. WORKING HOURS IN THE IT SECTOR IN IRELAND

The Quarterly National Household Survey data produced by the Irish Central Statistics Office provides information on those working in the IT sector (Nace 72, computing and computer services). Table 9.1 shows a breakdown of working hours both in the information technology sector and among the general Irish population.

The QNHS data shows that the numbers working 40 hours and over (48.3 per cent) in IT are only marginally greater than the numbers working less than 40 hours (42.7 per cent of employees). The time diaries I collected captured a similar picture, though the diaries reported less long-hours workers than found in the QNHS survey. The QNHS report that 48.3 per cent of computer workers work longer than a 40-hour week while the diaries record that 39.6 per cent of weeks recorded are longer than a 40 hour week. The QNHS data is gathered from the answer to the question "How many hours do you usually work at this job, including regular overtime, but excluding meal breaks?" Gershuny and Robinson (1994) found that questionnaires diverged from time data indicating that those working longer hours over-estimated the number of hours worked. That is, time-diary data tends to be more accurate in measuring the working hours of long-hours workers. However, taken together, they indicate that this is a sector in which long hours are prevalent but are not certainly the norm.

Table 9.1 also shows the usual working hours for all full-time employees in Ireland in 2000. The software sector does not have a higher percentage of workers working more than 45 hours than found in the general population (16.3 per cent are found in Nace 72, as opposed to 22.43 per cent of those working full-time in the general population). The European Labour Force Survey reports that in the UK in 1999 34 per cent of those in Nace 72 worked longer than 45 hours. This is double the percentage of those working in the same sector in Ireland.

Table 9.1: Hours Worked per Week

Hours	Nace 72 (2000 Q1) %	All Persons in Employment (ILO) %	Full-time Employment * %
1-9		1.7	
10-19	1.0	5.1	
20-29	2.0	9.1	
30-34		3.2	4.5
35-39	39.7	29.7	41.8
40-44	32.0	38.3	31.3
45 & over	16.3	22.3	22.4
Hours vary	8.7	16.0	
Not stated		12.8	
Total	99.7	100.0	100.0
Average hours per week	40.6	38	

*Time bands as % of those working over 30 hours a week

All persons in Employment includes persons aged 15 years and over in employment (ILO)

QNHS 2000 Q1 (special extraction) obtained from the Central Statistics Office www.cso.ie

Both the diary and QNHS results indicate that the perception of a long hours culture is only reality for some people working within the sector. This was also the result in the workplaces of those interviewed. Yet, respondents reported that there were a few individuals in their workplaces who worked long hours. What distinguishes one group from another? Why do some work over 45 hours a week, others less than 40?

Plantenga and Remery (2002) outline three areas which influence the organisation of working time in the information technology sector: the nature of the service being provided; the nature of the workforce; and flexibility requirements of the workforce. These factors are common to both the long-hours and short-hours groups. From the time diaries, the factor that accounts most for the differences is working hours of the different companies, separated by over seventeen hours a week in the sample.

3. COMPANY CULTURE

In these workplaces, the production of knowledge is an intangible process which makes it difficult to impose traditional hierarchical methods of management on knowledge industries. Those doing the work probably know more about the field than those supervising them. Even in situations where manager and worker both understand the particular area, neither can forecast how long it will take to solve a particular problem by, for example, writing a new program or debugging an existing program. Yet, management must ensure somehow that employees are working to their maximum ability without having a clear notion how that ability translates into timeslots on a schedule (Causer and Jones, 1996).

One solution to the problem is to manipulate workplace culture. Causer and Jones (1996) describe how the male dominated nature of computing recreates the "collegial" culture of universities. Control does not come from the top down, as in traditional workplaces, but from the side, from one's peers, co-workers, team-mates or customers. The employee has far more control over their work process than those working in traditional assembly line regimes or "McDonaldised" industries. They have control, but their commitment to the workplace is mobilised to operate in management's interests; in this case, commitment to organisational time and the temporal framework of organisational culture.

Creating a cultural of commitment is often done indirectly; however, direct methods of control are often also used. Participants spoke of being directly warned that they needed to come into work earlier. One of the long-hours workers was told she needed to work at the weekend, and that she should remember her review was coming up soon — directly linking promotions and career to working long hours.

A number of indirect strategies were also evident. Much has been written about the use of teams as a controlling mechanism in workplaces with a flattened hierarchy. For some respondents it was the gaze of their co-workers rather than the gaze of management that brought attention to their working time:

> If you come into work at half-ten and there's somebody who's been there since nine . . . you always get that feeling that they resent you because "I have to get up in the morning so why didn't you get up". I mean it hasn't cost them anything but sometimes people generally do feel resentful. It's one of the things I don't like about working with other people I guess or even not having my own office. (Joe 2: 120 — 38.5 mean working hours weekly (excluding lunch))

Participants in both groups described co-workers complaining about them arriving into work late or leaving too early (or if not complaining directly, teasing or exhibiting surprise). Some of the shorter-hours workers were in teams which contained members who were also the customer for the product being produced. One participant spoke of the pressure that came from customers expecting the product to be modified as it was produced, creating more work and more pressure to work longer. Finally pressure comes from the assumption that long hours are the expected norm.

Within the workplace, many spoke of the exceptional individuals who worked late in the night. These individuals act as Stakhanovites,[1] binding the image of the high-tech workplace with the long-hours worker. It is these isolated individuals who are the object of popular journalism. For example, I described above the story of the programmer who worked late, alone in his office; being a nudist, he worked naked. This individual provided the title to a book on software workers in Silicon Valley. Yet the

---

[1] Stakhanovites were workers in the Soviet Union who regularly surpassed production quotas and were specially honoured and rewarded.

author did not tell the story of the nudist co-workers who had all left the office, leaving our nudist alone. The exception is high-lighted, the majority disappear.

Orientations to Working Time

However, not all of the companies had a long hours culture. At the time of the study there was a strong labour market, and em-ployees could and did change workplaces in order to better their working conditions. The concept of orientations to working time helps explain why the long-hours workers did not take this op-portunity to move, instead accepting their working conditions. Orientations to working time are ways of thinking about working time which influence how the working day is structured. With a task orientation, the working day is as long as it takes to complete the task. With clock orientation, the length of the working day is determined by the time at which one clocks in and the time at which one clocks out (Thompson, 1991).

Traditionally the structure of the working day has been de-termined by the labour contract. The respondents' choices about their time still operate within the parameters set by the labour contract. However, there is a blurring of the edges, increasing variability with respect to length of working day (mean variation is 2.44 hours), and starting and finishing times. One does not clock in and out. Yet, the clock has not been replaced by the task.

In pre-industrial society, bouts of intense work alternated with bouts of leisure (Thompson, 1991). This type of task orientation is not evident here. One must still work every day, regardless of whether there are tasks to be completed or not. One must still turn up in the morning and leave in the evening, though the timing of the start and the finish are not clearly defined.

The contract still exists yet it is often ignored. Employees have an understanding that explicitly rejects clock-based discipline as being unfair and illogical. One is expected to stay in work until the task is completed. Yet, work has not become entirely task-based. Though tasks and deadlines increase the working day, this happens on an occasional basis and to a sub-section of the workforce. The task is not supremely important; some still finish work after counting eight hours. The task can and sometimes is ignored. This is an orientation that has elements of clock and task, where working time is defined by expectations of what is "normal" or "reasonable".

Expectations of what is normal have always played an important part in debates on working time. The clock orientation of the eight-hour day movement drew legitimacy by asserting the importance of non-working time over working time, driving towards establishing a clock. These workers' new orientation does not want fixed starting and finishing times; rather they want flexibility that fits the time of work into their lives.

As such, working time orientation in these workplaces revolves around highly contested definitions of what is "normal". Ideas about what is reasonable or fair with respect to working time come from the examples of managers, relationships with peers, institutional definitions of the working day and understandings of what is socially acceptable. Each attempts to legitimise what they consider to be normal.

Companies may draw on the task and the need for the project to meet a deadline, defining long working hours as normal. Employees were not able to draw on the task to shorten their hours, staying at work even when their task was completed. Instead, they drew on the clock, referring to length of time worked previously or their contracted hours. In some instances, they sought legitimacy for a decision to work shorter hours from the longer hours they worked earlier. Alternatively, some drew on the clock as defined within their contract, defining the eight-hour day as normal. Others determined their finishing times by counting forward from their starting times. If they came in earlier, it was not in response to management's desires, but in order to legitimately leave earlier. Some changed their working times to suit their non-working time. For example, women often drew on child-caring responsibilities to legitimate and shorten their working hours (although this choice comes with a cost in long-hours work cultures).

However, company culture is not a static entity; it must be continually created and re-created. There are spaces within which workers can exercise autonomy. At the same time, the autonomy of the individual and work teams operates alongside a framework set by management. Temporal autonomy operates sometimes inside and sometimes outside this framework. Workers' actions are not simply defined by management structure, resisting or acquiescing. While these responses can be seen, workers can also act independently of organisational frameworks and rhetoric, leading the organisation rather than following it.

4. THE LONG-HOURS GROUP

In the company with the longest working hours, "Cobh", many participants used the phrase "as long as the work gets done" to explain how they controlled their working time as long as they completed tasks they were given. This is explained below:

> A. I one hundred per cent control my own work pace although pressure is applied, but not through the normal mechanisms that pressures would be applied. It's just expected, it's expected that you'll stay to a minimum of six o'clock at night, nobody tells you, in fact if I left at three o'clock some day nobody would say it, that's because they know you are getting your . . . work done.

> Q. How do you know it's expected?

> A. The volume of work which is given to you and everyone performs to. If you compare your workload to your direct manager's workload, everybody performs to a minimum of 50 to a maximum of 90 hours a week so there is nobody left out of the equation, it's very much lead by example. (Conor 1: 52-56 — 52.08 mean working hours weekly (excluding lunch))

In assembly line organisations the pace of work is dictated by the speed of the line. In these knowledge workplaces, deadlines, shipping dates and management plans increase the amount of work to be done. Yet, the expectation is not to work long hours, but to finish one's work within certain deadlines. There is an expectation too that long hours will be worked by everyone within the company to meet by company's "volume of work". This is determined by the time frames allocated in the project planning process. The inability of the planning to deliver a 40-hour week has more to do with management design than any intrinsic aspect of the work process in the knowledge industry.

The workers in Cobh were very critical of this use of planning to make employees work longer hours:

> A. I think people can work a 50-hour week but that's going to have a long-term effect. I don't think a 50-hour week is feasible for very long. I know I worked [them] and the older you get the less feasible it is and the more responsibilities you have outside of work . . . I've worked effectively the last four years of my life in excess of 50 hours a week. The first year of that was 90-hour weeks with I suppose you could say with a lot of adverse affects. . . . It's unfeasible for a company to expect the bulk of its employees to do it. (Conor 2: 54 — 52.08 mean working hours weekly (excluding lunch))

> A. A properly run company doesn't depend on people working 60 hours a week. A properly run company is a company in which people work 48 hours a week and the work gets done. And if there is too much work to be done either you cut back on work or you increase the number of people. . . . There are people feeling like they are on this permanent — not death march 'cause things actually get done — but they are in a permanent state of crisis avoidance and although that has gone to a certain extent, there is still that feeling that people could be working longer hours. (Mike 3: 21-27 — 49 mean working hours weekly (excluding lunch))

These two quotes also show very different estimations of what are "normal" or "reasonable" working hours. For Conor a 50-hour week is evidence of bad planning and thus unacceptable, while for Mike a 48-hour week falls within his definition of "a properly run company" and hence is acceptable.

Even within this long-hours workplace, the temporal culture of the organisation was not stable and was at times challenged. One software worker commented, "the management are very good at keeping up the sense of crisis" (Mike 2: 112-116), creating an artificial sense of panic to heighten commitment to the workplace. Yet, there was also a growing cynicism amongst workers about the management of the culture.

There were also differences between senior and more junior level workers such as programmers. One senior programmer said he feels like he is letting his workmates down if he leaves at a "sensible time". He links this to his experience of working in college, being used to working long hours and being in the company from its early days when its working culture was similar to his college experiences. However, younger staff were resistant to that culture and did not share the view of the workplace as one where all levels of the hierarchy must co-operate together on an equal basis. He once defended his friend, a manager, from angry junior staff who did not want to put in the hours to meet a deadline: whether the deadline was met was the company's concern, not theirs. The junior staff also joined companies with large bureaucracies. Informal relationships between management and worker had been replaced by formal hierarchies and procedures, and workplace commitment undermined.

All but one of those working in Cobh worked longer hours than they wanted to. These Cobh workers were quite different from two long-hours workers, Nick and Johnny, who had moved from larger companies to start-ups, increasing their working hours. This is an example of one of the most enduring stories in information technology — the start-up, in which long hours are rewarded by promises of wealth and success. Nick and Johnny, at the beginning of that dream, were satisfied with the hours worked. For others in the start-up, the hope of a pay-off had re-ceded; all that remained were the long hours. One of these work-ers, Catherine, stated: "I fell for the whole routine, that [working extra] will come up in the review and you will be rewarded gen-erously" (Catherine 3: 41-55). After these interviews were con-ducted, these workers left the company: two to travel around the world, one to go to the US and one left the industry altogether. They used exit as a strategy to combat the temporal organisation of a time-greedy company.

5. THE SHORTER-HOURS GROUP

Half of the shorter-hours workers felt there was no expectation for them to work long hours. Mixed responses were often given when asked about the expectations of their company, many saying there was no expectation that they should work long hours and that a long-hours culture existed. For example, Aoife says the company is "reasonable" expecting "more than the minimum" while identi-fying people who worked longer hours:

> A. They expect about nine to half-five. Well that amount anyway but they expect you to be very flexible. They ex-pect you to work late if you have to. It's in your contract that you can't say no and you can't be paid for it. So it's ob-viously in the culture. They expect you to work weekends if you have to but in practice I think unless you have an un-reasonable manager they don't actually abuse [it] because they're so big and they have enough people to do the work. So I think to some extent people who work too much, it's because they don't mind. There's a lot of people who are very busy bodies and who want to work a lot, either for their career or because they enjoy it. But the company doesn't really force you. They ask a bit more maybe than the strict minimum or at least in theory you have to be pre-pared and you have to say you're prepared to do it but in practice I don't think they abuse you really. (Aoife 3: 270)

In terms of orientations to work, some explicitly did not draw their conception of what was reasonable from the working hours of those they worked with. Two types of strategies that limited working hours were evident. Thompson and Ackroyd show that work limitation practices have been frequently uncovered by researchers examining work organisations (Ackroyd and Thompson, 1999; Cunnision, 1964; Dalton, 1948; Goodrich, 1975; Lupton, 1963; Montgomery, 1980; Roy, 1952). In the short-hours workplaces, the employees' first strategy limited the working day rather than limiting work within the working day. The second strategy involved employees acting alongside the temporal organisation of work, not in response to the structures of the organisation. By organising working time according to their needs, these employees are not only "managing to resist" but also "managing management" (Collinson, 1992).

The shorter-hours workplaces had a number of similar features to, and outcomes arising from, the long-hours workplace. There was pressure to work from incorporating the customer into the work team; never-ending tasks; a cynicism that develops over time; and a withdrawal of personal commitment to the work process. However, the workers did more than vocally object at having to work late as in the example of the junior programmers above. The short-hours workers moved one step further: the team set the working time for itself. This has resonance with "soldiering" in the famous Hawthorn experiments in which a work group ensured the amount of work done by individuals was set by the group as a whole (Mayo, 1933).

This practice involved disengagement from the work process. Work time is placed under limits and the demands of the task are ignored:

Q. How do you cope with that, having too much work?

A. I just don't do it. It just means projects get backed up. It means our customers then complain to me and then complain to my boss and then complain to his boss and they say we want this work done . . . and [there is a] kind of constant tension over it, "why aren't they doing the work quickly enough" and obviously the idea is that maybe we should just work faster but everyone just has to work at their own pace but if you're constantly under pressure to have this work done it does kind of mean that you never really feel satisfied with what you're doing.

Q. At what point did you start getting cynical, how long were you working?

A. I suppose about two years in my previous job, when you know it doesn't really like help either yourself or your career if you allow yourself to be exploited, nobody really appreciates it. . . . That you might feel that you're building your career or you're showing that you're a really hard worker but really you're just showing yourself to be a bit of an idiot and people do look at it that way as well.

Q. How would you know?

A. Well if I took on somebody and they rushed to do everything they had to do and came in on the weekends in order to get extra work done, I wouldn't sort of feel inclined to say I must give that person a pay rise or I must promote that person really quickly . . . I would more take him aside and say "don't, you fool", no . . . I don't think it does actually work. Obviously it helps but it doesn't help just that easily. It doesn't add up. (Dermot 3: 16-31 — 36.53 mean working hours weekly (excluding lunch))

Dermot also described how the team agreed to come in at a particular time to be visible to the company as being in work. Here we see management's gaze influencing starting time. However, although they started early in order to be visible, they also left after eight hours, bring other team members into line if they deviated from this norm. Further, Dermot spoke of withdrawing his labour as he became cynical of management panics — a practice used by other respondents too. This de-prioritising the work task involved employees not caring whether the work was done or the deadline met, and of being willing to leave their work behind unfinished.

In the shorter-hours companies, flexibility was more likely to be granted in response to the demands of employees. Many identified the ability to determine their own starting time as an important aspect of the workplace. To those with child care responsibility, it was particularly important as it allowed greater manageability with respect to traffic and crèches. For most, this flexibility was not enshrined in their contracts; rather it became custom through informal practice. Some participants spoke of efforts by management to get them to arrive in on time, and how, after initially responding to these requests, they gradually re-introduced their practice of arriving at various times in the morning.

In these demands for flexibility, the de-prioritising of work tasks and work time is arranged around the demands of non-work time (such as the time of child care or time sleeping). In another workplace, software developers came and went as they chose. After attempts to regularise working hours failed, all were sent a memo granting official recognition to the practice. Such flexibility is emblematic of the new workplace, although the identification as something created by employee practices is less often highlighted.

Strategies more resonant of traditional industrial workplaces were also evident. A number of employees combined flexibility with clock watching. Arriving at a later time, they counted their hours, leaving eight hours after work started. This type of behaviour is most certainly not supposed to be occurring in these new autonomous workplaces. For two of these respondents — recent graduates — working long hours was not something to be valorised. One compared the experience of working in the US with that of working in Ireland, describing the American work ethic as "scary". He also noted the presence in this workplace of the Stakhanovite, the exceptional long-hours worker, whose example is rejected. Instead of a time determined by the task, these graduate workers still measured their time according to the clock.

6. CONCLUSION

The IT sector in Ireland has much in common with that in the US in terms of institutional frameworks. Working time is relatively un-regulated legally. Trade unions play almost no role in negotiating workplace conditions. Many companies are US in origin, sell to US markets or take their organisational cues from the working culture of Silicon Valley. In Ireland, as in the US, the project team is at the centre of the work organisation, and indeed many of the Irish teams stretch across the globe, including US based employees. As such, this study concurs with accounts of the production process drawn from Irish workplaces (O'Riain, 2002) and the US (Perlow, 1997) in which the intensity of work increases as deadlines are approached, and declines once deadlines are passed. Perlow describes an additional type of workplace, one in which a sense of continual urgency was evident. One of the workplaces in this study had a similar working culture.

Yet differences between Irish and US workplaces were also evident, especially in terms of working hours. A number of accounts from the US indicate that extremely long hours between 70 and 90 are worked (Bronson, 1999; Schor, 1991; Kidder, 1981; Perlow, 1997; Hochschild, 1997). Even the longest week noted within this study (65.6 hours) fell short of this number. CSO statistics also show that only a minority of those working in computers or computer services in Ireland work longer than 45 hours a week (16.3 per cent). In the US, Hochschild reported that 70 per cent of those she studied regularly worked overtime, while 49 per cent regularly worked weekends (1997). Further, Perlow noted that American "managers do not consider a late afternoon or Saturday meeting a serious infringement of engineers' time" (1997: 37). This study showed that many Irish software workers do view these as an infringement. The data highlights that long, short and normal are relative terms that must be considered with respect to national differences. Secondly, it highlights that in Ireland not all companies within the sector are time-greedy.

Perlow notes that in the US, the corporate assumption is that long hours are a consequence of global competition. This assumption is challenged by examining the alternative experiences of working hours found in the software sectors of other countries. The Irish experience is one in which a sizeable minority are working long hours (as in more than 45 hours a week) and sizeable minority are working "normal" hours (as in between 35-39 hours a week). These findings are mirrored in other European countries. Studies of working hours in the software sector in Denmark, the Netherlands, Germany and the UK also found that while a proportion of employees work long hours, a proportion do not (Plantenga and Remery et al., 2001). For example, in the UK 34 per cent of those in Nace 72 work longer than 45 hours a week, while 31 per cent work between 34 and 40 hours a week (Smith, 2001). While in Finland, a different temporal culture again is evident. Working hours are remarkably "normal", with 69 per cent of employees in Nace 72 working between 35 and 40 hour weeks.

These findings should make us critical of any discourse which seeks to identify long working hours as an intrinsic feature of the use of a particular type of technology, work organisation or economic form.[2] Such discourses divert us from understanding that time is of our own making. As Adam argues:

> It does make a difference to our lives whether we understand our social organisation by the clock and calendar as an inevitable fact of life, as a fact of history or as something we have created and imposed on ourselves and maintain by our daily actions. It constitutes the difference between having choices and seeing one's social life as determined (1994: 5).

This is important because a working culture rests very much on shared understandings and beliefs. If only the stories of those who work long hours are told, then these tales become the accepted

---

[2] In this respect I disagree with the Plantenga, et al. (2001) when they argue that "working in IT seems inextricably bound to working long hours".

norm. Similarly, it becomes an unquestioned assumption that non-working time is at the disposal of work time and a resource to be drawn on when required.

This chapter highlights the experience of the hidden majority of those who do not work long hours. Some of that experience is indeed coloured by the conception of the industry as being one in which long hours are worked. Whether or not an individual felt their employer expected them to work longer hours or not, they were always aware that long hours are part and parcel of working within the industry. The result of this is that those who are working long hours often see themselves as the rule rather than the exception within the industry.

This "Stakhanovite" effect may be what keeps those working more "normal" hours from reducing their hours further. Indeed what was interesting to note in this study is that despite control over one's working hours, and the flexibility of the work process (which surely implies that at some times there was very little to do) so few of the participants took the opportunity to work much shorter hours. Part of this may also be explained by company strategy. Thus, US research highlights the resistance to "family friendly" policies such as part-time work, job-sharing or tele-working (Perlow, 1997; Hochschild, 1997). Two of the participants in this study switched to part-time working, and one worked from home one day a week. However, their experiences would seem to be exceptional as CSO figures for the sector in general show that less than 3 per cent work less than 35 hours a week.

In the Irish workplaces studied, orientation to working time is highly contested with various actors attempting to legitimise claims that their particular definition of "normality" should apply. In this sense, there are many orientations to work each drawing on discourses of normality, acceptability, and fairness. Like previous contests about work orientation, the heart of this debate is the relationship between work and non-work time. The difference here is that interplay between flexibility and temporal autonomy has come to the fore. Flexibility minimises the importance of the company clock in regulating working hours. Since individuals have a degree of autonomy over their working hours, flexibility results in variations in the lengths of the working day, leading to the fragmentation of working time in this sector.

The result is that those working in a "long-hours" company culture can not draw on a universally accepted definition of what is normal to limit the expansion of their working hours. In industrial society trade unions challenged the current standard working time in an effort to re-introduce a new lower standard. Here there is no standard to challenge; instead, challenges come from employees' own orientations to working time. This lack of a standard, combined with an orientation that gives more priority to work/life balance, allows some workers freedom to vary their hours to reduce conflicts between working and non-working life, while others become the temporal Stakhanovites that colour the popular perception of work in the IT sector.

Chapter 10

THE LABOUR PROCESS REVISITED: TRAINING, SKILL, CONTROL AND THE CULTURE OF THE CUSTOMER IN THE RETAIL INDUSTRY

Tony Cunningham

1. INTRODUCTION

In the 1990s global capital privileged the Irish economy with an abundance of work and apparent prosperity. This period was characterised by an almost insatiable demand for labour, world-beating growth rates and the emergence of a wholehearted consumer society. Female participation in paid work expanded dramatically and the state moved from a net exporter of labour to a net importer. While many well-paid jobs were created, much of the new work was low-paid and part-time and could be characterised as "poor", especially in the service industry and in particular the retail industry. However, in the euphoria that surrounded this newly found prosperity, the presence of work was seen as an end in itself. According to the political and economic discourse that informs much of the debate, work, good or bad, is seen to provide dignity and the chance to participate in and contribute to society and the economy as a fully fledged consumer-citizen.

This understanding is underpinned by a strand of contemporary sociology suggesting that in high modernity we are disembedded from structure and free to pursue and construct reflexive narratives of the self (Giddens, 1991). The individual becomes involved in a "reflexive project of the self, which consists in the sustaining of coherent, yet continuously revised biographical narratives", requiring the acquisition and "reacquisition of knowledge and skills" (1991: 5, 7). In such a scenario, issues of class, gender and the labour process lose their importance to be replaced by concepts of risk, anxiety and work-life balance. As Lash and Urry (1994: 5) argue, "structural change in the economy forces individuals to be freed from the structural rigidity of the Fordist labour process". While this might be true for an elite section of the workforce, a large proportion is not privileged with such freedom — despite the emphasis on flexibility, autonomy, reflexivity and empowerment.

This chapter focuses on one such group — retail workers. It draws on a series of interviews with one male and seven female workers who were employed in department stores in the 1950s to 1980s, and who now work in self-service multiples such as Marks and Spencer and Dunne Stores or department stores like Arnott's. After "locating" the retail worker and the context wherein the labour process is played out, I explore the data arguing that issues of skill, deskilling, control and alienation are alive and well in the workplace. Further, I argue that the labour process is directed at the subjectivity of the worker with a view to rendering them complicit in the process and fostering a "culture of the customer" in the workplace.

2. LOCATING THE RETAIL WORKER

With the rise of the department store, sales people played a vital role in the selling process, promoting a culture of consumption and realising profit. The spectacle and grandeur of the department store was not designed for entertainment only but to expand consumption and profit. Within the department store, sales people were all powerful as far as the customer and selling process was concerned. While the customer was free to stroll and admire commodities on display, the store was a place of business in which one had to be served. This was underpinned by the store's physical layout where products were behind the counter or in a space controlled by a sales person. The sales person's job was to convert the stroller into a paying customer and "reliable consumer". As such, the retail worker played a vital part in the commodity chain (Leslie, 2002: 62), recognised in the commission system. For instance, Ronnie Nesbitt (1993: 107) of Arnott's described his sales staff as the company's most important asset, believing that "a process of education could produce stars of the future, or at least a well trained cadre of managers".

Alongside the department store, Marks and Spencer pioneered the multiple store in the UK. While these stores are laid out in "departments", the management structures and functions of the staff are very different from those of the department store. Unlike department stores such as Arnott's, which allowed a degree of autonomy to departments and staff, Marks and Spencer's management focus on the "requirements of the customer" displayed all the characteristics of Taylorism. All decisions relating to buying stock, distribution, design and layout of store are centrally controlled by head office with personnel management the only area delegated to local management, although recruitment policy and training are dictated by the head office (Drucker, 1974; Lancaster, 1995; Sieff, 1991; Tse, 1985).

While department stores were aimed at bourgeois elite consumption (Corrigan, 1997), Marks and Spencer's declared mission was to democratise consumption and to "to subvert the British class system" and address issues of poverty and welfare (Drucker, 1974: 96; Sieff, 1990: 12-13). As part of this social agenda managers were seen as welfare officers to a working class female staff (1990: 305). In 1967 Dunne Stores became a force in the Irish retail market and introduced the concept of self-service in the drapery trade. While they did not subscribe to the social agenda of Marks and Spencer they did subscribe to their philosophy of selling and work organisation. For example, customers were invited to become "sales workers" to themselves. However, alongside the re-definition of sales work, workers in multiples such as Marks and Spencer are involved in a process of "continuous learning" (Drucker, 1974: 147).

In recent decades, shopping and selling have become as much a recreational activity as a functional activity, and a way of giving expression to or constructing the self (Falk, 1997: 177-183). Further, Campbell argues that shopping and shopping space became feminised as a source of freedom and expression for women (1997: 166-175). Workers in the retail industry have also been subjected to a process of sexualisation or desexualisation (Adkins, 1995: 51). Training not only focuses on being friendly or helpful but also involves staff having "high personal standards" particularly in relation to appearance and hygiene (1995: 97). This concentration on appearance is not purely for aesthetic reasons but also relates to the control and regulation of the worker.

3. THE LABOUR PROCESS IN 2000

It is understandable that labour process analysis (Braverman, 1974) has fallen out of favour. When we look at work in Ireland today it is hard not to be grateful to global capital for delivering an abundance of work and affluence in the late twentieth century. As such, labour process analysis, with its emphasis on the exploitative nature of work in a capitalist society, the deskilling or degradation of work and the control of workers may, for some, seem churlish. The contention that this process results in the alienation of workers from the process of production, the product of their labour, their fellow workers and their own human potential would appear to be even more problematic.

It is even more unwelcome in the context of a new orthodoxy that suggests modern life is characterised by reflexive and empowered individuals (Giddens, 1991) involved in the aesthetic "construction of distinctive lifestyles" in all areas of life including work (Featherstone, 1991: 66-68). In the retail industry, Du Gay suggests that this "enterprising customer is placed at the moral centre of the market based universe" (1996: 76-78); while workers are encouraged to "stay close to the customer" and to imagine themselves as customers with individual needs and desires (as defined by corporate culture).

Rather than "devaluing" a labour process framework, this orthodoxy emphasises capital's more flexible and reflexive engagement with the labour process, cloaked in kinder and more caring managerial discourses and practices. In these flexible labour processes, control is articulated in diverse ways from direct supervision through surveillance to the appearance of autonomy and self-monitoring. The struggle over skill and knowledge extends to the subjectivity of workers, rendering workers complicit in their own exploitation and alienation. While resistance is not precluded, this process disguises the exploitative and alienating nature of the relationship. This is achieved by controlling the agenda, appropriating discourses of self-development, and shaping a norms and values embedded with the ethos of the market and morals of consumption.

4. The Labour Process in Action[1]

Changing Job Descriptions and the Deskilling of Work

In Irish department stores before the 1990s, workers were trained in many aspects of selling from colour co-ordination, pricing, display and knowledge of materials. However, the main task was selling. A good sales person knew their stock and customer intimately, using different strategies to achieve a sale. It was imperative to develop a personal trusting relationship with the customer in the short time available and to ensure that the customer left the shop with "suitable" merchandise only. Very often customers who had been well looked after and with whom a trusting rela-

---

[1] Note the data presented in the following sections are a composite representation of the interviewees' recollections and experiences.

tionship had been achieved, would become the sales person's "customer", or indeed recommend them to friends.

There was a pressure to sell and it was expected that once a customer entered the shop they would buy. Once the ritual greeting was offered the sales person then had to achieve a sale. Once a sale was achieved the customer was encouraged to buy another item to complement their first purchase. Different psychological and emotional techniques were used to gain the customer's trust. The women interviewed did not see their jobs as being skilled but rather saw them in terms of flair and talent. The one man interviewed drew on a particularly masculine discourse and saw his job in terms of skill and as something he had to work at rather than having a "natural" talent for sales.

The job description of the worker in the multiple in the 1990s was described in less complex terms. The floor staff have six basic tasks: checking customers and the merchandise into and then out of the fitting room; folding clothes tried on in the fitting room; re-displaying these goods; keeping the displays tidy and attending to till duties. The till is completely automated using a scanner and credit card checking facility. Workers are usually rotated during the day and assigned a variety of tasks. For instance, they might start on the till, move to the fitting room and finish the day tidying the display. Customers with queries should be directed to the customer service department.

Thus, retail work has been deskilled with the introduction of self-service multiples. Department stores offered "careers" and the opportunity to learn a trade that involved developing skills and talent. However, work in the self-service multiple is functional and Taylorised. In the traditional department store customer care was invested in the sales worker who provided service and advice. They served the customer's needs, making sure they only sold suitable high quality goods that would contribute to the customer's "happiness". They also had to build professional and personal relationships with the customer, drawing on intimate knowledge of the merchandise and the customer. This also involved reciprocal trust and faith between the buyer, management and sales staff.

However, customer care in the self-service multiple store means something different. It has been broken down into its component parts and removed from individual workers whose only requirement is to be pleasant and presentable in carrying out basic functions. In the multiple store, a customer service counter deals with exchanges and other customer queries. Beyond this, customer service revolves around aesthetics and access to goods on display. The offices and staff areas away from the shop floor are often known as the backstage, rendering the shop floor as both auditorium and stage. In the department store, sales staff were "performers" who were free to "ad lib", but within the confines of the company script. In the multiple store workers are little more than stagehands, ensuring props are present and the stage and auditorium ready for performing. The performance of buying and selling is external to the shop worker and invested in the "shopper" and the ambience of the store. The workers are functional components of the process, employed to carry out basic functions.

These companies rely on marketing, branding and ambience rather than sales workers. They value flexibility, efficiency and perception. Management has deconstructed the process of selling; the "knowledge" originally invested in workers has been reformulated in the marketing and "perception" of customer service. This process is accelerated and intensified through the introduction of new technologies that remove functions and control from the worker. As clerical duties, buying and stock control are relocated to sections away from the shop floor, the worker loses contact with the process of selling and becomes marginalised. The idea of service and quality is removed from the sales workers and invested in departments that dictate display, store layout and positioning of products. Workers lose further contact with the customer as marketing techniques, branding and the production of in house "life style magazines" supplant the workers knowledge as sales persons.

Alienation on the Shop Floor

While the concept of alienation can be seen as outdated, determi-
nistic and essentialist, I would argue that it is not necessarily any
of the above. Rather it points to an idea of good work that goes
beyond the material, where work is potentially meaningful, creative and where the worker has at least a degree of ownership of
the process. This is especially important in the context where the
subjectivity of the worker, as well as his or her labour, becomes
the target of the labour process. Of course there may be an argument to be made that these employees work for the money only
and have a purely instrumental orientation to work. However,
workers as individuals invariably try to make sense of their work
and lives, whether it is through compliance, resistance or an
awareness of the discourses and practices they are engaged in.
More importantly, given the fact that management seeks to engage the subjectivity of the worker with the aim of "governing the
soul" (Rose, 1999), alienation is an important symbolic tool. From
the above job descriptions, it is clear that a process of deskilling of
work and workers has taken place. As a result, it can be argued
that the workers become alienated in the classic sense articulated
by Marx.

For the department store worker it was essential to gain the
respect and trust of the customer. They had "their own" customers who returned to them year upon year. In some instances, special customers were contacted by phone when a new range might
be in stock. This "special" relationship with customers was a
source of pride and satisfaction. In the main they saw themselves
as part of a department sales team. Having said that, for those
working on an individual commission basis, there were many areas of tension arising from competition for sales especially when
conventions were broken by "sharks and grabbers". The introduction of pooled commission combated this but created other tensions where some staff sat back and "took it easy" or did not do
their fair share. However, these tensions were usually sorted out
or regulated within the group.

Interestingly, the department store workers regarded the merchandise in their assigned department as "their stock". They were also proud of "their" stock in terms of quality and indicated some attachment to it especially in the context of sending a customer away happy and "well dressed". This is underscored by the involvement of some of the staff in the display and fitting of merchandise, as well as the sales aspect. As such, these workers had, or imagined, a "real" relationship with the products and the satisfied customer. They also felt that that their input into the selling process contributed real value to the commodity. As such they had a sense of ownership of the process and indeed the products they were selling, something that was partially acknowledged by the commission system.

In the multiple stores there is no real contact with the customer. Despite the attention paid to promoting the merchandise at the induction, there appears to be no relationship with the merchandise other than as consumers. Because of the number of part-time staff and the flexible working conditions, few connections with other staff are possible. There is minor tension at times on the shop floor but this, more often than not, is between supervisor and staff. Temporary and part-time staff found that, because of the structure of their working hours and day, they had small breaks if any; although they may have only worked four hours, they felt they had worked a lot longer.

These workers are alienated from the product, the process, their fellow workers, their human potential and their own personality. They cede the "self" to the company, who reformulates it in a series of rules and regulations. These relate to physical aspects such as hygiene, the wearing of uniforms, rules on jewellery, personal grooming and posture, and personality aspects like "appearing" enthusiastic, smiling, being cheerful, expressing interest and being kind. This is underpinned by a management discourse that invites them to see themselves as customers. In this instance the alienation from the self is intensified, as not only is the physical labour directed by the company, but the emotional and psychological self is also subjected to the same process. Unlike most workers in the department store, these workers are not allocated to any particular area or "department" within the store. This flexibility in terms of time and space results in a fragmentation of their relationships with their work, the merchandise and their colleagues. Because of the surveillance and the short duration of breaks, contact with their peers is minimal. While these workers are functionally flexible, this arises from the degradation of work, the simplification of tasks, and the division of work conception from its execution.

This is not to argue that department store workers were not subject to alienation. While they had a degree of autonomy and could invest something of themselves in the process, there is a sense that they too ceded the "self" to the company. In many ways, their work could be described as "emotional" becoming part of the company image and the service the company offers. Further, whereas the uniformed worker in a self-service store is desexualised, the department store worker was sexualised through the wearing of the commodities they sell, becoming part of the display and thus commodified. However, because they had a degree of autonomy and control over the process, they constructed their work as "theirs" and as an outlet for their talents. The customers were "their" customers first and the company's second.

While this was not true, the important point is that work was organised to allow for this degree of worker autonomy and control over the process. This was reinforced by their involvement in buying functions, fitting and offering fashion etiquette advice. When a customer left the store well dressed and "looking good" it was often as a result of the attention and expertise of the sales person. On the other hand, the multiple-store worker has little control over or autonomy within the process and no real contact with customers, the stock or their fellow workers. The potential for alienation has been intensified and concretised for these workers and there is no room for self-expression or deploying their talent. This is reflected in the sorts of control exercised on the different shop floors.

Controlling the Shop Floor

From the 1940s to the 1960s the workplace was formal and a definite hierarchy existed, although it was relatively flat. In bigger stores owners delegated responsibility to the buyer in each department and as such each department was autonomous and somewhat self-contained. The buyer was directly responsible for the training and performance of the sales staff and took an active interest in all aspects relating to the shop floor. This was especially relevant to apprentices and junior staff. Sanctions were severe, ranging from a reprimand through to suspension without pay to dismissal. The buyer had an open office on the shop floor and observed the performance of the staff, correcting them on their appearance, punctuality, assessing their sales performance and general demeanour. However, once the position of senior sales person was achieved they were relatively autonomous and were more or less left to get on with the job of selling. Competition for bonuses and commission kept them focused, facilitating their autonomy. In later years they often had input into the operation of the department. While individuals competed for sales and commission, which could lead to conflict between the staff, there was a large element of teamwork and co-operation, especially where commission was pooled or a bonus system operated.

There was a great deal of self-regulation within departments, which revolved around a number of rituals and conventions. Convention dictated that each person took their turn and served one customer at a time. The ritual greeting of a customer laid claim to that customer. The ritual greeting was for the most part respected even if it broke one or other of the conventions. However, those who broke with convention were often ostracised and excluded from the group. It is important to point out that responsible autonomy in these stores emerges from a base of direct control over apprentices and junior sales people.

In the self-service multiple a strategy of direct control and surveillance is employed. Supervisors supervise the workers on the shop floor and are in turn supervised and report to the personnel department. Beyond collecting monies from the tills, their function is strictly supervision: informing individuals when they can take a break; when they are required to work; where they are to work; and giving permission for "toilet" break. Decisions on how work is organised and staffing levels are taken in the personnel department, in accordance with guidelines from head office. A system of "Personal Development Reports" is in operation. While the supervisor administers it, the worker assesses their effectiveness and personal development in conjunction with the supervisor.

In addition, "guest shoppers" test the alertness of workers to shoplifting by attempting to smuggle undeclared merchandise into the fitting room. Failure to detect this is reported to the supervisor, who offers a "gentle reprimand" to the guilty party to keep them on their toes. They are also required to sign a book acknowledging the indiscretion and the reprimand. The presence of security cameras, guest shoppers and the supervisors encouraged the workers interviewed to be self-monitoring and careful about talking to each other. One interviewee felt threatened by this lack of trust and was constantly on her guard. The others accepted this as a fact of life. Conditions were described as regimented and strong on discipline. Any deviation from the rules attracts a reprimand. Temporary, part-time staff complained that their temporary status, and the promise of permanency, was used to pressurise them into working unsociable or unsuitable hours.

There is no room for initiative and all work is directed and allocated by the supervisors, in accordance with the company rules. This extends to issues of personal appearance and interaction based on suggested "scripts" with the customers and enacted with an eye to encountering a "mystery shopper". In addition there appears to be little autonomy for many of the management or supervisory grades. Rather, control and conception is located within centralised departments within head office and the majority of grades are purely functional, focused on implementing the rules and regulations of the core management.

This approach is supplemented and informed by a "Human Resources Management" approach (Hourihan and Gunnigle, 1996). For instance, Marks and Spencer have a range of benefits and policies that address women's health issues in place. A company doctor, nurse, chiropodist and hairdresser are available and regular health checks encouraged. There is a subsidised canteen for the workers. All these benefits are in accordance with their principle of "social responsibility". However, there is an issue of control that is central to the principle of social responsibility. Attendance at work is ensured and malingering discouraged by the presence of the company doctor and nurse. This is an important factor in a situation where the minimum amount of labour is engaged, and reinforces the reliability of the flexible deployment of staff.

However, there is a wider benefit as such initiatives counteract the potential for conflict. This is reinforced by using other members of the staff as sponsors or "buddies" for new workers and begins the process of making the workers complicit. This process begins with the induction, where it is stressed how well the company looks after their staff and how good they are to work for. Rather than offering a career they offer a position within an apparently benign paternalistic organisation where their welfare and best interests are looked after. The continuous training offered and the perception of reskilling is central to this process and deflects any real interrogation of the nature of the work. In this way a pretence of equality is perpetuated and resistance deflected. Through an ethos of social responsibility, efficiency, customer service and flexibility, the purpose — to make a profit — is disguised.

This is underlined through the continuous training programmes that, in addition to acquiring new functional skills, are directed at the workers' understanding of themselves as customers rather than workers. It is instructive to compare the training these workers received as we can identify a shift to training as a form of control that is often directed at the workers' understanding of the process and the alienation that the degradation of their work involves.

Training and the Labour Process

Training is central to the labour process and paradoxically to the deskilling of workers. In the department store all the workers interviewed from the earlier period served an apprenticeship. The more exclusive stores operated a system where the apprenticeship had to be bought. Each apprenticeship lasted three years. As an apprentice they spent between three and six months in different departments within the store. Their duties were to familiarise themselves with the stock, keep the stock tidy, carry out stock checks and run the occasional errand. The apprentice operated as an assistant to the senior sales person and when not carrying out the other duties would spend their time "wrapping and packing". Initially, they could not address or serve customers but rather had to observe the senior sales people as they dealt with customers. As time progressed they were allowed to serve customers but they had to defer to senior sales staff. In addition to acquiring sales skills and knowledge of the merchandise and materials, they were trained in display, fitting, alterations and basic tailoring, depending on their interest or "flair". These skills were acquired informally from more experienced members of staff. Some of the workers who worked from the late 1960s on were also involved in clerical duties such as pricing and ordering.

Attendance at a technical college was required for one or two sessions a week, where the various attributes of materials and textiles and subjects such as colour co-ordination and the history of style, were studied. In the latter years the psychology of selling and basic accounting were also studied. At the end of the three years they were examined and certificates awarded to those who were successful. On completion of the apprenticeship a position of junior sales person was achieved and held for a period of two to five years. The apprenticeship system was designed to allow workers to develop and deploy a set of skills where they could take a degree of ownership of the process and have some control over conception as well as execution. A certain degree of training continued for senior sales people, albeit sporadically. The introduction of new technology required short but intensive training and often a degree of negotiation. Intermittent courses were attended in new sales techniques and refresher courses in old techniques.

Training in the self-service multiple is radically different. Initially it consists of up to two weeks of "intensive training". Much of this is repetitive and involves numerous "pep" talks where the "trainees" are shown a "nostalgia" video outlining the history of the company and the quality and value of the company merchandise in comparison to other firms. The training takes the form of induction and focuses on the "ethos" of the company. "Shopping workshops" take place to reinforce this. Issues surrounding customer care are stressed and central to these two weeks. They are to be pleasant, friendly and helpful to the customers at all times. Yet there is no room for initiative. This was underlined by an incident experienced by one of the respondents who had been trained in a department store but now works in a multiple store. A customer required an item in a particular size that was not available. She had noticed that the correctly sized item was on floor display and offered this to the customer. The removal of the item from display was noticed on the security camera and she was severely reprimanded after the customer had left. This would have been normal practice in a department store. This shows that adherence to rules and regulations are central to the operation of these stores.

Training also involves showing security footage of both customer and staff shoplifting. The benefits of working for the company are pointed out such as subsidised canteen facilities and access to the company doctor, nurse, chiropodist and hairdresser. Training is then directed to the shop floor. Each new worker is assigned to a "sponsor" for the first few weeks whose responsibility is to introduce the worker to the work and rules involved. Individual tasks are described and directions given and the workers left to learn by familiarising themselves with the tasks. The essential element is to build a familiarity with the layout of the store and the tasks themselves. After a number of weeks workers receive additional training on the "tills", the basic features of which are shown and explained in a four- to five-hour workshop.

Two booklets are issued to the staff. The first gives details of the type of products stocked and offers information similar to that found on the label. The second takes the form of a training hand-book, divided into modules, which deals with company rules, health and safety and relationships with the customer. There is an emphasis on appearance, enthusiasm, being pleasant, how to dress and hygiene. This is underpinned by the involvement of the workers in completing personal development reports.

However, depriving workers of the opportunity to make their work meaningful brings new problems in terms of creating and maintaining a committed, compliant work force and neutralising resistance. This brings the issue of worker subjectivity to the fore. In the absence of apprenticeship, training in the multiple is largely functional. Yet, a second strand runs parallel to the emphasis on functional skills, aimed at the subjectivity of the worker. Part of the "induction" element of the training programme in Marks and Spencer involves "shopping workshops". Thus, in the training manual, the workers are invited to imagine themselves as cus-tomers of the shop. For instance, in *Marks and Spencer: Initial Train-ing Programme Workbook* (1997) the Customer Service module be-gins with the following questions:

> 1a. What do you understand by "Customer Service"?
>
> 1b. What do YOU expect as a customer?
>
> 1c. Give two examples of good customer service: one that you've experienced yourself; one that you've heard about.

These questions and the suggested answers provided at the back of the manual begin to collapse the boundaries between the indi-vidual as worker and customer. This is captured by the final ques-tion in this section *"Who is your customer?"* And the answer — *"Your customers are external customers; internal customers i.e. other M&S staff in your own store and in other locations"*. This re-imagining of worker as customer is underpinned by a programme of self-improvement and self-assessment directed at the workers, supported by their trained invisibility on the shop floor, distancing themselves from the products on sale and the selling process.

In this regard, the handbook identifies 24 "qualities and skills" needed to give customer service. These range from enthusiasm, politeness, courtesy, cheerfulness, a positive attitude and self-motivation to adopting the right tone and facial expression, expressing interest and expressing concern (1997: 42). At the same time, the company suggests "We are all salespeople at heart. We've been selling our ideas, our opinions and our desires since we were children" (1997: 57). Workers are then invited to identify and rate their "own particular strengths" in terms of confidence, enthusiasm, courtesy, helpfulness, listening skills and assertiveness. Here the boundaries between customer and worker are collapsed and the worker is invited to strive for self-improvement through the auspices of the company ethos and the moral lens of the market.

The implication is that working for the company and "staying close to the customer" provides the means to achieve excellence in one's everyday life. In the words of Du Gay, they are offered the opportunity to "optimise the worth of their existence to themselves — by assembling a lifestyle, or lifestyles through personalised acts of choice in the marketplace" where they are "constituted as autonomous, self-regulating and self-actualising individual actors" (1996: 77). This emphasis on self-improvement is reinforced through the self-assessment procedures, the surveillance and the mystery shoppers. While most of the workers interviewed were sceptical of these exercises and were prepared to put down "very good" or "excellent", whether they thought it true or not, some "confessed" that they did not always live up to the standards expected but would try harder in future. Privately they all acknowledged that the exercises were, to some extent useful and did point to areas where they could lead "better" lives in the wider world.

Thus, while the "training" in Marks and Spencer is largely functional, there is a continuous emphasis on self-improvement drawing on ideas of the aesthetic self and the enterprising self as customer. This is reinforced through surveillance strategies, which in turn produce self-monitoring and even self-interpretation. As such, the labour process extends beyond the control of workers to their subjectivity and, in this instance, invites the workers to see themselves in terms of consumption rather than production.

5. CONCLUSION

In this era of flexibility and reflexiveness social relations have changed fundamentally. These changes are undeniable, yet we must ask the question: do they mark the arrival of a new era or are they as a result of the intensification of the processes that inform society? In particular we must ask: has the relationship between capital and labour changed fundamentally in the light of these changes? I have argued that the labour process still applies as a defining paradigm for informing and shaping society and the relationships therein. Indeed we can see that many of the changes that have come about have done so in the context of the labour process and that capitalism, as a hegemonic discourse, is more firmly embedded in the structures of society than ever before. In many ways it can be seen to be more benign than previously, or at least appears so.

Thus, despite the pessimism that is associated with the labour process approach, I believe there is basis for optimism. All too often the way we look at work is saturated with a blind optimism that ignores evidence to the contrary. To talk about the information society without investigating the nature of knowledge and those who exercise control over knowledge systems is inadequate. The same point can be made about reflexivity and the notion of choice. Rather than the freeing of agency from structure, we see the ultimate alienation of the agent — disengaged and disinterested, yet complicit and compliant! Are we to give meaning to our lives through mass aesthetic consumption only to lose sight of our human potential? Has our human potential been discarded in the dustbin of history along with Marx?

To provide a potential for real change, we must recognise these changes in the labour process as an intensification of a broader continuing process of unequal exchange and the pretence of equality. The modern discourses of flexibility and reflexivity, facilitated by spectacular technological advances, disguise deeper relationships and labour processes. While technology provides the opportunity for change, it is important to recognise who controls and implements technological changes. Technology is implemented and developed in accordance with the market to serve the needs of capital and perpetuate the social relations that it produces. Just as notions of skill are socially constructed by dominant discourses, so is technology deployed and designed to serve the same discourse.

The workers who participated in this research lead real lives and were engaged in real struggles over skill, knowledge and control of the labour process. They looked to work not just as a means to an end, but as something that was potentially creative and empowering. While this was to a certain extent informed by nostalgia for an idealised past, their stories demonstrated the impact and existence of the labour process and the importance of worker subjectivity therein. They understood and made a distinction between their different identities as workers who were experts in the art of selling and consumption and their identities as competent consumers. For them, work in the department store allowed a degree of control and creativity and ownership of the work. They saw that they played a vital and creative role in the realisation of value and the productive role they had in giving the commodities they sold value. Of course they also recognised that the work was hard and exploitative at times but lamented its passing and resented the degraded functional, unsociable work available in the self-service multiple. One of the underlying themes and resentments in their stories was their construction by management discourse as incompetent workers and indeed consumers. Management discourses of excellence and self-improvement tended to undermine their perceptions of themselves as competent self-actualised individuals and created anxiety and self-doubt. While they resisted some of the more absurd management discourses and practices this anxiety facilitated their compliance and complicity.

This research has shown that the labour process is a valid analytical framework though which to interrogate many of the changes at the heart of our society. By retrieving Marx from "the dustbin of history" a powerful interrogation of work and modernity can take place in conjunction with more "modern" approaches. This is all the more important as the subjectivity of the worker comes to the attention of the labour process and extends beyond the workplace to everyday life, where the "culture of the customer" infiltrates the area of work and indeed civil society.

Chapter 11

"ARE YOU BEING SERVED?": MIGRANT WORKERS, MULTICULTURALISM AND THE STATE

Tony Cunningham, İ. Emre Işık **and** *Niall Moran*

1. INTRODUCTION

In the last decade Ireland has moved from a position on the semi-periphery of Europe to one firmly embedded in the European core. During this transformation Ireland became a net importer of labour as the reserve army of labour (mainly female) was mobilised and largely exhausted. In the initial phase of spectacular growth, returning Irish emigrants from the US, the UK and mainland Europe satisfied much of the additional demand for labour. At the same time Ireland became a destination for economic migrants and asylum-seekers. This development elicited responses that were often characterised in terms of threat and informed by a deep ethnocentric and racist discourse that was facilitated by the absence of any coherent policy from the state.

In response to demands from global and local capital for labour to fuel the growth of the "tiger" economy, the government introduced a system of work permits, visas and authorisations to fill particular gaps in the market. There was a distinct pattern to recruitment. On one level, skill seemed to be the guiding factor.

Thus, nurses were recruited from the Philippines and high-tech workers from India and South Africa. However, the state also had a need to fill the many low-paid, low-skilled jobs that underpin the spectacle of "tigerish" affluence. Yet, while asylum-seekers from Africa and Romania were refused permission to work while they were "being processed", white Eastern Europeans were actively recruited to work in agriculture, service, retail and catering. The changed circumstances present particular problems for the state as it attempts to overcome its own ethnocentrism. While official state policy and rhetoric promotes multiculturalism or interculturalism, the framing of policy and its implementation does not. It appears not all cultures are welcome and for those that are their presence is conditional.

This chapter draws on the narratives of a selection of employers and migrant workers involved in the "main" street retail trade in Ireland. We contend that the situation of the migrant "other" in Ireland is shaped by exclusionist (one may argue even racist) policies operating within the state, where the decision-making process is based on collusion between state and business. Our research suggests that migrant workers on work permits are marginalised to the periphery of the labour market, denied the opportunity to use their cultural capital and are excluded from participation in civil society. In addition, they are silenced in a position of stasis within Irish society and thrust into competition or conflict for resources with other marginalised groups. This in turn may elicit or facilitate racist and ethnocentric responses to their presence. As such, the concept of multiculturalism proposed in the Irish context is set to fail. Instead, we must critically analyse the situation of migrant workers, tensions between the multicultural ideal and the neo-liberal market ethos that informs policy, and problematic notions of Irishness.

2. GLOBALISATION AND THE CULTURAL ECONOMY OF MIGRATION IN IRELAND

Contrary to popular opinion, the majority of the world's population stays put (Kivisto, 2002). Migration is a highly selective and structured process involving the relationship between home and receiving countries (Sassen, 1999). However, the migrant group's situation is determined by their position *vis-à-vis* other groups in the "host country". For Wolf (1982), the position of the migrant on arrival is not governed so much by his or her culture but rather by the mode of production, the structure of the labour market and spatial and temporal operations.

In today's societies, culture and economy have become inseparable. Yet, Touraine (2000) argues that an extreme dissociation of economy from culture is one of the major pathologies of the neo-liberal state, with only the economy influencing culture through consumption patterns. Such dissociation leaves two options for the social actor: succumb completely to the market or seek recourse in communitarian identities that, like nationalism, create self-definition through homogeneity and the exclusion of the "other". We suggest that a combination of the two is at work in Ireland today.

Politically, Peillon argues that the boundaries between the state and the business class have become blurred (Peillon, 2002), leading to collusion between the state and private enterprise in almost all aspects of decision-making processes. For Cronin, one result of these processes is that Ireland is now a society where speed is the essence of all activities, and migrant workers alongside the poor, disabled, and the disadvantaged find themselves trapped in "the slow lane of neglect and indifference" (2002: 62).

There are two ways of entry into Ireland as a non-EEA migrant worker: by work permit and by work visa or authorisation. Loyal (2003) points out that the majority of work permits have gone to non-African and non-Asian low-skilled migrants because of a racialised attempt by the state to regulate internal ethnic and religious diversity. Work visas and authorisations, which are more flexible than permits, were mainly given to high-skilled immigrants from countries like Australia, South Africa, the US, Canada and New Zealand (2003). Loyal also points out that Ireland's Celtic Tiger economy created a dual market structure in which secure, high-skilled well-paid jobs exist alongside unskilled badly-paid jobs.

From the early 1990s, the number of work permits in Ireland rose constantly to reach 47,551 by 2003. As migrant workers constitute only 2 per cent of the Irish labour force, it is nonsensical of the media and populist politicians to talk about an "invasion" of foreign workers. If anything, the recent phenomenon of in-migration to Ireland has been dominated by one specific group, namely returning Irish migrants who since 1999 have accounted for on average 40-45 per cent of all in-migration.

In Figure 11.1 we can observe the distribution of work permits across sectors for 2003. Of the total, 25,039 were renewals. Their distribution is heavily skewed towards the service, catering and agricultural and fisheries sectors. Figure 11.2 represents the breakdown of work permits issued by country where more than 1,000 permits were issued. The majority of work permits were issued to migrants from Eastern European countries. Where this "rule" is broken, the particular countries are targeted with the intention of procuring specific skills such meat industry workers in the case of Brazil.

Figure 11.1: Permits Issued/Renewed 2003

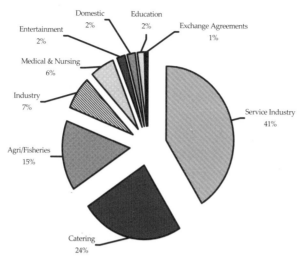

Source: Department of Enterprise, Trade and Employment

Figure 11.2: Permits Issued by Country, 2003

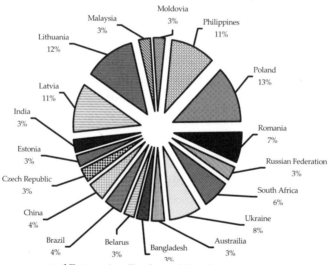

Source: Department of Enterprise, Trade and Employment

Conroy and Brennan (Equality Authority, 2003) show a very high turnover level of migrant workers from one year to another. Their report found that the majority of migrant workers were relatively satisfied with their circumstances and did not complain about low pay, long working days or isolation. The report suggests reasons for this silence. They found serious breaches of employment legislation including non-payment of wages, excessive working hours and below the minimum wage payment. Such breaches are compounded by the fact that employers have effective ownership of work permits. This affords employers a significant advantage in negotiations and facilitates the mistreatment of workers, who may end up "stuck" in a position of serious exploitation.

There exists little support structure either at the point of arrival or indeed within the workplace. As such, migrant workers, and particularly those who can be considered as performing "poor-work", are grossly unaware of their rights, both within the workplace and outside of it. Their access to the institutions of civil society and the state is severely limited due to language barriers and inadequate direction. More often than not, problems are presented to employers or colleagues. This has meant that many non-nationals have created autonomous "support" groups, based on nationality, where individual experience allows for fluid exchanges of useful and relevant information.

This presents a picture of a "silent worker": a seriously disempowered social actor with little access to Irish societal resources, unable to articulate their interests or have their rights communicated to. Since family reunification is also restricted, this "silent worker" is often isolated within Irish society, compounded by the fact that very little social integration takes place. Considering that migrant workers are an important element of the global labour market and Irish society, there is a need to move away from a situation where migration policy is informed through the lens of a neo-liberal market-driven ethos to one that recognises the complexities associated with the multicultural ideal.

3. EXCLUSION AS INTEGRATION:
MULTICULTURALISM AND IRELAND

The apparent commitment of the state to a multicultural Ireland disguises the plight of the migrant worker within the market place. Laguerre (2000) points to conflicting multicultural practices

in the context of globalisation. The first, "municipal multiculturalism", is practised to produce cultural harmony among various
ethnic groups in the name of patriotism and for love of country.
The second, "industrial multiculturalism", is achieved in the
name of the free market and for love of money; the third, "academic multiculturalism", is achieved in the name of participatory
and representative democracy and for love of freedom; the fourth
"congregational multiculturalism", is achieved in the name of religious life and for love of God. Finally, the fifth, "diasporic multiculturalism", is practised by the immigrant communities to
achieve parity and equality in racialised social life in the name of
social justice, and for love of homeland and country of residence.
The current Irish approach is most similar to the Industrial multiculturalism model in Laguerre's framework.

Writing on Ireland, Lentin and McVeigh theoretically "situate"
both Irish racism and anti-racism (2002). They suggest that Irish
racism is influenced by the Irish diaspora, their whiteness and Eu-
ropeanness and their involvement in racialised encounters
abroad. In contrast, they suggest Ireland is disempowered
through its colonial history, its history of emigration, economic
dependency and by the fact that Irish people throughout the
world experienced anti-Irish racism. They conclude that Ireland is
quintessentially "between two worlds" — both perpetrator and
survivor of racism, both thoroughly racist and determinedly anti-
racist (2002: 8).

Within the state's industrial multicultural approach, Lentin
identifies the strategy of the National Consultative Committee on
Racism and Interculturalism (NCCRI) as conservative multiculturalism based on assimilation into majority norms and values
(Lentin, 2002a). This conservative multiculturalism is important
when speaking of migrants in Ireland. Lentin suggests that what
is required is a "politics of interrogation". There is a need for "an
interrogation of Irishness as dominant, racialising and oppressive,
despite the history of anti-Irish racism and in the light of the racialisation of Irishness itself (Lentin, 2002a).

Fanning (2002) characterises Irish multiculturalism as a "weak multiculturalism" in the sense that a number of preconditions have not been met. He identifies the need to acknowledge and address racism and structural inequalities in Irish society with measures designed to combat racism. In addition to equality measures, there is a need to address institutional discrimination in accessing state services, markets and the voluntary sector if a strong multicultural society is to emerge (Fanning, 2002).

We can look at an ideal of a multicultural society through Parekh's definition of it as a numerical plurality of cultures which creates, guarantees, and encourages spaces within which different communities are able to grow at their own pace (quoted in Kaya, 1998). For Parekh, "multiculturalism is possible, but only if communities feel confident enough to engage in a dialogue and where there is enough public space for them to interact with the dominant culture". Multiculturalism has become a synonym for social integration in many countries. Its basic premise suggests that groups of different cultures can only live together when they learn to identify, understand and respect each other's cultural differences. More recently it has become tacit that a multicultural approach must be supplemented by a distinct anti-racism policy. For obvious reasons, racism, prejudice and xenophobia are perceived as a threat to the ideal of a multicultural society.

We have suggested that migratory processes into Ireland are controlled by a neo-liberal logic. The process of claiming the right to work and the subsequent experience of work, coupled with the simultaneous programme of multiculturalism and anti-racism, expose the contradictions and inadequacies of the Irish state. These inadequacies come to be embodied in the migrant "other" in Irish society as they are embroiled in a distinct process of racialisation and are constructed as scapegoats for social problems.

The Irish state has proved itself incapable of dealing seriously with the problem of racism. Its unwillingness to accept Jewish refugees during and after World War II and its mistreatment of various programme refugees thereafter are pertinent examples (Fanning, 2002). While contemporary state and institutional racism is most easily identifiable in the asylum process, the process through which the state attempts to hide or shun this reality is less well documented in the case of migrant workers. We argue that it is in the state's efforts to create a multicultural society that the chief schisms and contradictions of neo-liberal ideology can be seen most clearly.

As Pieterse shows, liberal democratic states are in many cases unable or unwilling to live up to the promise of a liberal multiculturalism that assumes "common citizenship and a commitment to individual rights" (2001). The backbone of any such conception of multiculturalism is the idea that the state can guarantee these individual rights, which are based on the reciprocal notion of citizenship. This assumption is made, however, without actually questioning or problematising the state itself. We contend that any multicultural policy constructed within the confines of the present state is riddled with inadequacies including a redundant form of democratic process and an overriding primacy of economic rationality, both of which are crucial in the perpetuation of the neo-liberal state.

There is a contradiction in how the asylum, refugee and work permit systems are operated and the Irish state's supposedly integrative policies that ultimately seek to assimilate the "other". A further aspect of this limitedness is captured in what Habermas refers to as the "dialectic of de jure and de facto equality" (1998). Equality enshrined in law, or promises of utopian social integration made in advertisements, do not necessarily transfer into equality in an individual's social experience. The Irish state is willing to fill jobs but unwilling to involve itself in the social problems and antagonisms surrounding work for economic migrants in contemporary Ireland like healthcare and welfare. Instead of recognising such problems and antagonisms as inherently products of the pre-existing state, the migrant Other, as conceptualised through anti-immigrant racism, becomes the embodiment or scapegoat of such problems.

The inability of the liberal state to provide equality to migrants in Ireland remains unchallenged. Thus, many economic migrants

— despite having a third-level education — are working in the secondary labour market in badly paid jobs with few benefits. Biological "difference" is no longer the sole justification for racism. Instead, the supposed threat to "Irish" majority norms, values and traditions by migrant minorities is often cited to justify racism. To prevent further incursions into the "Irish" cultural fabric, adherents of this viewpoint actively promote the exclusion or assimilation of minority cultures.

4. MIGRANT EMPLOYER AND EMPLOYEES' NARRATIVES

The following selection of narratives draw on a series of interviews conducted in a small town on the outskirts of Dublin. Like so many other towns a stroll through its main street displays many of the signs we might associate with a multi-cultural society and the orientation to speed that has come to characterise post-Celtic Tiger Ireland. Alongside the church, post-office, banks, doctors' surgeries, video store and traffic jams, Thai, Chinese, Indian, Italian and Irish-Italian restaurants jostle for the custom of the local consumer. An Afro-Caribbean shop nestles alongside an internet and international phone café and entertains a multi-ethnic audience, while the "Irish" pubs promise the delights of tradition and authentic Irish experience. Central to the life of these towns are the franchised "local" shops or supermarkets, increasingly staffed by migrant workers from Eastern Europe.

The greatest difficulty we encountered was gaining access to these migrant workers. In many cases they were reluctant to be interviewed and suspicious of interest. On the other hand, the employers were generally readily available for conversation. Yet, both sides of the story are important in understanding the changing nature of work and the workforce in Ireland.

An Employer's Narrative: Michael

Michael is a shopkeeper who owns and manages a franchised "local" shop. In addition to the usual stock of sweets, groceries, newspapers and cigarettes a substantial part of his business involves the preparation of food on site. At the busiest times of the day he requires five or six staff on the floor and a minimum of two at the quieter times. For the previous six months he has started work at 6.30 a.m. every day including Saturday and Sunday and did a double shift every week. Even when not in work his mind is there. We talked in the office above the shop and I was aware that he kept an occasional eye on the security images displayed on a computer. On a number of occasions members of staff trying to deal with what appeared to be relatively minor problems interrupted us. It appears all decisions, whether large or small, come to him.

Three years ago he felt he could not continue with the business as he could not get workers who would commit to a "career" in retail. The availability of workers from Latvia saved the business and he has not looked back since. While organising work-permits is a hassle it is worth it in the end as he has been able to secure a reliable compliant workforce who are committed to their work and earning money.

Most of our conversation revolved around his working life and history. This was enlightening in that two themes emerged. On one hand he saw a dramatic change for the worse in the attitude and commitment of potential Irish employees. On the other hand he identified with his Latvian workers as they reminded him of himself as a young man.

When Michael started work he was not happy as he would have preferred to work on the family farm but that was not possible. However, he recognised that he was lucky to have a job in a supermarket as unemployment was high and the family depended on his contribution. Work was a necessary evil and social circumstances dictated that he should persist with the job.

After a few years in the supermarket he migrated to America where he worked as an elevator attendant. While the work was low skilled and "poor" it was well paid in comparison to general income levels in Ireland. Not only was he able to have a reasonably good standard of living; he was able to save. However, his precarious status as an illegal worker meant that he was confined to the black economy and vulnerable to exploitation and a great degree of uncertainty. He missed the support his family and friends in Ireland provided and disliked the madness and excess that surrounded the Irish ex-pat networks in New York. His work ethic saw him through until he returned to Ireland and to his "old trade".

He became fully committed to his career in the grocery retail industry and when presented with the opportunity to acquire his own business he grasped the chance. Through hard work and investment he transformed the shop from a traditional slow-moving local shop into a thriving modern mini-market. Identifying a growing gap in the market for ready cooked meals, coffee and freshly made sandwiches, he expanded the business.

In the initial years there was no problem recruiting reliable committed staff. However, just as the growth in the economy and consumption fuelled his business it became increasingly hard to hold on to staff or to get any flexibility from them in terms of working hours. The abundance of retail work meant that workers began to dictate their own conditions of employment, often to suit desired lifestyles. If they did not like the hours or the work they could leave with no notice for a similar job elsewhere.

For Michael there is a problem of affluence — as a result of the dole and parental support young people have "too much money and no commitment". While they are reliable consumers, they make unreliable workers. The availability of work, the shortage of workers and the general atmosphere of affluence facilitated a culture of non-commitment and fecklessness from many potential Irish workers who are more interested in consumption than work. Michael can't understand this "new" attitude and appears to feel a distance between himself and the current generation, even though it is this culture of consumption and "fast food" that feeds his business and profitability.

On the other hand the Latvian workers are for the most part reliable and committed. Unlike their Irish counterparts they are usually available to provide "cover" at short notice. At the same time Michael is concerned that he does not exploit or abuse his workers' commitment. He pays them for the hours they work and makes sure they are not as tied to the shop as he is. He recalls his experience in America and how vulnerable he was as an undocumented worker. He recalled a period working with a local trader who made unreasonable demands on his time where he had to work late or extra hours most days but was not always paid for the extra work he did. Based on his own experiences he understands that it is counterproductive to mistreat or exploit workers' vulnerability and the uncertainty that surrounds their status. For the workers to be committed and reliable they need to feel comfortable and content in their work.

While Michael has no to desire to "own" any workers, the system of work permits places him in a position where he has an incredible amount of control over the workers' lives. They depend on him for the renewal of their permits and their continued "legitimate" presence in Ireland. Even though the process of securing and renewing work-permits is time-consuming and costly, Michael is prepared to put the effort in as it secures the viability of the business in providing continuity and a degree of reliability. He is a little concerned that the government has indicated a review of the work permit system and is concerned that he won't be able to continue to employ Latvian workers in the future. He hopes the accession of Latvia and the other proposed member states to the EU will resolve this dilemma. This fear is underpinned by a fear of having to depend on recruiting Irish workers again.

Michael admires the commitment of the workers especially when he sees a reflection of the work ethic and willingness to learn that he had in his younger years. This is especially true when he sees "potential to develop", learn the trade and progress. Of course his concern for their well-being was also a concern for his own well-being. If they were to return home prematurely, his investment of time and money would be wasted.

He appears to be grooming two of his Latvian workers as managers and gives them extra responsibility and is investing a degree of trust in them not available to other workers. As such he feels comfortable going on holiday for two weeks, the first time in a couple of years. The trust he has in them yet again appears to derive from the fact that the manner they have engaged with the work resembles his own commitment to the business, despite the fact that they have gone through third-level education at home and would belong to the middle class.

An Employee's Narrative: Katerina

Katerina was born and raised in a small city in Belarus. Since the collapse of the Soviet Union she has witnessed the large-scale deprivation of the masses, and seen the majority of capital fall into the hands of a few. In her own words, "there are only poor and very few people who have all the money, much much more [money] than the rich in Ireland". She came to Ireland three years ago with a college friend. After spending one month in Moscow waiting for her travel visa, she arrived in Dublin to a prearranged two-week English course. It was, she said, "strange, arriving and having to speak English" but within one week an event occurred which has shaped to a large extent her experience as both a worker and individual in Ireland. It was the chance meeting with two "lads" on a city-centre street. From here these networks afforded her and her friend permanent accommodation and the opportunity to work in a small-town convenience store. They quickly received their work permits and began to settle down to a new life. All this was accomplished independently of any institutional or national support structures. Chance and the early stages of friendship intervened to ensure a smooth transition for both Katerina and her friend.

She began work, moved into her new home and was happy. The money and the location seemed to be the prime movers. Although relative to a comparative Irish worker the money she received was little and the work "poor" it was generous compared to the situation in Belarus. She stresses how "everybody knows everybody". As we are speaking this point is proved. A lounge-girl drops two drinks to our table. We look at each other and think how could one of us have ordered them without the other noticing? She calls the lounge-girl over and we learn that a group of builders who have been coming into the shop for a while now had "sent them over". Life in a small suburban village life is quiet and social relations succinct.

As our conversation moves on she begins to speak of the downside of being an economic migrant in Ireland. Returning to the necessity of obtaining a visa to travel, she speaks of the intimidating requirements — medical reports, proof of her status as a student, proof of how much money she has, the list goes on. As she states herself, "I've done nothing wrong". The right to movement becomes a legal rigmarole where the onus is on the migrant to prove their worthiness. The same applies whenever she leaves Ireland for a destination outside of Belarus. Holiday plans to Spain are interrupted by a one-month process weighed down in the requirements of bureaucracy — payslips, bank statements, and letters from her employer. The irony is sharp when she goes on to say that nobody ever checks her documents as, according to her, a plane-full of Irish travellers arouses little suspicion among the Spanish emigration police. However, this process is just one way in which she differentiated from the "normal" Irish citizen.

She describes how little knowledge of her rights and entitlements she actually has. She has never been sick during her time here nor ever needed to access welfare resources. Still, should the case arise, she was unsure as to where to go. She had looked into completing the last year of her college education but the non-recognition of her educational achievements thus far and the high costs of fees were off-putting. She has been paying taxes now for three years but can see no direct benefits. She cites cases where friends have accessed resources and suggests that she could gain the necessary information from these people. She describes her position of mobility, from shop assistant to manager, in Ireland as being atypical. Most people she knows on work-permits are involved in poor-work which according to her is becoming ever more difficult to get. She thinks that too many people are coming, especially from Latvia and Lithuania, for whom entry to Ireland is much easier than for someone from Belarus. She has seen many friends decline promotions, usually because of the unpredictability of their length of stay in Ireland. She puts her success down to both doing what she is told and, importantly, doing it well.

The only sure way around these problems is to apply for and obtain citizenship. She intends to do this, but remains in limbo for another three years before application becomes possible. Even at this, she is unsure of her chances. She wants to stay in Ireland. There is nothing for her in Belarus. Yet, she misses family and friends and has returned twice to see them. The option of her family travelling here is a non-starter. Her status as a student and her proposed attendance at an English school were the only reasons she got here in the first place. Her family unfortunately cannot enter this way.

An Employee's Narrative: Nicola

Nicola is Romanian. She has worked in a small town take-away restaurant for the past year as a waitress and she also prepares food. Her Romanian husband also works there. She considers herself lucky to have found work in Ireland and to have received a work permit. She is from a middle class background and has completed a degree in law in Romania. However, she sees no viable future for herself and her husband back home. In Ireland she earns enough money to have a decent standard of living, to socialise with her friends when she has time off and to save for the future, something that would be impossible in Romania. She works six seven-hour shifts a week, many of which are late night shifts where she might not finish until 2:00-3:00 a.m. Her employer arranges that these coincide with those of her husband.

Working in a take-away was a bit of a culture shock for both of them, especially when the pubs close and "the drunks" arrive in on their way home. They cannot believe how much the Irish drink when they go out. However, they have settled into the work and have got used to the customers and their banter. Nicola has a high regard for her employer, or "patrone" as she called him, and when the issue of being tied to one particular job was raised she expressed a degree of surprise and declared that she was very happy where she was and would not want to work for anybody else.

This can be partially explained given the circumstances of her getting her work permit. Both Nicola and her husband attended a local English college for three months. Before their return to Romania her husband got to know the owner of the business and discovered that he was recruiting foreign workers. An agreement was reached and their employer applied for a work permit for her husband. While he returned to Ireland to take up employment she remained in Romania. When another vacancy came up the employer organised a work permit for her, reuniting the couple. In addition he helped to find them accommodation and became a guarantor for them.

Nicola misses her family but not Romania. She is sad that they will not be able to join her in the near future but she hopes that when Romania joins the EU things will get easier. She was somewhat consoled that her permit allowed her to visit home without jeopardising her status. She hopes to apply for Irish citizenship after five years. Like many other workers she does not appear to be fully aware of her rights and entitlements or the implications of her non-citizenship. For the time being, she is happy to live here and has not encountered any particular problems as a result of her status.

Despite the long and unsocial hours that work demands she has a satisfactory social life, mainly with other young Romanians in the city and with her friends from college and work whom she also sees regularly. At some time in the future she would like to return to her studies and develop the sort of career she could have had in Romania. However, for the time being that can only remain a distant aspiration due to her lack of confidence in English and her non-citizenship. Yet, life in Ireland doing "poor work" is a better option for Nicola and her husband than pursuing a career in Romania where her peers earn between €200-€300 per month. Despite the cost of living in Ireland, which she finds expensive, she has a better life-style, more financial security and hope for the future.

5. CONCLUSION

At first glance the above narratives appear to present a rosy picture of the situation of the migrant worker in Ireland. The employers are benign and satisfied with their workers while the
workers appear to be happy and contented with their lot. Indeed
one employer reunited one couple and thus helped overcome the
family restrictions the work permit system imposed, albeit in the
context of his requirement for labour. However, the imbalance
between the employer's narrative and those of the workers is telling. While all our interviewees were self-monitoring the workers
were much more guarded and largely confined themselves to
praising their employers and expressing gratitude for the opportunity to work, earn money and save. Yet when questions of their
status and rights were raised they were largely ignorant of them
and appeared uncomfortable talking about them, as if to do so
was a betrayal of their employers' commitment.

Under the work permit system employers are put in a position
of unenviable power. In practice, not only have they the power to
hire and fire, they are also given the power to determine the
worker's right to stay in the country. Despite their declared
awareness that their employees could be abused and exploited
such dependency on the employer renders the worker helpless
and beholden. Workers are not only silenced; they are removed
from the potential mobility and exercise of choice enjoyed by most
Irish citizens. This is underlined in the employer's narrative. Here
the migrant workers are valued for their commitment to hard
work, reliability and dedication. They provide continuity and
flexibility in a manner that many contemporary Irish employees
do not. However, this is not a reflection of Irish workers' laziness
but rather a reordering of the power of workers in an era of near
full employment. In the context of a more affluent society where
the indigenous reserve army of labour is nearing exhaustion, the
low-skilled worker has more choice and can pick and choose
when and where he or she works, and remove themselves from
situations where conditions are exploitative or oppressive. There-

fore, not only is the migrant worker confined to the secondary labour market, their dependence on the employers' goodwill marginalises them in relation to native workers, thus moving them to a position on the periphery of the secondary labour market.

While these workers are involved in low-skilled and poor work it is important to recognise that they are well-educated, middle class; as such they are not low-skilled workers but rather deskilled workers. However, under the current regime the cultural capital they possess is discredited and reduced to a form of social capital where their whiteness and middle class discipline allows them conditional access to the labour market based on their potential to do low-skilled labour. Not only are they marginalised within the labour market; they are excluded from wider participation in society. In addition, the stasis and marginal position in the labour market thrusts them into competition with other marginalised groups that in itself encourages or facilitates racist responses.

It is clear from our ongoing research that it is not just refugees and asylum-seekers, but also migrant workers who, despite paying taxes and helping the economy, lack basic civil rights and benefits. The existing dual market structure and immigration policy together operate against the migrant workers. Their exclusion from basic rights such as changing jobs with little control over working hours, pay and union membership is a result of the dominant neo-liberal ideology operating in the Republic. The effect of this collusion on the fate of migrants is very clear as both state and business decide together who enters the country, how they enter, how long they stay and what rights they have. As such, primacy within certain legislature processes is placed upon the economic aspects of life to the detriment of cultural and social practices.

The state's traditional role in the establishment of border controls and immigration policy is no longer organised and driven only by internal state dynamics, but is in fact mainly governed by the transnational dynamics of the capitalist global order. The effect on migrants of course extends far beyond the time of entry, it also governs their way of life in the country. It is no slave trade, but the situation, in terms of basic rights for certain migrant workers, is not desirable. The collusion between state and business is the most visible reflection of this ideology, and the organisation of migration policies within this neo-liberal framework leaves us with serious questions. The existing condition of and attitudes towards migrants create a moral problem neglected in the *de facto* market relations that determine legislation in the state. As Mac Éinri states:

> One has to wonder how the distinction between work visas for the well educated, high-skilled migrant, and work permits for the less fortunate, can be justified (2001).

One great political discourse is centred today on the control of migration within the EU. This is clearly visible in the rise of parties of the extreme right, who are using such jargon in their search for power and the promotion of racist sentiments. The EU, in erasing internal borders, is becoming more and more suspicious of immigration and furthermore, is contradicting its own assumptions regarding human rights, democracy and cosmopolitanism. This idea of immigration control, based on combating and controlling economic immigrants, attempts to legitimise various actions by the states with regard to all types of migration. Jacques Derrida speaks of the growing resemblance the EU bears to a police state, with this being evident nowhere more than in its treatment of asylum-seekers, refugees and migrant workers (Derrida 2002).

In this respect, Ireland is not trying to be different. We argue that it is impossible to address these problems within the framework of a confusing concept of multiculturalism as articulated by the state in collusion with business. Multiculturalism, in this context, only serves to invent or reinvent the "other" as other and to facilitate racism. As such, migration policy cannot solely be formulated through the ethos of the market. Rather there is a need to reinsert the social and cultural and in doing so to engage in "a politics of interrogation" which not only renders migration problematic but also renders Irish society problematic.

Chapter 12

IS THE GRASS GREENER? EXPERIENCES OF REFUGEES AND ASYLUM-SEEKERS ON THE IRISH LABOUR MARKET

Catherine Conlon, Sara Parsons **and** *Joan O'Connor*

1. INTRODUCTION

Over the past decade Ireland has experienced a substantial rise in non-Irish immigration, mostly from other European Union countries and a smaller but significant rise in non-EU immigrants. The latter group have come as immigrant workers on permits or visas or as asylum-seekers and programme refugees. Since the mid-1990s, then, Ireland has become for the first time both a net immigration country and a refugee-receiving country.

Employment is one of the most important factors assisting the integration process for immigrants, including refugees, into the host society (DJELR, 1999; British Refugee Council, 2001). It assists integration by increasing economic independence, self-esteem and contribution to the host country. This chapter looks at the experiences of refugees seeking to enter the Irish labour market. It is based on a study undertaken in 2002 in three urban centres in Ireland that involved a survey of 149 refugees and qualitative interviews with a sub-set of the surveyed group.

Refugees experienced exclusion from and marginalisation in the Irish labour market through unemployment and under-employment. The research identified structural and cultural barriers to the refugees' integration into the labour market. These barriers ranged from a lack of English language skills and evidence of qualifications achieved prior to arrival in Ireland to more complex and harder to redress issues such as ethnically based discrimination, an unfamiliar job search culture and problems associated with childcare. These barriers led to a sense of discouragement among refugees about their access to and participation in the Irish labour market. In this sense, the grass has not been greener on the other side when considering the employment prospects and realities of refugees who have come to Ireland.

2. LOCATING REFUGEES IN IRISH IMMIGRATION POLICY

Ireland's immigration policies have been criticised for being limited in relation to both restrictions on entry as well as the absence of any developed policies on integration. Fanning (2001) points out how the administration of immigration in Ireland has had the effect of stratifying immigrants (on the basis of being either immigrant workers, immigrants with Irish-born children,[1] people with refugee status and people seeking asylum) in relation to their entitlements relating to employment, education and training. According to Mac Éinri, Ireland's immigration policies increasingly reflect a pragmatic and market-led approach with the introduction of special work visas and authorisation programmes for certain high-skills immigrants and the widespread use of short-term work permits for other immigrant workers (Mac Éinrí, 2002).

---

[1] Non-national parents of a child born in the state were eligible to apply for residency to stay in the country based on the parentage of an Irish child before 1 January 2005. Following implementation of the Irish Nationality and Citizenship Act in December 2004 a child may only become an Irish citizen if at least one of its parents has been legally resident here for more than three of the preceding four years. The Act thereby removed the right of non-national parents to make such applications from this date.

Organisations such as the Immigrant Council of Ireland and the Irish Refugee Council argue that there are significant failings in the immigration system as a whole and assert the need for an integrated, transparent, rights-based immigration policy (Immigrant Council of Ireland, 2003). Instead, the Irish Government's Immigration Act of February 2004 is limited to the control of entry into the state, the duration and conditions of stay and obligations while in the state for non-nationals, falling far short of an integrated immigration policy (Immigrant Council of Ireland, 2004).

With respect to the Irish labour market, research by the Irish Business Employers' Confederation (IBEC, 2000b) concluded that, while certain issues are particular to refugees and asylum-seekers like legal status, displacement and trauma, others such as retraining, adaptation to the Irish workplace and the need for supports in accessing and progressing in employment are relevant to all immigrants. Ireland's stratifying market-led approach to immigration does not adequately address these legal, socio-cultural and economic issues of integration for immigrants in general and refugees in particular.

Before discussing the study on refugees and the Irish labour market, it is useful to consider the recent patterns of refugee applications relative to overall immigration flows in Ireland. The following table presents numbers of applications for declaration as a refugee from 1993–2004.

Table 12.1: Applications for Declaration as a Refugee, 1993–2004

93	94	95	96	97	98	99	00	01	02	03	04
91	362	424	1,179	3,883	4,626	7,724	10,938	10,325	11,634	7,900	4,766

Source: Office of the Refugee Applications Commissioner, Department of Justice, Equality and Law Reform.

As is evident from the table, the number of people seeking refugee status in the early 1990s was minimal, beginning to increase from 1996 onwards, and peaking in 2002 with 11,634 applications. In the subsequent year, 2003, the number declined by 32 per cent to 7,900 and this trend continued in 2004 with a further 40 per cent drop to 4,766. While Woods writing in 2001 noted that the trends between 2000 and 2002 were more towards a stabilising of numbers rather than a sustained drop, the figures for 2003 and 2004 indicate that this drop has now occurred.

While the numbers seeking asylum in Ireland grew almost threefold between 1997 and 2002, the increase was slower than that of other immigrants (Woods and Humphries, 2001). The number of asylum-seeking applicants constitutes only a small proportion of overall immigration into Ireland. Between April 2002 and April 2003 immigration into Ireland numbered 50,500 (CSO, 2003) while the number of applications for asylum in the same period numbered 11,880 constituting 23 per cent of immigrants. Trends indicate that this proportion continues to decrease in size. Alongside this an extremely high rate of refusal for refugee status has occurred over the past number of years indicating that other adequate immigration routes for people do not exist.

3. THE STUDY OF LABOUR MARKET NEEDS AND EXPERIENCES OF REFUGEES IN IRELAND

The overall aim of the research reported on here was to explore the labour market experiences of minority ethnic groups, including refugees, and to identify ways to facilitate labour market access and participation among the group. This entailed the following objectives:

- To explore the aspirations and experiences of refugees in relation to participarting in the Irish labour market;

- To identify barriers to accessing the labour market, including labour market programmes, from the perspective of refugees and that of programme providers;

- To identify the core issues that need to be addressed to secure labour market outcomes for refugees; and

- To assess the implications of the research findings for the design and delivery of measures under employment and human resources policy.

The research was conducted in three separate locations in Ireland — Dublin, Ennis and Waterford — over a period of 10 months from December 2001 to September 2002. The research comprised unstructured, qualitative interviews with 34 participants across the three sites; survey interviews with 149 respondents across the three sites; and one-to-one interviews with key informants from within the policy-making process and service providers at national and local level.

The purpose of the qualitative component of the study was to generate an in-depth understanding of the experiences and needs of refugees in relation to the labour market taking account of the wider social, economic, political, legal and cultural context of their lives. A total of 34 interviews were carried out comprising 30 face-to-face interviews each with one participant (N=30); 2 face-to-face interviews with two participants (N=4); and 2 focus groups with members of the Roma Community (N=11). In the face-to-face interviews there was an equal number of women and men (17 female and 17 male) in the final sample. Of the eleven participants of the focus group, 5 were male and 6 female.

This stage of the study generated a contextualised understanding of the labour market needs and experiences of refugees and minority ethnic groups in Ireland. It also provided the basis for a questionnaire to be used in the survey phase of the study.

For the survey element the only viable sampling strategy was that of purposive sampling; a target population was defined and as many respondents who fitted within the target as possible were identified and included in the survey. The final sample size was 149 respondents, 58 per cent from Dublin, 21 per cent from Waterford, 17 per cent from Ennis and 3 per cent from the pilot survey all of which took place in Dublin. The gender breakdown of participants fitted closely with the national pattern of asylum applications, the majority being male, 65 per cent, and slightly over one third female. Also the nationality of respondents broadly reflected the breakdown in applications for asylum. The achieved sample comprised 57 per cent African nationalities, 26 per cent Eastern

Europeans including Russians and 15 per cent from other countries.[2]

4. RESEARCH RESULTS

Employability of Refugees on Arrival

By "employability" we mean the education, qualifications, skills
and work experience refugees brought with them to Ireland and
the Irish labour market. Many studies have shown that refugees
tend to have a high level of educational attainment on arrival in
the host country with many drawn from amongst the intellectual
elite in their home country (Krahn et al., 2000; IBEC, 2000b; Peabody Trust, 1999; ECRE, 1998; O'Regan, 2000; Bloch, 1999; Zena
Project, 1996; Brink, 1997). In Britain, Bloch's study of refugees in
Newham, London in 1996 found that three-quarters of all participants had a qualification on arrival, including 22 per cent who
had attended university. In fact members of the refugee community arrived with higher levels of academic qualifications than
those achieved by people from minority ethnic communities as a
whole in the area studied (Bloch, 1999: 192). Similarly in Ireland a
number of studies have shown that many refugees have high levels of educational attainment, with the majority holding third-
level qualifications of some kind (Faughnan and Woods, 2000;
IBEC, 2000b; Begley et al., 1999). However, differences in educational background by gender and country of origin have been observed. In some studies refugee women were educationally disadvantaged in relation to secondary education and in further
training (Zena Project, 1996; Bloch, 1999; Kofman et al., 2000).

The findings of this study confirmed the high levels of educational attainment of refugees arriving in Ireland. Of those surveyed 77 per cent had attained a college diploma or certificate before they came to Ireland. A bachelor's degree, postgraduate

---

[2] The largest single nationality of the "other" group are Iraqis, 12 out of 22, other
nationalities (beginning with the most prevalent) are Vietnamese, Libyan, Azer-
baijani, Afghan and Pakistani.

qualification or doctoral degree had been achieved by 27 per cent of the sample. Gender differences were observed in educational attainment. Up to the point of third-level education there were only marginal differences between men and women. In third level and above the male respondents were more highly educated than the females, 33 per cent of the men had a degree or higher qualification compared 17 per cent of the women.

In all 29 per cent had some kind of professional qualification. These included engineers, medical practitioners, teachers and accountants. A further 10 per cent had acquired a trade before arriving in Ireland. These included the trades of carpentry, welding, electrician, printing, hairdressers/beauticians, bricklaying, locksmith, mechanic, caterer and professional trader.

As well as education and training, work experience contributes to the assets a person brings to the labour market. Over 80 per cent of those surveyed had worked before coming to Ireland. The main economic sectors of employment represented among the group were retail trade, education and health and financial and other business services. The youngest age group, 15 to 30 years, had spent an average of just under 2.5 years in employment. As expected, the older age group had spent longer in employment on average just under 13.5 years. Those who had never worked were predominantly within the younger age group and female.

5. Refugees' Proficiency in English on Arrival

Alongside qualifications and work experience, language proficiency is crucial for the prospects of a migrant on the host country labour market (Pittaway, 1990; O'Regan, 1998; Zena Project, 1999; Bloch, 1999; British Refugee Council, 2001). Analysis of the survey data on self-reported rankings of English understanding, speaking, reading and writing abilities demonstrated significant differences in the abilities of respondents of African origin with those from Eastern European and other countries of origin. Only 5 per cent of respondents of African origin indicated they had little or no ability to communicate in English on arrival. The Eastern European and other nationality groups did not rank their English language skills so highly. Forty per cent ranked themselves as having very little or no English at all and, in a complete reversal of the findings for the African nationalities, only 6 per cent expressed the opinion that they had very good or complete fluency in English when they first arrived in Ireland.

Across the study sites English language provision for refugees varied. At the time of the study it was only programme refugees who benefited from a reception programme, which included organised English language training. This was reflected in the findings of the survey. Numbers that had participated in any kind of English language training varied considerably across the survey locations even when allowances were made for those who were already fluent in English and so did not require further training. In total fewer than half, 44 per cent, had availed of some kind of English language training while in Ireland, 33 per cent had not accessed any English language training. The remaining 24 per cent stated that they were already fluent in English and training was not needed.

6. LOCATION OF REFUGEES ON THE IRISH LABOUR MARKET

When the labour market status of the 149 refugees surveyed in this study was broken down, 30 per cent were in employment when surveyed, 32 per cent were unemployed, while 39 per cent were in education or training. A general feature of the employed group was that they had both been in Ireland and had the entitlement to work for longer. The group also had participated in a range of education and training in Ireland. However, the jobs secured by participants frequently entailed under-utilisation of their qualifications and skills and downward occupational mobility.

While 30 per cent were employed when surveyed, in total 44 per cent of the study group had worked in Ireland at some time. The figure below details the sectoral location of those participants who had ever been in employment in Ireland:

Figure 12.1: Principal Employment Sector of Participants

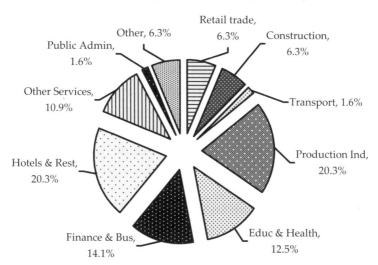

The largest employment sectors for the group before they came to Ireland had been retail trade, 15 per cent, and education and health, also 15 per cent. When the refugees entered the labour market in Ireland, the distribution shifted towards production industries (20 per cent) and hotels and restaurants (20 per cent). The findings for the study sample were compared with the sectoral location of the entire Irish employed population as detailed in the Quarterly National Household Survey (QNHS) for the period corresponding to the period of data collection. The study group was over-represented within production industries, by 3 per cent, and in the hotels and restaurants sector by 14 per cent. Further, another sector emerged, that of "other services", which absorbed 5 per cent more refugees than of the general population. All the respondents in this category of sector for whom data was available were cleaning and security staff. Thus the respondents were over-represented in the more menial and lower status employment sectors. The sectors in which the study group was concentrated are also those sectors that are particularly vulnerable to economic downturn.

The higher proportion of refugees within the hotels and restaurants sector is particularly striking. The study group's level of participation in this sector before they came to Ireland, 7 per cent, was only marginally above the overall participation in Ireland, 6 per cent. Yet when in Ireland their participation in this sector is three times that of the overall population. The major shift towards this sector could be a sign that the hospitality industry is more open to a multi-cultural workforce. It is probably more likely, however, that the refugee population has less choice. Hence they are more likely to find themselves in a situation where they are offered positions that employers are unable to fill from the host population, becoming a residual source of labour for the Irish economy.

In an attempt to provide a more meaningful comparison, the general occupation category of the respondents was considered. This provided an insight into the level and seniority of the post held. A breakdown of the occupations within each category was obtained from the CSO to ensure accurate recoding of the data. Two sample columns are included in the table; one shows the percentage of refugees in each category of those who were working at the time of the survey; the other shows the principal category of all those in employment at the time in Ireland.

Table 12.2: Categories of Employment Held by Irish Population Compared with Survey Respondents (%)

	QNHS Q2	Study Group (n=63)
Managers and Administrators	17.6	6.3
Professional	10.8	7.9
Ass. Prof. and Technical	8.8	12.7
Clerical and Secretarial	12.8	14.3
Craft and Related	12.8	1.6
Personal and Protective Services	9.6	17.5
Sales	8.2	7.9
Plant and Machine Operatives	10.5	12.7
Other	8.9	19.0

These figures confirmed that respondents were working within lower seniority and status areas. Their under-representation in higher occupation categories was reflected in their predominance in personal and protective services, plant and machine operatives and other occupations. This category of other occupations typically includes labourers, trades peoples' mates, porters, domestic staff and cleaning personnel. Again, a negative picture is cast of the employment experiences of refugees when compared to the general Irish population.

When the occupation category of the positions held by participants on the Irish labour market were compared with the occupation categories they held in their country of origin further evidence of underemployment of the study group is revealed. Of all those currently working in Ireland 40 per cent of respondents were working in occupations of a lower ranking than they had before they came to Ireland. One third, 33 per cent, had gained employment at a level equivalent to their previous occupational status while only 14 per cent had managed to move up the classification scale since they came to Ireland.[3]

Finally, the quality of the work of those who had ever worked in Ireland was considered. The survey explored this issue by attempting to quantify the appropriateness, prospects and security of employment respondents had held. When asked to rate how well matched they thought their experience, skills and qualifications were to those needed to carry out the work involved in their current job, only 17 per cent felt there was an appropriate match. The vast majority of respondents in employment felt they had more or a lot more experience, skills and qualifications than were needed for their current positions.

The prospects and security of work were measured in terms of assessing whether work was permanent or temporary and by respondents' opinions on opportunities for promotion. Of the respondents who had worked in Ireland, only 37 per cent were in permanent posts and 56 per cent indicated they had been em-

---

[3] All percentages total slightly over 100 due to rounding.

ployed on a temporary basis.[4] Their overall opinions on their
prospects for promotion were fairly evenly split with 30 per cent
feeling promotion was likely or very likely and 29 per cent believing it to be unlikely or very unlikely. The combination of these
two factors rather than each in isolation provides the most insight-
ful view as to security and prospects within the working environment. The permanent workers had a higher opinion of their
opportunities for promotion than the temporary workers. Permanent work gave respondents a more positive view of the future
regardless of the appropriateness of their experience, skills and
qualifications. Of those who had the right amount or not enough
experience, skills and qualifications and had permanent work, 44
per cent stated that they felt promotion was likely or very likely
compared with just 25 per cent of temporary workers who gave
their capabilities the same rating.

7. FACTORS CONTRIBUTING TO REFUGEES' RISK OF EXCLUSION AND MARGINALISATION

Analysis of the experiences of refugees on the Irish labour market
revealed a range of barriers to securing quality employment.
While participants held high levels of qualifications, the experiences of those who sought to enter employment directly on being
granted the entitlement to work, demonstrated how the resources
people had accrued in their home countries in the form of education, skills and experience held little or no currency on the labour
market in Ireland. For the majority of participants of this study,
displacement had the effect of reducing their employability with
respect to their qualifications, skills and experiences. Therefore
the group was left in a position similar to Irish labour market en-
trants after second-level school or in some cases to those who had
left school early. Many also had the added barrier of English as a
second language. In addition, the group reported a perception of
some form of discrimination by employers against minority ethnic

---

[4] Data was missing in 5 (7.9 per cent) cases.

groups as well as lack of clarity among employers about the rules governing entitlement to work.

The education and skills profile of the respondents prior to arrival in Ireland and their past economic activity demonstrates high levels of employability and employment among the group in their home country. We next examine the extent to which their education and skills were recognised as currency for employment in Ireland. From the literature the main difficulties faced by refugees in utilising their education and skills obtained in their country of origin on the jobs market of the host country are: recognition of these qualifications and low numbers actually attempting to have their qualifications recognised; no documentation or proof of qualifications; and the transferability of their qualifications (Bloch, 1999; O'Regan, 1998; Krahn et al., 2000).

For most qualifications there are no formal systems in place in Ireland to recognise participants' qualifications obtained abroad. No system of accreditation for prior learning has been implemented to date at national level. Nor are there any systems of training or education to supplement the qualifications, skills or experiences participants brought with them to tailor them to the Irish labour market. The Interdepartmental Working Group on the Integration of Refugees in Ireland noted in its 1999 report that there is no specific co-ordinated scheme in place for assessing or recognising skills and overseas qualifications and that this could result in many refugees remaining unemployed or being under-employed. They recommended that a system of assessing and recognising existing skills, qualifications and the experience of refugees must be established in co-operation with the National Qualifications Authority, Chambers of Commerce, employers' groups, FÁS, the Civil Service and Local Appointments Commissions and professional bodies (DJELR, 1999). As yet no such system has been developed.

Many refugees also have the added barrier of English as a second language. Poor English language skills were identified as a principal barrier in both the survey and qualitative elements of the study. Language difficulties represented a barrier to accessing employment at all or could cause a person to have to rule out the possibility of being able to practise the profession they had followed in their country of origin. While some people were able to get a job with low language skills these were in low skill areas and made for very difficult work situations for participants. A need for employees for whom English is not their first language to be supported in the workplace with English language training schemes was evident. Thus while the current model of "front-loaded" English language training is important for accessing employment there appeared to be a further need for continued language-support schemes while in employment.

Ethnic-based discrimination was the second principal barrier to accessing employment identified by study participants. Their perceptions varied to include discrimination on basis of nationality, ethnicity, colour, legal and immigrant status. The identification of discrimination as a barrier varied according to country of origin with African participants more likely to report experiencing discrimination than participants from Eastern Europe or elsewhere. Two Muslim Arab participants felt particularly targeted in the political climate of the time. There were some cited instances of employers operating a discriminatory recruitment policy. One explanation given by respondents for this was the negative attitudes to minority ethnic groups in society generally; another was a lack of confidence in minority ethnic groups' abilities. Participants highlighted the lack of visibility of black and minority ethnic groups in Irish workplaces as an indication that discriminatory practices were at work. Participants perceived that the only jobs offered to minority ethnic groups were low-paid, low-skilled jobs conveying an impression of them as being a residual source of labour to take up positions not wanted by the indigenous workforce when labour supply was tight. At the same time, participants who were in employment did not tend to experience direct discrimination.

An unfamiliar and different job search culture also represented a barrier to accessing employment for refugees newly arrived onto the Irish labour market. Participants described how they found the system of job-seeking in Ireland unfamiliar on arrival and highlighted how they needed information to help them negotiate it. This indicated a need for a structured system of support to familiarise refugees with the Irish labour market system and job-seeking culture. To meet the demands of an intercultural society this should incorporate familiarisation of immigrants with Irish job-seeking practices and familiarisation of employers and employees with cultural practices of minority ethnic groups in relation to job-seeking and work culture.

Child care emerged as a further barrier contributing to women being over-represented in the unemployed group, reflecting their caring responsibilities and difficulties accessing child care. This issue arose in the qualitative analysis also where women spoke of not being able to participate in education or training because of difficulties finding a child care place, even in situations where they had secured a place on a course that included a child care allowance. Those contemplating employment felt that private crèche places were prohibitive due to the high cost of child care in Ireland to the extent that one parent would have to stay at home. The most common source of child care used by participants in employment and education or training was other family members. However, as we would expect, many participants were separated from their extended family and so did not have this support network available to them.

8. STRATEGIES TO ENHANCE OPPORTUNITIES FOR REFUGEES ON THE IRISH LABOUR MARKET

A detailed analysis of the extent to which measures under the Employment and Human Resources Development Operational Programme (EHRDOP) of the National Development Plan can address the barriers experienced by refugees and minority ethnic groups in relation to the labour market was undertaken as part of this research. This was based on the qualitative and survey interviews with refugees and asylum-seekers as well as interviews carried out with policy makers and programme providers at national and local level. Four types of support measures were identified: targeted supports; job-seeking supports; employment support services; and education and training supports. The targeted supports in place were limited to English language training for asylum-seekers and refugees. The latter three refer to mainstream measures and our assessment focused on their capacity to meet the specific needs of minority ethnic groups, particularly refugees identified over the course of this study.

Analysis of the targeted supports demonstrated fragmented and variable levels of delivery from across the three sites. The Dublin model comprised a refugee language training service integrated into mainstream vocational training services with a bridging component into further education or training and parallel career guidance. The Ennis model comprised a language training service with a career guidance element that advised people on options for mainstream education or training but without a bridging programme. The Waterford model comprised a package of measures for the reception of a group of programme refugees but with no provision for the general population of refugees and asylum-seekers in the area. As expected, the Dublin model was perceived to be the most successful from the perspective of both the community and the programme providers and developers. Under this model formal language assessments were undertaken on application to the programme. Where an applicant's level of English was determined to be insufficient to enable them participate on a skills training course they were referred to English language training. The bridging component comprised of pre-vocational training incorporating applied language training and computer skills together with career guidance usually leading to entry onto a skills training programme.

Of the two types of supports, the targeted supports were found to be the most effective. However this appeared to be related more to the operation of the mainstream programmes than their capacity to address the needs of refugees and asylum-seekers. Of the mainstream job-seeking, employment and education and training supports, low levels of awareness and use of these services were reported by survey respondents. When reasons for not accessing such services were explored lack of awareness was the most commonly cited. A number of programmes aimed at supporting entry onto the labour market determined eligibility on the length of time an applicant had been unemployed. Time spent by refugees who were in enforced labour market inactivity due to not having the entitlement to work during the asylum-seeking process was not taken into account when calculating length of time unemployed.

Of the mainstream programmes, the Local Employment Service (LES) which operates on a case-load basis (i.e. intensive one-to-one assessment and support) was found to offer the best range of services and supports to the study group. This was because it was able to address the barriers in relation to accessing the labour market, i.e. unfamiliarity with job-search culture, not having a reference from an Irish employer to accompany a job application and lack of information about labour market supports and welfare entitlements. As the LES case-worker took on the role of advocate for their client they would then provide references for employers, seek out information tailored to their skills and interests and provide orientation on job-seeking and workplace culture.

Recommendations were made for the provision of extended targeted supports addressing language skills in particular with an integrated bridging component leading into mainstream vocational training services and parallel career guidance. Crucially, a set of recommendations were put forward addressing the process of integrating policies and procedures to respond to the issues raised by a migrant and multicultural job-seeking community in the design and delivery of all labour market programmes and support schemes.

9. ETHNIC DIVERSITY AND THE LIMITATIONS OF EMPLOYMENT POLICIES

Kirton and Greene's (2000) argument that workplace and labour market inequality cannot only be an employment policy issue is strongly supported in the conclusions to the study. Inequality in the labour market reflects inequality throughout society and the effects of wider societal attitudes on the labour market. This research highlighted various ways in which the attitudes prevalent in Irish society contributed to the exclusion and marginalisation of minority ethnic groups within the labour market.

As well as the effect of legal status on participants' risk of exclusion and marginalisation, their experiences seemed to vary according to the ethnic origin of participants. The effect of gender on labour market access in the form of increased risk of exclusion and marginalisation for women in the general population certainly held true for this group. Comparisons across the three study sites demonstrated that targeted provision for refugees does enhance their chances on the Irish labour market. However, across the three sites studied the availability of supported programmes varied greatly. The need also emerged for culturally specific programmes for those within the refugee community with an even greater risk of exclusion. From this study the Roma community emerged as a group in need of culturally specific programmes of support to overcome the effects of exclusion they have experienced in previous countries of residence as well as in Ireland.

All of the social partners, other statutory led initiatives and bodies including the Equality Authority, the National Consultative Committee on Racism and Interculturalism and NGOs including the Irish Refugee Council, as well as all members of Integrating Ireland are important partners in the process of fostering wider societal attitudes that will challenge the exclusion and marginalisation of minority ethnic groups on the Irish labour market. In particular there is a need for strong political leadership on this issue. The myth that abounds suggesting that Ireland is being overwhelmed by people seeking asylum needs to be challenged. Information about the factual situation of immigration into Ireland is required. There is also a need to generate awareness and understanding about the factors that cause people to flee their countries of origin and seek asylum, and the difficult circumstances under which this takes place. More broadly a comprehensive immigration policy is needed within which the obligations and responsibilities of the state as a signatory to the 1951 UN Convention on Refugees can be set out clearly.

Mac Éinri (2001) considers that current frameworks for integration are specifically focused on refugees referring in particular to the Interdepartmental Working Group on the Integration of Refugees in Ireland. He argues that such an exclusive focus carries a danger that other labour market immigrants and their needs are not being attended to at all. Primarily the absence of a proper framework for the reception and integration of all non-Irish workers in the Irish labour market can lead to considerable difficulties for individuals and can perpetuate a variety of hidden, implicit and explicit forms of exclusion and/or discrimination against such individuals. Other organisations have also argued for a comprehensive immigration policy including the Irish Refugee Council, IBEC and ICTU. The findings of this research endorse the support for the formulation of such a comprehensive immigration policy.

Chapter 13

THE LIMITS OF IRISH
NEO-LIBERALISM AT WORK

Gerry Boucher **and** *Gráinne Collins*

1. INTRODUCTION

The preceding chapters have outlined the changing face of work
and the life-work nexus. Both of these have been shaped under a
neo-liberal framework and in this last chapter, we discuss the
possible limits of Irish neo-liberalism. In particular we draw attention to the themes of gender in the workplace and at home, the
issues created by global workplaces and the role of immigrants in
the Republic of Ireland. The "loosely coupled" structure of the
Irish state, particularly with regard to gender relations, workplaces and immigration means that policy is often contradictory
and results in families, informal work groups and individuals carrying much of the burden in adapting to the new types of work
and workplaces.

2. THE "LOOSELY COUPLED" IRISH NEO-LIBERAL STATE

In an analysis of welfare states, Hemerijck and Schludi distinguish
between loosely and tightly coupled ideal types (2000). Loosely
coupled welfare states are characterised by a relative lack of co-
ordination between policy structures and decision-making in

which "crosscutting spillover" from one policy-making area to another is often spontaneous and "typically takes place without design", and "adjustment takes place through local adaptation" (2000: 136–7). Tightly coupled welfare states are identified by "decision-making institutions that enable policy makers to co-ordinate policy interdependencies" leading to "co-ordinated change and issue linkage across different policy areas (136–7).

More recently, Boyle (2005) has applied this typology to the Irish state in an empirical study of FÁS and active labour market policy in Ireland. Boyle characterises "policy making institutions in Ireland" as loosely coupled in that "there is often considerable capacity for autonomous intervention, but little capacity for joined-up government and co-ordination of policy across subsystems" with the "partial exception" of the "centralised financial authority exercised by the Department of Finance" (2005: 20). There are at least three other partial exceptions: the role of the IDA Ireland in the country's economic development; the National Development Plans to implement EU funding; and the National Agreements arising from the social partnership process. These exceptions require some explanation.

Like other former British colonies, particularly in the Anglosphere, the Irish state developed initially along "liberal" lines, inheriting and institutionalising a configuration based on a minimal "*laissez-faire*" state with, as Boyle suggests, expenditure centrally controlled by the Department of Finance. From the early 1930s to the late 1950s, the state shifted from a *laissez-faire* market economy to one in which the state selectively intervened to promote a policy of import substitution industrialisation (ISI). This period also saw the gradual low-level building of a "liberal" minimal welfare state with some Catholic and continental corporatist features depending on the social policy area (Boucher and Collins, 2003).

The failure of the ISI policy to successfully develop the country led to it being progressively jettisoned from the mid-1950s in favour of an export-led industrialisation (ELI) policy based on opening the economy and attracting foreign direct investment (FDI). This gradual economic opening involved: first, joining a free trade area with the UK in 1965; second, entering the now EU in 1973 with the UK (and Denmark); and third, increasing integration into the global economy from the late 1980s largely through American high technology and to a lesser extent financial services multinational corporations (MNCs).

Of increasing importance was the role of the relatively autonomous (from 1969) IDA to both attract the "right" MNCs for Ireland's level of development and to "crosscut spillover" with other state institutions. These have been instrumental in Ireland's successful economic development (Mac Sharry and White, 2000). Yet, IDA Ireland is the main organisational exception in the Irish state with its high degree of operational, personnel and financial autonomy and its quasi-business structure and strategies, even if its "employees" are often motivated by Irish economic nationalism (Mac Sharry and White, 2000).

From the 1960s to the late 1980s, Ireland's economic opening up was accompanied by a fairly rapid expansion of the welfare state largely along the already established liberal corporatist institutions and policy areas (Boucher and Collins, 2003). This expansion also involved the addition of new policy areas and institutions such as the creation of a system of Regional Technical Colleges (now Institutes of Technology) controlled directly by the state through the Department of Education (White, 2001).

However, the growth in size of the Irish state during this period, its increased capacity to act and its (apparent) greater autonomy from other domestic collective actors did not result in the tighter coupling of decision-making institutions and policy makers across policy areas. Instead, the Irish liberal corporatist state of this period remained loosely coupled with a low degree of co-ordination between decision-making institutions across policy areas.

The major exception here is the First Programme for Economic Expansion (a precursor to the later National Agreements and to a lesser extent the EU-mandated National Development Plans) in 1958. The First Programme presented a short integrated planning model for Ireland's economic development from 1959–64 (Lee,

1989: 344–53). The economic growth that followed during the period of the plan led to two further, although not very successful plans, the Second Programme for 1964–70 that was dropped in 1967 and the Third Programme that was abandoned in 1971 (Lee, 1989: 353).

Ireland's first period of economic "catch up" continuing through the 1960s and 1970s was spurred by factors such as FDI, initially from the UK and increasingly from the US, and EEC funds, particularly from the Common Agricultural Policy (CAP) to farmers and agro-industry, from the mid-1970s. Latterly, it was fuelled by profligate public expenditure in the late 1970s and early 1980s that heavily indebted the country, contributing to the prolonged economic recession from 1981 to 1986. Despite the beginning of social partnership in 1987 and the first National Development Plan for 1989–94, the consensus of the late 1980s and even early 1990s was that the now comparatively large and rather unwieldy Irish state had failed to effectively use its capacity and autonomy to implement policies to achieve its socio-economic goals (Breen et al., 1990; Lee, 1989; Mjøset, 1992).

The six social partnership agreements from 1987 to 2005 and the three National Development Plans from 1989 to 2006 have significantly increased the tight coupling of the Irish state relative to its previous very loose coupling. This is particularly evident in the incorporation of an "elite community of social partners" (Boucher and Collins, 2003: 302–3) in the decision-making process and the greater co-ordination across policy domains in both the national agreements and development plans.

Nonetheless, the state's enhanced capacity for decision-making and implementation has been only partially and selectively effective depending on the policy area and the cluster of policies involved. Thus, the social partnership agreements have been most effective, at least until the late 1990s, in achieving the cluster of quantitative macro-economic objectives, tax reductions and social policy reforms that form the core of all the agreements. They have been much less effective in achieving objectives in the cluster of "quality of life" issues such as life-work balance, child care, relative poverty, income inequality, workplace democracy, racism, immigration and infrastructure. The differences between Ireland's economic development and its quality of life have also been detailed statistically through comparative national progress indicators (CSO, 2005).

Likewise state failure has occurred in the policy areas of regional and local development planning, land use and property development, housing, transportation, infrastructure, social space and environmental protection. This state failure can be seen as failing to intervene to provide adequate public goods or failing to intervene to counter the power of private monopolies. As such, the tighter coupling of the Irish state in terms of economic efficiency can be contrasted with a continued loose coupling and relative ineffectiveness of state capacity to effectively address social issues. This has generated the economic dominance over society analysed in the introductory chapter, and the gendered, global workplace and immigrant life-work imbalances examined in the empirical chapters of this book.

3. TRANSFERRING THE BURDEN OF LIFE-WORK IMBALANCES

Yet, the loosely coupled Irish state has not had exactly the same impact on the three thematic areas covered in this book. Instead, there has been differential impact in each of these areas, resulting from failures of policy-making and implementation, coverage and exclusion. However, the overall social result is similar: families, informal work groups and individuals end up carrying the bulk of the burden in adapting to the structural and policy constraints of these various life-work imbalances. Put more bluntly: the individual carries the can for the failure of the state.

Thus, the chapters by Fine-Davis and Richardson highlight the continued gendered nature of the life-work imbalances resulting from the relative failure of policy-makers, including the social partners, to effectively address this important policy issue. This is in spite of a growing number of (partially) implemented agreements and a not insubstantial expenditure of public funds. Further, the chapters by Collins and Browne, Greco, and Preston and MacKeogh show how the state (and social partnership) failure at the national level transfers issues of gendered life-work imbalances, first to the management of public and private sector firms in terms of company policy and management prerogative, and ultimately to families and individuals that have to adapt living to work.

Especially for women with children, transferring the burden of adapting to gendered life-work imbalances to the family and individual level often means that in practice women still have to choose between advancing in their career and taking care of their family. That this stark choice exists, even for women with the most highly developed skills, does not bode well for the long-term competitiveness of the Irish economy, more reliant on the increased participation of skilled women than ever before. While the marriage bar has long since ended, an informal care bar has seemingly emerged to take its place in the governance gap between state failure and market dominance.

The chapters by Collings et al., Doherty, O'Carroll, and Cunningham examine globalised workplaces in American MNCs and the Irish ICT, financial, public and retail sectors. These show limits of policy coverage, for instance, in workplace representation and democracy, despite social partnership. This is particularly the case in non-unionised American MNCs and Americanised Irish companies such as those in the information and communication technology (ICT) sector. In these non-unionised companies, relatively autonomous company cultures operate almost as "total institutions" (Goffman, 1961). These encompass the whole workplace, while transferring the burden of middle management to individualised work teams and lower management to the self-managed individual employee. Even in the partly unionised retail sector, Cunningham details company practices that proceed much further than standard human resource management policies, encouraging the employee's subjective transformation into an aesthetic and enterprising self as consumer.

While the unionised public and less-unionised financial sectors are directly incorporated into the social partnership process through the national agreements, Doherty reveals that employees report more stress and insecurity, and feel under threat from more powerful employers. In the public sector, the continuing neo-liberalisation of the state through policies such as deregulation and privatisation heighten these fears and insecurities, transferring emotional burdens to the individual level of the employee. At the same time, trade unions are viewed contradictorily as being more relevant and yet less effective in addressing the key issues of working life, leading to informal industrial action against the binding commitments of the national agreements. As such, enhanced trade union capacity and autonomy at the national level is seemingly counterbalanced by decreased union capacity and autonomy at the workplace.

Thus, even in unionised workplaces, employee resistance has been either largely reduced to informal work groups or individualised. Both of these resistance strategies are perhaps best exemplified in O'Carroll's chapter on the non-unionised software companies in the Irish ICT sector. At the individual and group levels, O'Carroll identifies a number of personal strategies such as: hardening cynicism; commitment withdrawal from the workplace; vocally objecting as a group to working late hours; and the work team setting working time for itself regardless of official company policy. While the latter informal group strategies are more positive examples of workplace resistance, they also reveal the glaring gap in policy coverage between enhanced participative democracy in the social partnership process and the lack of participative (or even representative) democracy in many Irish globalising workplaces.

The chapters by Cunningham et al. and Conlon et al. concerned with immigrants highlight the exclusionary impact of Irish policies with regard to issues like labour market access and citizenship rights. Like other neo-liberal states in the Anglo-sphere such as Australia, the US and the UK, the Irish variety of neo-liberalism is characterised by a contradictory focus on opening markets in the economy and (increasingly) the polity, while at the same time emphasising greater regulation of society in areas such as individual behaviour, crime and immigration. In terms of the latter policy area, the Irish state is especially contradictory, pro-claiming an employer-led, market-driven immigration policy that is in fact highly regulated by the state.

Specifically, Ireland's current asylum-seeker and refugee poli-cies exclude the former from labour market access in spite of the country's continuing low unemployment rate, employer demand for unskilled and skilled labour, and the relatively high education and skill levels of many asylum-seekers upon arrival in Ireland. This is not an employer-led, market-driven policy at all, but a po-litical strategy to pressurise individuals and families of asylum-seekers to voluntarily leave (before being deported at cost to the state) or become part of the informal economy (again eliminating costs to the state). In both cases, the burden of exclusion from the formal labour market is borne by the individual or families of asy-lum-seekers. This strategy also has an external demonstration ef-fect, attempting to encourage potential asylum-seekers to apply as legal migrant workers instead of as asylum-seekers (yet again re-ducing costs to the state).

Further, Conlon et al. show that even if an asylum-seeker is of-ficially recognised as a refugee, the individual encounters a range of structural, cultural and organisational barriers to quality em-ployment in Ireland including lack of recognition of qualifica-tions, poor English language skills and discrimination. In this case, however, the state does operate a market-based approach to integration, largely transferring the burden of overcoming these barriers to the individual refugee or family (once again reducing costs to the state).

Finally, Cunningham et al. reveal through employees' narra-tives the burden of powerlessness that many migrant workers on temporary work visas experience, given their condition of almost bonded servitude to their employer. As with Irish asylum policy, there is no free-market basis for severely curtailing the rights of migrant workers to change their job. It benefits many low-wage, low-skill employers, though, to have migrant workers tied to their job for a specified period, given the tight labour market in which most native Irish workers no longer want (or have) to do menial labour. This strategy is also an additional control mechanism, allowing the state to keep tabs on temporary migrant workers through their employer and to clear these sectors of the labour market more quickly should the state decide that labour supply outstrips demand.

Ireland now has the economic growth so desperately needed and wanted, but this has left the state and Irish people with several problems of co-ordination and adaptation. However, these problems are known elsewhere. Other states have faced these problems and gone forward, creating societies where men and women can work and enjoy a family life, where the individual is protected at the workplace, where there is flexibility and where migrants are incorporated without assimilation into society. What is lacking in the Irish case is a vision of what we want Ireland to look like in the twenty-first century.

REFERENCES

Acker, J. (1990), "Hierarchies, Jobs, Bodies: A Theory of Gendered Organisations", *Gender and Society* 4: 139-158.

Acker, J. (1998), "The Future of Gender and Organizations: Connections and Boundaries", *Gender, Work and Organization*, 5(4): 195-206.

Ackroyd, S. and Thompson, P. (1999), *Organisational Misbehaviour*, London: Sage.

Adams, R. (2003), "Why American Workers are so Disorganised", *Human Resources and Employment Review*, 1(1): 11-36.

Adkins, L. (1995), *Gendered Work: Sexuality Family and the Labour Market*, Buckingham: Open University Press.

Adnett, N. (1996), *European Labour Markets: Analysis and Policy*, London: Longman.

Allen, K. (1997), *Fianna Fáil and Irish Labour: 1926 to the Present*, London: Pluto Press.

Allen, K. (2000), *The Celtic Tiger: The Myth of Social Partnership*, Manchester: Manchester University Press.

Alvesson, M. and Billing, Y. (1997), *Understanding Gender and Organizations*, London: Sage.

Arora, A. Gambardella A. Torrisi S (2001), *In the Footsteps of Silicon Valley? Indian and Irish Software in the International Division of Labour*, Stanford University: Stanford Institute of Economic Policy Research (SIEPR), Discussion Paper No. 00-41.

Arthur, M. and Rousseau, D. (eds.) (1996), *The Boundaryless Career*, Oxford: Oxford University Press.

Asheim, B. (2000), *The Learning Firm in the Learning Region: Workers Participation as Social Capital*, Denmark: DRUID Summer 2000 Conference.

Auer, P. (2001), *Employment Revival in Europe: Labour Market Success in Austria, Denmark, Ireland and The Netherlands*. Geneva: International Labour Office.

Bacon, N. and Storey, J. (1993), "Individualisation of the Employment Relationship and the Implications for Trade Unions" *Employee Relations* (15)1: 5-17.

Bacon, N. and Storey, J. (1996), "Individualism and Collectivism and the Changing Role of Trade Unions" in P. Ackers, C. Smith and P. Smith (eds.), *The New Workplace and Trade Unionism*, London: Routledge.

Barling, J. Fullagar, C. and Kelloway, E. (1992), *The Union and its Members*, New York: Oxford University Press.

Barrett, A. Callan, T. Doris, A. O'Neill, D. Russell, H. Sweetman, O. and McBride, J. (2000), *How Unequal? Men and Women in the Irish Labour Market*, Dublin: Oak Tree Press.

Barry, F. (ed) (1999), *Understanding Ireland's Economic Growth*. London: Macmillan.

Barry, F. (2002), "FDI and the Host Economy: A Case Study of Ireland", Unpublished Paper presented at National University of Ireland, Galway, 8 November.

Beck, U. (1992), *Risk Society: Towards a New Modernity*, Cambridge: Polity.

Beck, U. (2000), *The Brave New World of Work*, Cambridge: Polity.

Beck, U. (2002), *Individualisation: Institutionalised Individualism and its Social and Political Consequences*, London: Sage.

Becker, G. (1981), *A Treatise on the Family*, Cambridge: Harvard University Press.

Begley, M. Garavan, C. Condon, M. Kelly, I. Holland, K. and Staines, A. (1999), *Asylum in Ireland: A Public Health Perspective*, Dublin: University College Dublin.

Bennett, F. (2002), "Gender Implications of Current Social Security Reforms", *Fiscal Studies* 23(4): 559-584.

Bird, S. (2001), "Men's Social Relations and Intimacy in Men's Work Lives: Issues and Implications" *Gender Work and Organisation Conference*, Keele University, 27–29 June 2001.

Black, J. Green, A. and Ackers, P. (1997), *The Demise of Collectivism: Implications for Social Partnership*, Wolverhampton: Wolverhampton Business School Working Papers Series.

Blackwell, J. (1989), *Women in the Labour Force*, Dublin: Employment Equality Agency.

Bloch, A. (1999), "Refugees in the Job Market: A Case of Unused Skills in the British Economy" in A. Bloch and C. Levy (eds.), *Refugees, Citizenship and Social Policy in Europe*, Britain: Macmillan.

Boucher, G. and Collins, G. (2003), "Having One's Cake and Being Eaten Too: Irish Neo-Liberal Corporatism" *Review of Social Economy* (61)3: 295-316.

Bourdieu, P. (1977), *Outline of a Theory of Practice*, Cambridge: Cambridge University Press.

Bourdieu, P. (1984), *Distinction: A Social Critique of the Judgement of Taste*, London: Routledge and Kegan Paul.

Bowlby, S. and Preston, P. (1985), "Women's Employment in the New IT Sector in Britain: New Technology Systems and Changing Gender Roles", Paper to Institute of British Geographers, Annual Conference, January.

Boyer, R. (1988), *The Search for Labour Market Flexibility: The European Economies in Transition*, Oxford: Clarenden.

Boyle, N. (2005), *FÁS and Active Labour Market Policy 1985-2004*, Dublin: The Policy Institute at Trinity College Dublin.

Brandth, B. and Kvande, E. (2001), "Flexible Work and Flexible Fathers", *Work Employment and Society* 15(2): 251-267.

Braverman, H. (1974), *Labour and Monopoly Capital: The Degradation of Work in the Twentieth Century*, New York: Monthly Review Press.

Breen, R. Hannan, D. Rottman, D. and Whelan, C. (eds.) (1990), *Understanding Contemporary Ireland*, Dublin: Gill and Macmillan.

Brink, M. (1997), "The Labour Market Integration of Refugees in the Netherlands" in P. Muus (ed.), *Exclusion and Inclusion of Refugees in Contemporary Europe*, Utrecht: European Research Centre on Migration and Ethnic Relations.

British Refugee Council (2001), *Refugee Employment in Europe*, London: British Refugee Council with the support of the European Commission.

Bronson, P. (1999), *The Nudist on the Late Shift and Other Tales of Silicon Valley*, London: Secker & Warburg.

Brown, J.S. and Druguid, P. (1991), "Organisational Learning and Communities of Practices. Towards a Unified View of Working, Learning and Innovation", *Organisation Science* 2: 40-56.

Campbell, C. (1997), "Shopping, Pleasure and the Sex War" in P. Falk and C. Campbell (eds.), *The Shopping Experience*, London: Sage Publications.

Carter, B. (2004), "Unions, Civil Service and the State: State Restructuring and Union Renewal" *Work, Employment and Society* (18) 1: 137-157.

Castells, M. (1996), *The Rise of the Network Society*, Cambridge, Mass: Blackwell.

Castells, M. (2000), *The Rise of Network Society Volume I* (second edition), Oxford: Blackwell.

Causer, G. and Jones, C. (1996), "Management and the Control of Technical Labour", *Work, Employment and Society* 10(1): 105-123.

Central Statistics Office (various) *Quarterly National Household Survey*. Dublin: CSO.

Central Statistics Office (2003), *Population and Migration Estimates*, Dublin: CSO.

Central Statistics Office (2005), *Measuring Ireland's Progress 2004*, Dublin: CSO.

Clinch, P. Convery, F. and Walsh, B. (2002), *After the Celtic Tiger: Challenges Ahead*, Dublin: O'Brien Press.

Collins, G. and Wickham, J. (2004), "Inclusion or Exploitation? Irish Women Enter the Labour Force", *Gender, Work and Organization*, 11(1): 26-46.

Collins, G. and Wickham, J. (2001), *What Childcare Crisis? Irish Mothers Entering the Labour Force*, Employment Research Centre: Trinity College Dublin.

Collinson, D. (1992), *Managing the Shopfloor: Subjectivity, Masculinity and Workplace Culture*, Berlin: William de Gruyter.

Collinson, D. and Hearn, J. (eds.) (1996), *Men as Managers, Managers as Men: Critical Perspectives on Men, Masculinities and Managements*, London: Sage.

Conley, H. (2002), "A State of Insecurity: Temporary Work in the Public Services" *Work, Employment and Society* (16)4: 725-737.

Conroy, P. and Brennan, A. (2003), *Migrant Workers and Their Experiences*, Dublin: Equality Authority.

Cook, K. (ed.) (1987), *Social Exchange Theory*, Newbury Park: Sage Publications.

Corrigan, P. (1997), *The Sociology of Consumption*, London: Sage Publications.

Coulter, C. and Coleman, S. (eds.) (2003), *The End of Irish History? Critical Reflections on the Celtic Tiger*, Manchester: Manchester University Press.

Crompton, R. (ed) (1999), *Restructuring Gender Relations and Employment: The Decline of the Male Breadwinner*. Oxford: Oxford University Press.

Crompton, R. (2002), "Employment, Flexible Working and the Family", *British Journal of Sociology* 53(4): 537-558.

Crone, M. (2002), *A Profile of the Irish Software Industry*, Belfast: Northern Ireland Economic Research Centre.

Cronin, M. (2002), "Speed Limits: Ireland, Globalisation and the War against Time" in P. Kirby, L. Gibbons and M. Cronin (eds.), *Reinventing Ireland*, London: Pluto Press.

Crouch, C. (1999), *Social Change in Western Europe*, Oxford: Oxford University Press.

CSO (2003), *Quarterly National Household Survey — Childcare Fourth Quarter (2002*, Dublin: Central Statistics Office.

CSO (Various) *Labour Force Surveys*, Dublin: Central Statistics Office.

Cunnision, S. (1964), *Wages and Work Allocation*, London: Tavistock.

D'Art, D. (2002), "Managing the Employment Relationship in a Market Economy", in D. D'Art and T. Turner (eds.), *Irish Employment Relations in the New Economy*, Dublin: Blackhall.

D'Art, D. and Turner, T. (eds.) (2002), *Irish Employment Relations in the New Economy*, Dublin: Blackhall.

D'Art, D. and Turner, T. (2002), "An Attitudinal Revolution: The End of "Them and Us" in Irish Industrial Relations" in D. D'Art, and T. Turner (eds.), *Irish Employment Relations in the New Economy*, Dublin: Blackhall.

Dalton, M. (1948), "The Industrial Rate Buster", *Applied Anthropology* 7(1): 5-23.

Department of Education and Science *(1999), Ready to Learn — White Paper on Early Childhood Education*, Dublin: Stationery Office.

Department of Justice, Equality and Law Reform (1999), *Integration, A Two Way Process*, Dublin: Department of Justice, Equality and Law Reform.

Department of Justice, Equality and Law Reform, 4 March 2005, Press Release, http://www.justice.ie.

Department of the Taoiseach (2000), *Programme for Prosperity and Fairness*, Dublin: Stationery Office.

Derrida, J. (2002), *Cosmopolitanism and Forgiveness* (trans. M. Dooley and M. Hughes), London: Routledge.

Dickens, L. (2004), "Problems of Fit: Changing Employment and Labour Regulation" *British Journal of Industrial Relations* (42) 4: 595-605.

Djelic, M. (1998), *Exporting the American Model: The Post War Transformation of European Business,* Oxford: Oxford University Press.

Drew, E. Humphreys, P. and Murphy, C. (2002), *Off the Treadmill: Achieving Work/Life Balance*, Dublin: National Framework Committee for the Development of Family Friendly Policies.

Drucker, P. (1969), *The Age of Discontinuity: Guidelines to Our Changing Society*, London: Heinemann.

Drucker, P. (1974), *Management: Tasks, Responsibilities, Practices*, New York: Harper and Row.

Drucker, P. (1988), "The Coming of the New Organisation", *Harvard Business Review*, Summer: 53-65.

Du Gay, P. (1996), *Consumption, Work and Identity*, London: Sage.

Dunn, W. (1994), *Public Policy Analysis: An Introduction*, Englewood Cliffs, N.J: Prentice-Hall.

Eagly, A. (1987), *Sex Differences in Social Behaviour: A Social Role Interpretation*, Hillsdale, NJ: Erlbaum.

EC (European Commission) (1994), *Europe and the Global Information Society: Recommendations to the European Council* ("Bangemann Report"). Brussels: CEC.

EC (European Commission) (2002), *"Towards a Knowledge-based Europe: The European Union and the Information Society*, DG for Press and Communication (Accessed from "Europa" website, Nov. 2002).

EC (European Commission) (2002), *Employment in Europe. Recent Trends and Prospects*, Brussels: EC.

Economist, The (1997), "Green is Good: Advantages of Ireland as a Host for FDI", 17 May, 343(8017): 21-4.

Edwards, T. and Ferner, A. (2002), "The Renewed 'American Challenge': A Review of Employment Practices in US Multinationals", *Industrial Relations Journal*, 33(2): 94-111.

Enderwick, P. (1986), *Multinational Business and Labour*, London: Croom Helm.

Esping-Andersen, G. (1996), *Welfare States in Transition. National Adaptations in Global Economies*, London: Sage.

Esping-Andersen, G. (1990), *Three Worlds of Welfare Capitalism*, Cambridge: Cambridge University Press.

Esping-Andersen, G. (1999), "Politics Without Class? Postindustrial Cleavages in Europe and America" in H. Kitschelt, P. Lange, G. Marks and J. D. Stephens (eds.), *Continuity and Change in Contemporary Capitalism*, Cambridge: Cambridge University Press.

European Consultation on Refugees and Exiles (ECRE) (1998), *Report of Conference on Integration of Refugees in Europe*, Antwerp 12–14 November 1998, Antwerp: ECRE.

Expert Group on Future Skill Needs (2000), *Second Report of the Expert Group*, Dublin: Forfás.

Expert Working Group on Childcare (1999), *National Childcare Strategy — Report of the Partnership 2000 Expert Working Group on Childcare*, Dublin: Stationery Office.

Fagnani, J. (1998), "Recent Changes in Family Policy in France: Political Trade-Offs and Economic Constraints" in E. Drew, R. Emerek, and E. Mahon (eds.), *Women, Work and the Family in Europe*, London: Routledge.

Fahey, T. and FitzGerald J. (1997), "The Educational Revolution and Demographic Change" in D. Duffy, J. FitzGerald, I. Kearney, and F. Shortall (eds.), *Medium Term Review*: 1997-2003. No. 6: 7-33, Dublin: Economic and Social Research Institute.

Falk, P. (1997), "The Scopic Regimes of Shopping" in P. Falk and C. Campbell (eds.), *The Shopping Experience*, London: Sage Publications.

Fanning, B. (2001), "On No Man's Land: Asylum Seekers in Ireland and the Limits of Social Citizenship", Paper presented to the *Irish Social Policy Annual Conference*, Trinity College Dublin, 27 July.

Fanning, B. (2002), *Racism and Social Change in the Republic of Ireland*, Manchester: Manchester University Press.

Faughnan, P and Woods, M. (2000), *Lives on Hold, Seeking Asylum in Ireland*, Dublin: Social Science Research Centre, University College Dublin.

Featherstone, B. (2003), "Taking Fathers Seriously", *British Journal of Social Work* 33(2): 239-254.

Featherstone, M. (1991), *Consumer Culture and Postmodernism*, London: Sage.

Ferguson, K. (1984), *The Feminist Case against Bureaucracy*, Philadelphia: Temple University Press.

Ferner, A. (1997), "Country of Origin Effects and HRM in Multinational Corporations", *Human Resource Management*, 7(1): 19-37.

Ferner, A. (2000), *The Embeddedness of US Multinational Companies in the US Business System: Implications for HR/IR*, Occasional papers number 61, Leicester, De Montfort University Business School.

Ferner, A. and Hyman, R. (1998), *Changing Industrial Relations in Europe*, Oxford: Blackwell.

Fine-Davis, M. (1983a), "Mothers' Attitudes towards Childcare and Employment: A Nationwide Survey" in *Working Party on Childcare Facilities for Working Parents*, Report to the Minister for Labour, Dublin: Stationery Office, pp. 73-168.

Fine-Davis, M. (1983b), *Women and Work in Ireland: A Social-Psychological Perspective*, Dublin: Council for the Status of Women.

Fine-Davis, M. (1988), "Changing Attitudes to the Role of Women in Ireland: 1975-1986, Vol. I: Attitudes toward the Role and Status of Women, 1975-1986" in *First Report of the Second Joint Oireachtas Committee on Women's Rights* (Pl. 5609), Dublin: Stationery Office.

Fine-Davis, M. and Clarke, H. (2002), "Ireland and Cross-National Comparisons" in M. Fine-Davis, H. Clarke, and M. Berry (eds.), *Fathers and*

Mothers: Dilemmas of the Work-Life Balance — Conference Proceedings, Dublin: Centre for Gender and Women's Studies, Trinity College.

Fine-Davis, M. Fagnani,, J. Giovannini, D. Hojgaard, L. and Clarke, H. (2002), *Fathers and Mothers: Dilemmas of the Work-Life Balance — Final Report to the European Commission and Irish Dept. of Justice, Equality and Law Reform*, Dublin: Centre for Gender and Women's Studies, Trinity College.

Fine-Davis, M., Fagnani, J., Giovannini, D., Hojgaard, L. and Clarke, H. (2004), *Fathers and Mothers: Dilemmas of the Work-Life Balance — A Comparative Study in Four European Countries*, Dordrecht, Boston and London: Kluwer Academic Publishers.

Flood, P. and Toner, B. (1997), "How do Large Non-Union Companies Avoid a *Catch 22*", *British Journal of Industrial Relations*, 35 (2): 257-77.

Forfás (2002), *International Trade and Investment Report 2001*, Dublin: Forfás.

Forfás (2003), *National Survey of Vacancies in the Private, Non-Agricultural Sector*, Dublin: Forfás.

Forfás (2004), *International Trade and Investment Report 2003*, Dublin: Forfás.

Fosh, P. (1981), *The Active Trade Unionist*, Cambridge: Cambridge University Press.

Fosh, P. (1993), "Membership Participation in Workplace Unionism: The Possibility of Union Renewal" *British Journal of Industrial Relations* (31) 4: 577-591.

Fosh, P. and Cohen, S. (1990), "Local Trade Unionists in Action: Patterns of Local Democracy" in P. Fosh and E. Heery (eds.), *Trade Unions and Their Members*, London: Macmillan.

Foucault, M. (1971), *L'Ordre du Discours*, Paris: Gallimard.

Fynes, B., Morrissey, T., Roche, W., Whelan, B. and Williams, J. (1996), *Flexible Working Lives: The Changing Nature of Working Time Arrangements in Ireland*, Dublin: Oak Tree Press.

Geary, J. and Roche, W. (1995), "The Attenuation of 'Host Country Effects'? Multinationals, Industrial Relations and Collective Bargaining in Ireland", Unpublished Working Paper, Dublin: University College Dublin.

Geary, J. and Roche, W. (2001), "Multinationals and Human Resource Practices in Ireland: A Rejection of the 'New Conformance Thesis', *International Journal of Human Resource Management*, 12 (1): 109-27.

Gershuny, J. and Robinson, J. (1994), "Measuring Hours of Paid Work: Time Diary vs Estimate Questions", *Bulletin of Labour Statistics*: xi-xvii Geneva: ILO.

Gibbons, M., Limoges, C., Nowotny, H., Schwartzman, S., Scott, P. and Trow, M. (1994), *Production of Knowledge: The Dynamics of Science and Research in Contemporary Societies*, London: Sage Publications.

Giddens, A. (1991), *Modernity and Self Identity*, London: Polity Press.

Giddens, A. (1998), *The Third Way: The Renewal of Social Democracy*, Malden, MA: Polity Press.

Giovannini, D. (2002), "The Italian Experience" in M. Fine-Davis, H. Clarke, and M. Berry (eds.), *Fathers and Mothers: Dilemmas of the Work-Life Balance — Conference Proceedings*, Dublin: Centre for Gender and Women's Studies, Trinity College.

Goffman, E. (1961), *Asylums: Essays on the Social Situation of Mental Patients and Other Inmates*, Garden City, NY: Anchor Books.

Goldthorpe, J., Lockwood, D., Bechhofer, F. and Platt, J. (1968), *The Affluent Worker: Industrial Attitudes and Behaviour*, Cambridge: Cambridge University Press.

Goodbody Economic Consultants (1998), *The Economics of Childcare in Ireland*, Dublin: Goodbody Economic Consultants.

Gooderham, P., Nordhaug, O. and Ringdal, K. (1999), "Institutional and Rational Determinants of Organisation Practices: Human Resource Management in European Firms", *Administrative Science Quarterly*, 44: 507-31.

Goodrich, C. (1975), *The Frontier of Control: A Study of British Workshop Politics*, London: Pluto.

Gray, A. (ed) (1997), *International Perspectives on the Irish Economy*, Dublin: Indecon Economic Consultants.

Greco, L. (2002), *Industrial Redundancies*, Aldershot: Ashgate.

Green, F. (2001), "It's Been a Hard Day's Night: The Concentration and Intensification of Work in Late Twentieth-Century Britain", *British Journal of Industrial Relations*, 39(1): 53-80.

Groot, W. and Van den Brink, H. (2000), "Education, Training and Employability", *Applied Economics* 32(5): 573-581.

Guest, D. (1990), "Human Resource Management and the American Dream", *Journal of Management Studies*, 27(4): 977-87.

Gunnigle, P., Collings, D. and Morley, M. (2005), "Exploring the Dynamics of Industrial Relations in US Multinationals: Evidence from the Republic of Ireland", *Industrial Relations Journal*, 36(3): 241-56.

Gunnigle, P., Collings, D., Morley, M., McAvinue, C., O'Callaghan, A. and Shore, D. (2003), "US Multinationals and Human Resource Management In Ireland: Towards a Qualitative Research Agenda", *Irish Journal of Management*, 24(1): 7-25.

Gunnigle, P., McCurtain, S. and Morley, M. (2001), "Dismantling Pluralism: Industrial Relations in Irish Greenfield Sites", *Personnel Review*, 30(3): 263-79.

Gunnigle, P., Morley, M. and Turner, T. (1997), "Challenging Collectivist Traditions: Individualism and the Management of Industrial Relations in Greenfield Sites", *The Economic and Social Review*, 28(2): 105-34.

Gunnigle, P., O'Sullivan, M. and Kinsella, M. (2002), "Organised Labour in the New Economy: Trade Unions and Public Policy in Ireland", in D. D'Art and T. Turner (eds.), *Irish Employment Relations in the New Economy*, Dublin: Blackhall.

Gunnigle, P., Turner, T. and D'Art, D. (1998), "Counterpoising Collectivism: Performance-related Pay and Industrial Relations in Greenfield Site", *British Journal of Industrial Relations*, 36(4): 565-79.

Habermas, J. (1998), *The Inclusion of the Other: Studies in Political Theory*, Cambridge, Mass: MIT Press.

Hall, E. and Rodrigues, M. (2003), "The Myth of Post-Feminism", *Gender & Society*, 17(6): 878-902.

Hall, P. A. and Soskice, D. (eds.) (2001), *Varieties of Capitalism: The Institutional Foundations of Comparative Advantage*, Oxford: Oxford University Press.

Harbison, F. and Myers, C. (eds.) (1959), *Management in the Industrial World: An International Analysis*, New York: McGraw-Hill.

Hardiman, N. (1988), *Pay, Politics and Economic Performance in Ireland 1970-1987*, Oxford: Clarendon.

Hardiman, N. (2000), "Social Partnership, Wage Bargaining, and Growth" in Nolan, B., P. O'Connell and C. Whelan (eds.), *Bust to Boom: The Irish Experience of Growth and Inequality*, Dublin: IPA.

Harney, M., July 2000, Address at a Meeting of the American Bar Associates, Dublin: Law Society of Ireland.

Hartley, J. (1996), "The "New" Service Sector: Employment Status, Ideology and Trade Union Participation in the UK." in P. Pasture, J. Verberckmoes and H. De Witte (eds.), *The Lost Perspective? Trade Unions Between Ideology and Social Action in the New Europe*, Aldershot: Avebury.

Harvey, D. (1990), *The Condition of Postmodernity*, Oxford: Blackwell.

Harzing, A. and Sorge, A. (2003), "The Relative Impact of Country of Origin and Universal Contingencies on Internationalization Strategies and Corporate Control in Multinational Enterprises: Worldwide and European Perspectives", *Organization Studies*, 24(2): 187-214.

Haughton, J. (2000), "The Historical Background" in J.W. O'Hagan (ed.), *The Economy of Ireland: Policy and Performance of a European Region*, Dublin: Gill and Macmillan.

Heery, E. and Kelly, J. (1994), "Professional, Participative and Managerial Unionism: An Interpretation of Change in Trade Unions" *Work, Employment and Society* 8(1): 1-22.

Hemerijck, A. and Schludi, M. (2000), "Sequences of Policy Failure and Effective Policy Responses" in F. Scharpf and V. Schmidt (eds.), *Welfare and Work in the Open Economy, Volume 1*, Oxford: Oxford University Press.

Hirst, P. and Zeitlin, J. (1990), *Flexible Specialisation Versus Post-Fordism: Theory, Evidence and Policy Implications*, London, Birbeck Public Policy Centre Working Paper.

Hochschild, A. (1997), *The Time Bind: When Work Becomes Home and Home Becomes Work*, New York: Metropolitan Books.

Hofstede, G. (1980), *Culture's Consequences, International Differences in Work Related Values*, Beverly Hills, CA: Sage.

Hojgaard, L. (2002), "The Danish Experience" in M. Fine-Davis, H. Clarke, and M. Berry (eds.), *Fathers and Mothers: Dilemmas of the Work-Life Balance — Conference Proceedings*, Dublin: Centre for Gender and Women's Studies, Trinity College Dublin.

Hourihan, F. and Gunnigle, P. (1996), "H.R.M. and Trade Unions: Marks and Spencer (Ire) Ltd" in A. McGoldrick, F. Hourihan and P. Gunnigle (eds.), *Cases in Human Resource Management*, London: Pitman.

Hughes, C. and Kerfoot, D. (2002), "Editorial: Rethinking Gender, Work and Organization", *Gender, Work & Organization* 9(5): 473-82.

Humphreys, P., Drew, E. and Murphy, C. (1999), *Equality in the Civil Service*, Dublin: Institute of Public Administration.

Humphreys, P., Fleming, S. and O'Donnell, O. (2000), *Flexible Workingin the Public Service*, Dublin: Institute of Public Administration.

Hutton, W. (1996), *The State We're In*, London: Vintage.

Hyman, R. (1999), "Imagined Solidarities: Can Trade Unions Resist Globalisation?" in P. Leisink (ed.), *Globalisation and Labour Relations*, London: Edward Elgar.

Hyman, R. (2004), "Varieties of Capitalism, National Industrial Relations Systems and Transnational Challenges", in A.W. Harzing and J. van Ruysseveldt (eds.), *International Human Resource Management*, London: Sage.

IBEC (2000a), *Flexibility and Working Time Arrangements*, Dublin: IBEC.

IBEC (2000b), *Employment of Non-EU Nationals/Refugees in Ireland, Employers' and Refugees' Experience*, Dublin: IBEC.

IBEC (2003), *A Business Vision for Ireland: The Next Decade*, Dublin: Irish Business and Employers Confederation.

Immigrant Council of Ireland (2003), *Labour Migration into Ireland*, Dublin: Immigrant Council of Ireland.

Immigrant Council of Ireland, Irish Council for Civil Liberties, Irish Refugee Council and Migrant Rights Centre (2004), *Joint Response to the Immigration Bill*, Dublin: Irish Council for Civil Liberties.

Industrial Development Authority (2001 & 2003), *Annual Report*, Dublin: IDA.

Inglis, T. (1998), *Moral Monopoly: The Rise and Fall of the Catholic Church in Modern Ireland*, Dublin: University College Dublin.

International Social Survey Programme (2002), Family and Changing Gender Roles III, http://www.data-archive.ac.uk (accessed 15 April 2005).

Irish Congress of Trade Unions (1999), *Delivering Gender Equality: Fourth Equality Programme 1999-2000*, Dublin: ICTU.

Irish Congress of Trade Unions (2002), *Congress Report on Survey of Childcare Practices*, Dublin: ICTU.

Irish Congress of Trade Unions (2002), *Identifying Members' Childcare Needs*, Dublin: ICTU.

Irish Times (2001), "Childcare here costs working parents more", 17 May 2001: 3.

Jacoby, S. (1985), "American Exceptionalism Revisited: The Importance of Management", in S.M. Jacoby (ed.), *Masters to Managers: Historical and Comparative Perspectives on American Employers,* New York: Columbia University Press.

Jacoby, S. (1997), *Modern Manors: Welfare Capitalism Since the New Deal,* New Jersey: Princeton University Press.

Kanter, R. (1977), *Men and Women of the Corporation,* New York: Basic Books.

Kaya, A. (1998), "Multicultural Clientelism and Alevi Resurgence in the Turkish Diaspora: Berlin", *New Perspectives on Turkey* 18: 23–49.

Kelly, A. and Brannick, T. (1985), "Industrial Relations Practices in Multinational Companies in Ireland", *Journal of Irish Business and Administrative Research,* 7: 98-111.

Kelly, J. (1998*), Rethinking Industrial Relations: Mobilisation, Collectivism and Long Waves,* London: Routeledge.

Kelly, J. and Heery, E. (1994), *Working for the Union,* Cambridge: Cambridge University Press.

Kerfoot, D. and Knights, D. (1996), "The Best is Yet to Come?: The Quest for Embodiment in Managerial Work", in D. Collinson and J. Hearn (eds.), *Men as Managers, Managers as Men: Critical Perspectives on Men, Masculinites and Managements,* London: Sage.

Kerfoot, D. and Knights, D. (1998), "Managing Masculinity in Contemporary Organizational Life: A 'Managerial Project'", *Organization* 5(1): 7-26.

Kerr, C., Dunlop, J., Harbison, F. and Myers, C. (1973), *Industrialism and Industrial Management,* Harmondsworth: Penguin.

Kessler, I. (2001), "Reward System Choices", in J. Storey (ed.), *Human Resource Management: A Critical Text second edition,* London: Thompson.

Kidder, T. (1981), *The Soul of a New Machine,* New York: Avon Books.

Kiely, G. (1995a), "Paid and Unpaid Work in Families in Ireland" in T. Willemsem, G. Frinking and R. Vogel (eds.), *Work and Family in Europe: The Role of Policies,* Tilburg: Tilburg University Press.

Kiely, G. (1995b), "Fathers in Families" in I. McCarthy (ed.), *Irish Family Studies: Selected Papers,* Dublin: Family Studies Centre, University College Dublin.

Kirby, P. (2002), *The Celtic Tiger in Distress: Growth with Inequality in Ireland*, Basingstoke, Palgrave.

Kirby, P., Gibbons, L. and Cronin, M. (2002), *Reinventing Ireland: Culture, Society and the Global Economy*, London: Pluto.

Kirton, G. and Greene, A. (2000), *The Dynamics of Managing Diversity: A Critical Approach*, Oxford: Butterworth-Heinemann.

Kivisto, P. (2002), *Multiculturalism in a Global Society*, Oxford: Blackwell.

Klandermans, B. (1992), "Trade Union Participation" in J. Hartley and G. Stephenson (eds.), *Employment Relations: The Psychology of Influence and Control at Work*, Oxford: Blackwell.

Klandermans, B. (1996), "Ideology and the Social Psychology of Union Participation" in P. Pasture, J. Verberckmoes and H. De Witte (eds.), *The Lost Perspective? Trade Unions Between Ideology and Social Action in the New Europe*, Aldershot: Avebury.

Kleiner, M. and Ham, H. (2003), "The Effects of Different Industrial Relations Systems in the United States and Europe on Foreign Direct Investment Flows", in W.N. Cooke (ed.), *Multinational Companies and Global Human Resource Strategies*, Westport, CA: Quorum.

Kochan, T. and Osterman, P. (1994), *The Mutual Gains Enterprise*, Boston: Harvard University Press.

Kochan, T., Katz, H. and McKersie, R. (1986), *The Transformation of American Industrial Relations*, New York: Basic Books.

Kofman, E., Phizacklea, A., Raghuran, P. and Sales, R. (2000), *Gender and International Migration in Europe*, London: Routledge.

Korpi, W. (2000), "Faces of Inequality: Gender, Class, and Patterns of Inequalities in Different Types of Welfare States", *Social Politics* 7(2): 127-191.

Krahn, H., Derwing, T., Mulder, M. and Wilkinson, L. (2000), "Educated and Underemployed: Refugee Integration into the Canadian Labour Market", *Journal of International Migration and Integration* 1(1): 59-84.

Laguerre, M. (2000), *Global Ethnopolis*, Macmillan: London.

Lancaster, B. (1995), *The Department Store: A Social History*, London: Leicestershire University Press.

Lane, C. (1993), "Gender and the Labour Market in Europe: Britain, Germany and France Compared", *Sociological Review* 41(2): 274-301.

Langford, S. (1999), *"The Childcare Challenge" Proceedings of the SIPTU National Women's Forum — 1999 — The Legal, Social and Economic Position of Women on the Verge of a New Century and Millennium*, Dublin: Equality Unit, SIPTU.

Lash, S. and Urry, J. (1987), *The End of Organised Capitalism*, Cambridge: Polity.

Lash, S. and Urry, J. (1994), *Economies of Signs and Space*, London: Sage.

Lee, C. and Duxbury, L. (1998), "Employed Parents' Support from Partners, Employers, and Friends", *Journal of Social Psychology* 138(3): 303-322.

Lee, J. (1989), *Ireland 1912-1985, Politics and Society*, Cambridge: Cambridge University Press.

Legge, K. (1998), "Flexibility: The Gift-Wrapping of Employment Degradation" in P. Sparrow and M. Marchington (eds.), *Human Resource Management: The New Agenda*, Harlow: Financial Times/Prentice Hall.

Leidner, R. (2002), "Fast Food in the United States of America" in T. Royle and B. Towers (eds.), *Labour Relations in the Global Fast Food Industry*, London: Routledge.

Leijnse, F. (1996), "The Role of the State in Shaping Trade Union Policies" in P. Leisink, J. Van Leemput and J. Vilrokx (eds.), *The Challenges to Trade Unions in Europe*, London: Edward Elgar.

Lentin, R. (2002a) "Introduction: Intercultural Education for the University of Tomorrow?" in *Working in a Multicultural University*: Proceedings of a Workshop Held in Trinity College Dublin pp. 6-22.

Lentin, R. (2002b), "At the Heart of the Hibernian Post-Metropolis: Spatial Narratives of Ethnic Minorities and Diasporic Communities in a Changing City" in *City: Analysis of Urban Trends, Culture, Theory, Policy, Action* 6(2): 229-249.

Lentin, R. and McVeigh, R. (2002), "Situated Racisms: A Theoretical Introduction" in R. Lentin and R. McVeigh (eds.), *Racism and Anti-Racism in Ireland*, Belfast: Beyond the Pale Publications.

Leslie, D. (2002), "Gender, Retail Employment and the Clothing Commodity Chain", *Gender, Place and Culture* 9(1): 61-76.

Lind, J. (1996), "Trade Unions: Social Movement or Welfare Apparatus?" in P. Leisink, J. Van Leemput and J. Vilrokx (eds.), *The Challenges to Trade Unions in Europe*, London: Edward Elgar.

Lodovici, M. (1999), "The Dynamics of Labour Market Reform in European Countries" in G. Esping-Andersen and M. Regini (eds.), *Why Deregulate Labour Markets?* Oxford: Oxford University Press.

Loyal, S. (2003), "Welcome to the Celtic Tiger: Racism, Immigration and the State" in C. Coulter and S. Coleman (eds.), *The End of Irish History? Critical Reflections on the Celtic Tiger*, Manchester: Manchester University Press.

Lupton, T. (1963), *On the Shop Floor: Two Studies of Workplace Organisation and Output*, Oxford: Pergamon Press.

Mac Éinrí, P. (2001), "Immigration into Ireland: Trends, Policy Responses, Outlook" Cork: Irish Centre for Migration Studies. (http://migration.ucc. ie/irelandfirstreport.htm).

Mac Éinrí, P. (2002), "The Implications for Ireland and the UK arising from the Development of Recent European Union Policy on Migration" in *Migration Policy in Ireland: Reform and Harmonisation*, Dublin: National Consultative Committee on Racism and Interculturalism.

MacSharry, R. and White, P. (2000), *The Making of the Celtic Tiger: The Inside Story of Ireland's Boom Economy*. Cork: Mercier Press.

Madsen, M. (1997), "The Relationship Between Working Life and Individualisation: A Study among Danish Trade Union Members" *Work, Employment and Society* (11)2: 197-217.

Mahon, R. (2002), "Child Care: Toward what Kind of 'Social Europe'?" *Social Politics* 9(3): 343-379.

Malpas, N. and Lambert, P. (1993), *Europeans and the Family: Results of an Opinion Survey*, Brussels: Commission of the European Communities.

Marks and Spencer (1997), *Marks and Spencer: Initial Training Programme Workbook*, London: Marks and Spencer.

Martin, A. and Ross, G. (1999), *The Brave New World of European Labour*, Oxford: Berghahn.

Mayo, E. (1933), *The Human Problems of an Industrial Civilisation*, New York: Macmillan.

McIver Consulting (1998), *Manpower, Education and Training Study of the Software Sector*, Dublin: FAS.

McKeown, K., Ferguson, H. and Rooney, D. (1998), *Changing Fathers? Fatherhood and Family Life in Modern Ireland*, Cork: The Collins Press.

McKeown, K., Ferguson, H., Rooney, D. (1998), "Fathers: Irish experience in an international context — an abstract of a report to the Commission on the Family" in *Strengthening Families for Life: Final Report of the Commission on the Family to the Minister for Social, Community and Family Affairs*, Dublin: Stationery Office.

Mjøset, L. (1992), *The Irish Economy in a Comparative Institutional Perspective* National Economic and Social Council Report No. 93, Dublin: NESC.

Montgomery, D. (1980), *Workers' Control in America: Studies in the History of Work, Technology and Labour Struggles*, London: Cambridge University Press.

Nesbitt, R. (1993), *At Arnotts of Dublin 1843-1993*, Dublin: A & A Farmer.

Newell, S. Robertson, M. Scarborough, H. and Swan, J. (2002), *Managing Knowledge Work*, New York: Palgrave.

Nolan, B., O'Connell, P. and Whelan, C. (eds.) (2000), *From Bust to Boom? The Irish Experience of Growth and Inequality*, Dublin: Institute of Public Administration.

O'Carroll, A. (2003), *In the Shadow of the Clock: Working Time in the Irish Software Sector*, Trinity College Dublin: Unpublished Ph.D Thesis, Department of Sociology.

O'Connell, M. (2001), *Changed Utterly: Ireland and the New Irish Psyche*, Dublin: The Liffey Press.

O'Connell, P. (2000), "The Dynamics of the Irish Labour Market in Comparative Perspective" in B. Nolan, P.J. O'Connell and C. Whelan (eds.), *Bust to Boom: The Irish Experience of Growth and Inequality*, Dublin: ESRI.

O'Connor, P. (1998), *Emerging Voices: Women in Contemporary Irish Society*, Dublin: Institute of Public Administration.

O'Dwyer, C. (2003), *Do Irish Fathers Father? An Identification of the Attitudes towards the Implementation of Family-Friendly Policies, Especially of Fathers in Dublin Bus*, Unpublished Thesis, Department of Sociology, Trinity College Dublin.

Ó Gráda, C. (1997), *A Rocky Road: The Irish Economy since the (19(20s*, Manchester: Manchester University Press.

O'Hearn, D. (1998), *Inside the Celtic Tiger: The Irish Economy and the Asian Model*, London: Pluto.

O'Hearn, D. (2001), *The Atlantic Economy: Britain, the US and Ireland*. Manchester: Manchester University Press.

O'Higgins, E. (2002), "Government and the Creation of the Celtic Tiger: Can Management Maintain the Momentum?", *Academy of Management Executive*, 16(3): 104-120.

O'Regan, C. (2000), "Immigration and Resettlement in Ireland: Planning Services, Supporting People" in M. MacLachan and M. O'Connell (eds.), *Cultivating Pluralism*, Dublin: Oak Tree Press.

O'Toole, F. (2003), *After the Ball*, Dublin: TASC/New Island.

O'Riain, S. (2002), "High-Tech Communities: Better Work or Just More Work?", *Contexts* 1(4): 36-41.

O'Sullivan, M. (2000), "Industrial Development: A New Beginning?" in J.W. O'Hagan (ed.), *The Economy of Ireland: Policy and Performance of a European Region*, Dublin: Gill and Macmillan.

OECD (1999; (2000), *International Direct Investment Statistical Yearbook*, Paris: OECD.

Osterman, P. (2000), "Work Reorganisation in an Era of Restructuring: Trends in Diffusion and Effects on Employee Welfare", *Industrial and Labor Relations Review* 53(2): 179-196.

Parsons, T. and Bales, R. (eds.) (1955), *Family, Socialization and Interaction Process*, New York: Free Press.

Pattinson, B. (2001), "Multinational Companies and Human Resource Management: A Case Study of an American Pharmaceutical Company in Ireland", Paper Presented at the *Conference on Multinational Companies and HRM: Between Globalisation and National Business Systems*, DeMontfort University Graduate School of Business, 12–14 July.

Peabody Trust (1999), *Refugee Skills-Net, The Employment and Training of Skilled and Qualified Refugees*, Britain: Peabody Trust.

Peillon, M. (2002), "Culture and State in Ireland's New Economy" in P. Kirby, L. Gibbons and M. Cronin (eds.), *Reinventing Ireland*, London: Pluto Press.

Peillon, M. (2002), *Welfare in Ireland: Actors, Resources and Strategies*, London: Praeger.

Perlow, L. (1997), *Finding Time: How Corporations, Individuals, and Families Can Benefit from New Work Practices*, London: ILR Press.

Pieterse, J. (2001), *Development Theory: Deconstruction/Reconstruction*, London: Sage.

Pittaway, E. (1990), "We want help, not charity: refugee women in Australia speak about their own resettlement needs", prepared for Expert Group Meeting on Refugee and Displaced Women and Children, 2–6 July 1990, Vienna, Australian Consultative Committee on Refugee Women (ANCCORW) PO BOX K 359, Haymarket 2000, Australia.

Plantenga, J. and Remery, C. (2002), "Organisation of Working Times in IT", *Transfer* 3(2): 347-468.

Plantenga, J., Remery, C., Csonka, A., Boll, J., L. Antilla, T. Natti, J. Voss-Dahm, D. and Smith, M. (2001), "New Forms of Employment and Working Time in the Service Economy (NESY): The case of information technologies" in E. Mermert and S. Lehndorff (eds.), *New Forms of Employment and Working Time in the Service Economy*, Brussels: European Trade Union Institute (ETUI): 1-59.

Prahalad, C.K. and Hamel, G. (1994), *Competing for the Future*, Boston: Harvard Business School Press.

Preston, P. (2001), *Re-shaping Communications: Technology, Information and Social Change*, London and Thousand Oaks, California: Sage Publications.

Putnam, R. (2001), *Bowling Alone: The Collapse and Revival of American Community*, London: Simon and Schuster.

Regini, M. (1999), "The Dilemmas of Labour Market Regulation" in G. Esping-Andersen and M. Regini (eds.), *Why Deregulate Labour Markets?* Oxford: Oxford University Press.

Regini, M., Kitay, J. and Baethge, M. (2000), *From Tellers to Sellers: Changing Employment Relations in Banks*, Cambridge, MA: MIT Press.

Reich, R. (1991), *The Work of Nations*, New York, Vintage Books.

Report on the National Forum for Early Childhood Education (1998), Dublin: Stationery Office.

Roche, W. (1998), "Between Regime Fragmentation and Realignment: Irish Industrial Relations in the 1990s", *Industrial Relations Journal* 29: 112-25.

Roche, W. (2001), "The Individualisation of Irish Industrial Relations?", *British Journal of Industrial Relations* 39(2): 183-206.

Roche, W. and Ashmore, J. (2001), "Irish Unions in the 1990s: Testing the Limits of Social Partnership", in G. Griffin (ed.), *Changing Patterns of Trade Unionism: Comparisons Between English Speaking Countries*, London: Mansel.

Roche, W. and Geary, J. (2002), "Collaborative Production and the Irish Boom: Work Organisation, Partnership and Direct Involvement in Irish Workplaces" in D. D'Art and T. Turner (eds.), *Irish Employment Relations in the New Economy*, Dublin: Blackhall.

Rose, N. (1999), *Governing the Soul: The Private Shaping of the Self*, London: Free Association Press.

Roy, D. (1952), "Quota Restriction and Goldbricking in a Machine Shop", *American Journal of Sociology* 60(3): 255-66.

Royle, T. and Towers, B. (eds.) (2002), *Labour Relations in the Global Fast-Food Industry*, London: Routledge.

Ruhs, M. (2003), *Emerging Trends and Patterns in the Immigration and Employment of Non-EU Nationals in Ireland: What the Data Reveals.* The Policy Institute at Trinity College Dublin: Working Paper 06.

Rupp, L. (2001), "Is Feminism the Province of Old (or Middle-Aged) Women? A Sociological Analysis of the Politics of the Women's Liberation Movement", *Journal of Women's History*, 12(4): 164-173.

Sassen, S. (1999), *Guests and Aliens*, New York: New Press.

Sassen, S. (2000), *Cities in a World Economy*, London: Pine Forge.

Schor, J. (1991), *The Overworked American: The Unexpected Decline of Leisure*, New York: Basic Books.

Shaver, S. (2002), "Gender, Welfare, Regimes, and Agency", *Social Politics* 9(2): 203-211.

Sieff, M. (1991), *Management the Marks and Spencer Way*, London: Fontana.

Smith, C. and Meiskins, P. (1995), "System, Society and Dominance Effects in Cross-National Organisational Analysis", *Work, Employment and Society*, 9(2): 241-267.

Smith, M. (2001), *Information Technologies in the United Kingdom: New Forms of Employment and Working Time in the Service Economy*, Brussels: ETUI.

Soskice, D. (1999), "Divergent Production Regimes: Coordinated and Uncoordinated Market Economies in the 1980s and 1990s" in H. Kitschelt, P. Lange, G. Marks and J. D. Stephens (eds.), *Continuity and Change in Contemporary Capitalism*, Cambridge: Cambridge University Press.

Stone, K. (2001), "The New Psychological Contract: Implications of the Changing Workplace for Labor and Employment Law" *UCLA Law Review* 48: 519-661.

Streeck, W. (1999), *Competitive Solidarity: Rethinking the European Social Model Cologne*, MPIfG Working Paper 99/8.

Sweeney, P. (1999), *The Celtic Tiger: Ireland's Continuing Economic Miracle*, Dublin: Oak Tree Press.

Sweeney, P. (2004), *Selling Out? Privitisation in Ireland*, Dublin: TASC/ New Island.

Tansey, P. (1998), *Ireland at Work: Economic Growth and the Labour Market, 1987-1997*, Dublin: Oak Tree Press.

Teague, P. and Donaghey, J. (2003), "European Economic Government and the Corporatist" *Industrial Relations Journal*, Vol. 34: 104–18.

Thompson, E. P. (1991), *Time and Work Discipline: Customs in Common*, Middlesex: Penguin.

Thompson, P. (1989), *The Nature of Work: An Introduction to the Debates on the Labour Process*, Basingstoke: MacMillan Education Ltd.

Thompson, P. (2003), "Disconnected Capitalism: Or Why Employers Can't Keep Their Side of the Bargain" *Work, Employment and Society* (17)2: 359-378.

Timonen, V. (2003), *Irish Social Expenditure in a Comparative Context*, Dublin: Institute of Public Administration.

Touraine, A. (2000), *Can We Live Together: Equality and Difference* (trans. David Macey), California: Stanford University Press.

Travers, J. (2001), *Driving the Tiger: Irish Enterprise Spirit*, Dublin: Gill and Macmillan.

Tse, K. (1985), *Marks and Spencer: Anatomy of Britain's Most Efficiently Managed Company*, Oxford: Pergamon Press.

Turner, T., D'Art, D. and Gunnigle, P. (2001), "Multinationals and Human Resource Practice: A Rejection of the 'New Conformance' Thesis: A Reply", *International Journal of Human Resource Management*, 12(1): 128-33.

Van der Veen, G. (1996), "Trade Union Participation in the Netherlands"in P. Pasture, J. Verberckmoes and H. De Witte (eds.), *The Lost Perspective? Trade Unions between Ideology and Social Action in the New Europe*, Aldershot: Avebury.

Waddington, J. and Hoffman, R. (2000), *Trade Unions in Europe: Facing Challenges and Searching for Solutions*, Brussels: ETUI.

Waddington, J. and Whitsun, C. (1996), "Collectivism in a Changing Context: Union Joining and Bargaining Preferences Among White-collar Staff" in P. Leisink, J. Van. Leemput and J. Vilrokx (eds.), *The Challenges to Trade Unions in Europe: Innovation or Adaption*, Cheltenham: Edward Elgar.

Wajcman, J. (1996), "Desperately Seeking Differences: Is Management Style Gendered?", *British Journal of Industrial Relations* 34(3): 333-349.

Wallace, J. (2003), "Unions in 21st Century Ireland — Entering the Ice Age?", IRN Annual Conference, University College Dublin, 27 February.

Wallace, J., Gunnigle, P. and McMahon, G. (2004), *Industrial Relations in Ireland. Theory and Practice*, Dublin: Gill and Macmillan.

Wenger, E. (1998), *Communities of Practice: Learning, Meaning and Identity*, New York: Cambridge University Press.

Wheeler, H. and McClendon, J. (1998), "Employment Relations in the United States" in G. J. Bamber and R. D. Lansbury (eds.), *International and Comparative Employment Relations*, London: Sage.

Whelan, C.T. and Fahey, T. (1994), "Marriage and the Family" in C.T. Whelan (ed.), *Values and Social Change in Ireland*, Dublin: Gill and Macmillan.

White, T. (2001), *Investing in People: Higher Education in Ireland from 1960 to 2000*, Dublin: Institute of Public Administration.

Whitley, R. (1999), *Divergent Capitalisms: The Social Structuring and Change of Business Systems*, Oxford: Oxford University Press.

Willemsen, T. and Frinking, G. (eds.) (1995), *Work and Family in Europe: The Role of Policies*, Tilburg: Tilburg University Press.

Willemsen, T., Jacobs, M. and Frinking, G. (1998), *Do Policies Influence the Gender Division of Work? Empirical Evidence from Two Different Approaches*, Tilburg: WORC, Tilburg University Press.

Wolf, E. (1982), *Europe and the People Without History*, Berkeley: University of California Press.

Woods, M and Humphries, N. (2001), *Seeking Asylum in Ireland, Statistical Update*, Dublin: Social Science Research Centre, University College Dublin.

Working Party on Childcare Facilities for Working Parents (1983), *Report to the Minister for Labour*, Dublin: Stationery Office.

Working Party on Women's Affairs and Family Law Reform (1985), *Irish Women: Agenda for Practical Action*, Dublin: Stationery Office.

Wren, M-A. (2003), *Unhealthy State: Anatomy of a Sick Society*, Dublin: New Island.

Wunderink-van Veen, S. (1997), "New Home Economics: Children and the Labour Market Participation of Women" in A. Geske Dijkstra and Janneke Plantenga, *Gender and Economics: A European Perspective*, London and New York: Routledge, pp. 17-35.

Zena Project (1999), *Report of a Survey, Barriers and Needs of Bosnian Refugee Women with Regard to Education, Employment and Social Inclusion*, Dublin: Zena Project.

Zoll, R. and Valkenburg, B. (1995), "Modernisation, Individualisation and Solidarity: Two Perspectives on European Trade Unions Today" *European Journal of Industrial Relations* (1)1: 119-144.

INDEX